Lakota Hoops

Critical Issues in Sport and Society

Michael A. Messner, Douglas Hartmann, and
Jeffrey Montez de Oca, Series Editors

Critical Issues in Sport and Society features scholarly books that help expand our understanding of the new and myriad ways in which sports is intertwined with social life in the contemporary world. Using the tools of various scholarly disciplines, including sociology, anthropology, history, media studies, and others, books in this series investigate the growing impact of sports and sports-related activities on various aspects of social life as well as key developments and changes in the sporting world and emerging sporting practices. The following series authors have produced groundbreaking research that brings empirical and applied work together with cultural critique and historical perspectives, all written in an engaging, accessible format.

Rachel Allison, *Kicking Center: Gender and the Selling of Women's Professional Soccer*

Jules Boykoff, *Activism and the Olympics: Dissent at the Games in Vancouver and London*

Diana Tracy Cohen, *Iron Dads: Managing Family, Work, and Endurance Sport Identities*

Cheryl Cooky and Michael A. Messner, *No Slam Dunk: Gender, Sport, and the Unevenness of Social Change*

Jennifer Guiliano, *Indian Spectacle: College Mascots and the Anxiety of Modern America*

Kathryn E. Henne, *Testing for Athlete Citizenship: Regulating Doping and Sex in Sport*

Jeffrey L. Kidder, *Parkour and the City: Risk, Masculinity, and Meaning in a Postmodern Sport*

Alan Klein, *Lakota Hoops: Life and Basketball on Pine Ridge Indian Reservation*

Michael A. Messner and Michela Musto, eds., *Child's Play: Sport in Kids' Worlds*

Jeffrey Montez de Oca, *Discipline and Indulgence: College Football, Media, and the American Way of Life during the Cold War*

Joshua I. Newman, Holly Thorpe, and David L. Andrews, eds., *Sport, Physical Culture, and the Moving Body: Materialisms, Technologies, Ecologies*

Stephen C. Poulson, *Why Would Anyone Do That?: Lifestyle Sport in the Twenty-First Century*

Nicole Willms, *When Women Rule the Court: Gender, Race, and Japanese American Basketball*

Lakota Hoops

Life and Basketball on Pine Ridge
Indian Reservation

ALAN KLEIN

Rutgers University Press

New Brunswick, Camden, and Newark, New Jersey, and London

ISBN 978-1-9788-0405-0 (cloth)
ISBN 978-1-9788-0404-3 (paperback)
ISBN 978-1-9788-0406-7 (epub)

Library of Congress in Publication Control Number: 2019037918

A British Cataloging-in-Publication record for this book is available from the British Library.

♾ The paper used in this publication meets the requirements of the American National
Standard for Information Sciences—Permanence of Paper for Printed Library Materials, ANSI
Z39.48-1992.

www.rutgersuniversitypress.org

Manufactured in the United States of America

For the Lakota, who reminded me of the importance of family and humility. For my family, who reminded me of the importance of the Lakota. And for humility, in whatever form it should take.

Contents

Photographs follow chapter 5.

Lakota Hoops

Introduction

January in Pine Ridge

Not having seen me since summer, Brad Piper felt inclined to chide my tardiness, "You finally came! Basketball season's already started, and you *know* how passionate we are about basketball around here." For the Lakota Nation out on Pine Ridge Indian Reservation, winter is the most important time of the sports year. "It's January, Brad. Why else would I come two thousand miles to South Dakota," I pushed back. "And, hey, are those today's scones?" The Higher Ground coffee shop has the best coffee and baked goods on the reservation, as well as an unexpected Seattle-coffeehouse feel. Very seductive to coastal wayfarers like me. Brad works for his mother, Belva Thunder Hawk, who started it in 2005.

We talk basketball a lot at Pine Ridge, sometimes—depending on who's around—for hours. I may be an outsider—an older, white, male anthropologist from the East Coast—but because Lakota basketball is such a passion at Pine Ridge, getting all kinds of people to talk with me about it couldn't have been easier. Still, this morning it's bitter cold outside, and I'm just waiting for whoever is coming in to close the door!

I drove over an hour to get here, and this morning Route 18, the main road in was dry. What a terrible name for the scenic two-lane road that snakes through Pine Ridge. It's a road filled with opposing forces, at once gentle and wild, undulating plains and jutting mesas, welcoming and deadly.

Like a wild mustang trying to shed its first rider, the road seems to simultaneously move up, down, and sideways, explosively yet dreamily. My car hugs the road as it negotiates the curves, rises, and dips. And always, the sky is daubing this endless landscape in a breathtaking light.

In the few years that I've made this seasonal "run" to catch these games, I've seen how treacherous the January weather can be, going from above freezing and sunny to whiteout conditions in just a few hours. "White-knuckling" best describes the driving in these sudden storms. Unable to see a thing beyond my windshield, I can't go further. And being forced to stop on one of the most deadly roads in the country I'm terrified of being plowed into from behind. There's not even a shoulder for me to seek safety on. So basically, I'm immobilized in a box, fearful and cursing January. Route 18 definitely needs a name.

Pine Ridge Indian Reservation is home to about 30,000 Oglala Lakota, the largest of the seven bands or "council fires" making up the Lakota tribe or nation. The other six bands are the Miniconjou, Hunkpapa, Brule, San Arc, Blackfoot, and Two Kettles. The Lakota tribal flag depicts this confederation as a circle of seven white teepees on a red background. The reservation's almost 3,500 square miles of plains encases parts of the Badlands, white-cliffed mesas, and rippling terrain, and it sits just east of the Black Hills and Mt. Rushmore which is a chronic reminder of land stolen from the Lakota.

At this time of year, you can drive to any reservation in the state, or in the Great Plains region for that matter, and experience the Indian mania for "hoops." Along with powwows, basketball, many would argue, is the preferred expression of modern culture for the Lakota. On all six of their reservations in South Dakota, high school gyms are packed, and everyone—boys and girls, young and old, traditional and modern—is excited. Part of their fixation with the sport is the distinctive style of play seen all over Indian Country: called rez ball, it is a fast-paced "run-and-gun" style of play, mixed with an uber-aggressive defense and transition game. Don Wetzel Jr., a Crow Indian in Montana, has a solid sense of rez ball. The son of Montana legend Don Sr. (the first Montana Native to play Division 1 basketball), Don Jr. defines the game as "controlled chaos . . . run, run, run . . . and not one guy, but five guys out on the break, over and over again. If the opponents can't handle the ball, they fall apart."[1]

But by itself, rez ball doesn't come close to conveying how pervasive the sport is in Lakota culture. For many Lakota, basketball is not simply played;

it's lived. The Oglala have subtly woven it into their lives so that it's expressed in a wide range of ways from the simple joy of watching players excel, to off-setting the sting of poverty and racism, and in everything between.

So long a target of government suppression and missionary hubris, their culture has been tenaciously guarded by generations of Lakota. Today, they continue to take every opportunity to safeguard their culture—by nourishing it from within and distancing it from outside threats. This simple game of "hoops" has been retrofitted to help shore up areas of their social life that need tending. As in their nineteenth-century horse raids, the Lakota have stealthily slipped off the game's cultural tether, driving basketball (as they once did horses) back to their camps. Once, safely nested within the confines of Pine Ridge, the game has been integrated into Lakota life as an elixir—at once pleasurable, medicinal, and transformative. Soul-crushing winters, with long, biting cold nights are interrupted by the warmth and light emanating from high school gyms around the state. People in communities everywhere bundle up and head for basketball games in the hopes that their school, their community will get to compete for a state title. They call it, simply, "States." The Lakota covet this title as much as anyone, but they have also taken the game in new directions, far from the quest for championship. When they gather in a gym to watch their high school teams play, they are not simply parents, students, and boosters looking for a win; rather, they are also the Lakota nation, the *oyaté* filling the air with Lakota sounds and the gyms with their presence.

Retrofitting Hoops to Lakota Context

Writing about sports and culture comes with its own challenges. For example, how much weight should one give to sport as opposed to culture? As a game, sport is socially designed to be both distinct from the "real world" yet ubiquitous. Its core ethos creates a democratic social setting, "a level playing field" and an environment of sameness that allows players to recognize and respond to the game itself, with minimal outside social interference. At my first Pine Ridge game, that ethos seemed intact. Hip-hop music blared as teams ran in and immediately formed layup lines. I might have been in any high school gym. But at game time, the color guard marched out, presenting a slight wrinkle. Instead of carrying only the American flag, along with a state or school flag, the Pine Ridge Thorpes Color Guard added one I'd never seen—the Lakota flag: seven white teepees in a circle against a red background. Then the crowd stood, and I anticipated the singing of the national anthem. A husky, six-foot-five ball player moved to the scorer's table. Picking up the mic, he closed his eyes and took a deep breath. But instead of hearing "'Oh, say can you see?" in the empty space that anthems typically fill, I heard a high-pitched a cappella song come out of this burly baritone's body. And, it wasn't the Lakota version of the U.S. national anthem; it was the Lakota anthem—their flag song, in their language. As the evening progressed, I discovered that the culture and basketball are entwined in smaller ways, too, such as when an announcer might slip into Lakota-isms like "*Ohichi mani*, White River's basketball!" (meaning a traveling violation and a change of possession) or "*Yamini!*" (Lakota for "Three!" indicating a 3-point shot). Through that I began to realize that they intentionally sought to remake this game as their own just as they did with most outside influences. Culture would matter in basketball as well.

Lakota Hoops Looking Inward

It's an oft-told tale—people from hard-pressed backgrounds using sports to escape (or at least ease) harsh conditions. But what makes Lakota basketball specifically worthy of being looked at are the stories of resilient people who have used the game to craft an added measure of joy and meaning to their lives. These are narratives of using the game to fashion a meaningful direction in their lives. For some Lakota girls, for instance, playing on their high school teams has given them enough of an identity to both ease their adolescent ordeals and propel them into adulthood, giving them the strength to weather crises and maybe even a willingness to finish school and to give back to their communities. And for boys stumbling into manhood, practicing for countless hours and traveling to various places to play difficult games can give them a template for taking on the responsibilities of being husbands, fathers, and brothers (both biological as well as declared—the latter of which are called *kolas*). For players of either gender, the game can make them resolute enough to try again following each of the many disappointments they will face.

Often, in modern America, where old ways are thought of as obsolete, we only tolerate tradition. Native American societies, however, have a special reverence for the past and tradition, one born of the efforts of the U.S. government and Christian missionaries to eradicate their cultures. For a chunk of the twentieth century, the Lakota had to conceal their treasured practices and beliefs in the folds of other benign cultural garments, hidden from a judgmental and prying "white gaze." Thus, for Lakota, traditions are not merely quaint; rather, they are practices and ways of thinking that had to be fought for. Tradition isn't old and nodded at; tradition is victory.

Thus, the Lakota and other tribes have bent modern practices in ways that help them hold onto older beliefs and ways of life (see chapters 2 and 3). As such, the Lakota have used the game of basketball, traditionally identified with contemporary urban black America, as a bridge between tradition and modernity. Whether it's a game announcer using a Lakota phase such as "*Hoka hey!*" ("Come on!" or "Let's go!"), family members taking players to sweat lodges to be spiritually cleansed before a game, or players being honored at halftime with quilts draped over their shoulders, tradition is intentionally brought out to stamp the event as being "theirs," as being authentic Lakota.

The Lakota Nation Invitational (chapter 3) is the premier basketball tournament in Lakota Country and a powerful example of this constructive fusion of tradition and modernity. In their pre-reservation days, buffalo-hunting, nomadic Plains Indians regularly scattered into smaller groups, so the Lakota have always looked forward to larger gatherings, viewing them as important expressions of their cohesiveness as a society. Traditionally, events that brought together disparate bands, such as the large summer buffalo hunt or the Sun Dance, were eagerly anticipated expressions of tribal solidarity. Basketball games continue this tradition into the twenty-first century.

And so on winter nights, a myriad of community members from far-flung areas of the reservation congregate at the high school basketball court. The parking lot fills, and the gym is packed with just about anyone who's ever gone to the school, even those who have dropped out, along with their kids, parents, and spouses. Home-cooked chili or jerked-pork sandwiches allow people to break bread, and the staples—popcorn, hotdogs, and, of course, fry bread—are never far away. These games are today's versions of the buffalo-hunt gatherings of 150 years ago.

There are, however, points of contention between basketball and traditional Lakota life.

The North American preoccupation with individual accrual of statistics and glory doesn't fit well with Lakota traditions around modesty (see chapter 7). Further, the benchmarks for success in the Lakota community are a bit different from those in middle-class North America. At Pine Ridge, wealth and influence are immediate goals for only a few, while family, culture, and safety are the key objectives for most. In other words, Lakota who strive for Success with a capital *S* (college degrees, positions of influence, wealth) can be found, and they live lives that we outsiders understand; however, most people on the reservation draw on Lakota daily practices—whether that be "sweats" (Sweat Lodge ceremony), helping someone repair their car's brakes, or going to get cheese at the "commod store" (commodity store where people can get access to certain government issued foods)—things that provide meaning and context to one's life. Having enough to provide for your family, putting smiles on your children's faces, and keeping a large stockpile of family members nearby, both to feed and to be fed by, all constitute success. These are the small and treasured jewels of life that we tend to take for granted in defining success, but on Pine Ridge Indian Reservation they loom large.

Race Relations in South Dakota

Indians and whites share little except a mutual disdain and a love of basketball. The land has divided them since the beginning. Both fought bitterly either to keep it or take it. As successful interlopers, whites have wrested most of Lakota country from the tribe and continue to operate with the arrogance of conquerors. But, the Lakota have relentlessly taken the fight to them out onto the open plains, into schoolrooms, onto the streets, as well as "in" the courts. Indeed, the longest-lasting land-claims case in U.S. history (the *Black Hills* case) is a Lakota battle. They have also faced off "on" the basketball court. As such, games can have a special resonance as partial enactments of centuries of acrimony. While any Lakota can recount experiences of varying forms of racism, basketball games are a favored site for whites to heap racist abuse on Pine Ridge athletes. In chapter 9, we will see unique acts of Lakota defiance centered on the game.

And often, these racially charged on-court dramas extend beyond the game. Racism is so much a part of the fabric of Lakota life that even casual conversations of basketball away from the court invariably morph into a commentary on whites. This is standard in people who have endured trauma. For instance, while at Big Bat's gas station at the main crossroad in the town of Pine Ridge, I ran into two men who I'd come to know. Not surprisingly, a history lesson ensued: "Do you know where the 'fast break' (a basketball play) we use in Indian Country came from?" asked one. Not waiting for an answer, he continued, "Came from right here. There was a white teacher come up here from Alabama who was teaching at segregated black schools there. They [the black players] started that style, and he brought it up here. Our boys sure can run. Next thing you know, those white boys look like they had their basketball shoes nailed to the floor. They're going, 'What happened!' We were making those white boys look bad." His words were punctuated with a smile of satisfaction.[2] A narrative that began by addressing how the Lakota adopted a style of play morphed into a commentary about the joy of thrashing whites.

Whites are the primary source—*the* reference for Lakota trauma and animosity—and besting them in sports is a surrogate retribution for all of the offenses Lakota have suffered at their hands. Corey Shangreau, who played at Little Wound High School, implied this sense of social reversal and retribution in sports terms when he said, "We felt really different when we played whites. I'd get so fired up to play their schools. We wanted to prove we could beat those white kids. We wanted to beat them real bad."[3]

A Grim Context

So much for the more lyrical and cultural qualities of the game. There's a sobering side to Lakota hoops as well. Most Pine Ridge residents find life hard-going. Just the basics—food, housing, fuel, and a modicum of safety—prove challenging. If you google "Pine Ridge," just about every result that comes up immediately lets you know that Oglala Lakota County is one of the poorest counties in the United States. Unemployment figures are regularly quoted at anywhere between 40 to 85 percent. We don't even need to put that into any relative context to know that it's a devastating statistic. News stories and other accounts of the reservation relate mind-numbing figures and picture of squalid living conditions.

By extension, the overall health of people on Pine Ridge is alarming, with rates of diabetes, obesity, heart problems, alcohol and drug addictions, abuse, and other conditions being at least several times higher than the national average (e.g., the rate of diabetes on the reservation is reported to be 800 percent higher and the rate of teen suicide 150 percent higher than the U.S. national averages).[4]

Maybe not surprisingly, the source of much of Lakota poverty lies in its historically compromised social position in the state of South Dakota. From the onset, when whites trespassed en route to the Northwest, through the century and a half of their taking Lakota land, the racial history is abysmal. Ever mindful of overgeneralizing, while there most certainly are whites in the region that hold genuinely progressive views of Indians, the majority of white views fall somewhere between bare tolerance and raw bigotry.

Rosebud Reservation member Dana Lone Hill summed it up when she said, "I live in the . . . state most racist against American Indians, hands down. . . . To live in South Dakota, especially west of the Missouri River near the Black Hills, and be an Indian, is definitely a struggle."[5] This informs a highly publicized, but by no means unusual, incident in 2015, in which a group of Lakota elementary school children attending a hockey game in Rapid City, South Dakota were verbally assaulted with racist language while having beer poured on them by drunk white fans. Such attitudes are also found on the streets of Rapid City, where relations between the police and the Indian community are badly frayed, or in border towns, where Lakota children are routinely targeted in schools. For these children, any misbehavior can result in their being dismissed or even having police brought into the school.

Most informed Americans have only a vague sense that this is the lot of many Indian communities, and reversing these trends appears to be out of the question, at least in the foreseeable future, even with all of the federal programs, charity donations, hosted benefits, and weeks spent on reservations by well-intended whites with any of the scores of NGOs (nongovernmental organizations) that were created to help.

But one would think that escaping these conditions would be forefront in the minds of those who are aware of the realities—that is, of those living on the reservation. And it is certainly something that many young boys and girls on the reservation talk about. But as the experience of some rez ball players illustrates, leaving the reservation is complicated.

Basketball prowess, in the form of college scholarships to play, could offer the most gifted athletes a chance to leave, succeed in getting a degree, and either moving off the rez or getting one of its few coveted jobs. But few do so. The factors that derail most such efforts are predictable: lack of academic preparedness, discomfort in white settings, and minimal interest by college coaches to find and keep Native players. Most athletes I've talked with also note that missing their families weighs heavily on them, causing them to return prematurely. This longing to return to family is, at times ironically, mixed with the need to protect younger siblings from threats caused by their own family members. And it's not the western "nuclear family" of dad, mom, and unmarried children that Lakota have in mind when they talk about pining for family; rather, it's the large extended family—the *tiyospayé*—that typically surrounds an individual on the reservation. At the bottom, the family can be the source of both joy and pain. That the game is played by and for people who navigate such waters means that, just beneath the elation of a win or a beautiful play, is a soberness brought on in exiting the gym.

Conversely, one must avoid the tendency to see the Lakota life as "poverty porn," and to do so, one must appreciate the areas of Lakota life that are filled with joy, warmth, and humor, all of which are doled out daily and are a part of the strange stew that constitutes life on Pine Ridge. And basketball has a role to play in this.

The Tension between Hurt and Hope

As meaningful as the game is for the Lakota, not everything around the game reflects the best of Lakota life on Pine Ridge. And it would be especially naïve to think that such a hard life as most people there live wouldn't take a toll on their psyche and solidarity. As such, envy, pettiness, and backbiting are in evidence, both in Lakota life and the game. These toxic expressions erode cohesiveness and have always been antithetical to Lakota values, but they have also always been present. And in modern reservation life, with all of its hardships, this spitefulness may loom larger than ever. Thus, this book examines Lakota efforts to contain these harmful social expressions, through the efforts of people to hold on to traditional practices that feature sharing and humility, and through organizations working on behalf of the *oyaté*.

In the Ken Burns series on the Vietnam War there's an interview with a Viet Cong soldier who, in the final days of the war, fought in a battle in which he was wounded three times. It would be several days before his men could come to his rescue, during which time his only concern was survival. That soldier could just as easily have been a wounded American GI with the 101st Airborne Division or the 9th Marine Regiment. Remarkably, he tended to the bleeding, pain, and insect infestation of his wounds by blocking out his present condition and focusing on the future—on being rescued. It was only then that he fully acknowledged the pain and suffering of his excruciating injuries.

Similarly, I'm looking at how and when the Lakota bear up. Do they, like that soldier, block out their social wounds, staying positive and focusing on hope and the future? Or do they give into the pain associated with their everyday lives, squabbling, hating, and losing hope? Lakota journalist Brandon Ecoffey captured the spirit of this tension between present and future when writing about a particular weekend tournament:

> I have always seen this hope expressed by our youth when they lace up their shoes and step on the hardwood. The reality facing many of our young people is that too many of them understand that when this weekend is over, they will return home to a house where their family can only sometimes afford propane to heat their home, a warm meal after school. . . . Despite these realities, however, these children wake themselves each day, eat what they can, and honor their commitments to their families and teammates to not only make it to rural practice facilities, but to live a lifestyle where they are successful in the classroom.[6]

It seems some Lakota can marshal their will to blot out the demons that would drag them down, but by no means can all of them do so. Thus, that overriding tension is also a theme of this work.

Careful Where I Walk

There's an old joke that goes something like this: Jesus, Moses, and St. Peter are in a boat sailing across the ocean. Suddenly, the boat stops, and they see a small island ahead. Jesus looks around, then gets out of the boat and walks across the water toward the island. St. Peter then stands up, carefully steps out of the boat, and walks after Jesus. Moses looks puzzled. He stands up and steps out of the boat only to fall into the water. Soaked and confused, he gets back into the boat. All the while, Jesus and St. Peter are watching from shore. Jesus laughs and whispers to St. Peter, "Do you think we should tell him where the rocks are?"

In writing this book, I really wanted to have that sense of where the rocks are. I realized that footing may come in the form of things I want badly to show, like how the game can be a creative cultural force, or in things I want to avoid, like romanticizing the game's importance. Either way, I knew needed a number of them to avoid getting wet.

Thus, the work and views of certain people, such as Vine Deloria Jr. and Sherman Alexie, became my rocks. I was fortunate enough to have served on a panel at the American Anthropological Association with Vine and was around him just long enough to be aware of what a presence he was. Soft-spoken but strong, it was Vine Deloria Jr. who called anthropologists on the carpet here in North America. His manifesto, *Custer Died for Your Sins,* did not spare the discipline of anthropology, which he saw simultaneously as being his own and being alien. In scathing tongue-in-cheek prose, Delo-ria characterized the discipline as a culture-crushing infestation that occurs each summer when universities adjourn.[7] In this spirit, I hoped to straddle the worlds of Pine Ridge and anthropology, to avoid the pitfalls of myopic small community social worlds while also sidestepping the sometimes artificial pretense at pure objectivity.

Though I don't know him, I also kept Sherman Alexie's work in mind. Much of his writing reflects on race and culture. One work, in particular, bore directly on my own: in a review of a book by Ian Frazier, *On the Rez,* Alexie laid out issues that any outsider dealing with Indians would do well to carefully consider.[8] In particular, Alexie took Frazier to task on the grounds of cultural appropriation and racial hubris. As a white man, Frazier com-mitted a cardinal sin in his writing about the Lakota at Pine Ridge: he inad-vertently claimed them as "his." Further, Frazier thought he could justify this attitude by admitting to having an affinity for Lakota culture. By claim-ing a lifelong attraction to their ways of life, Frazier fell prey to romanticiz-ing both the Lakota and his relationship with them. For Alexie (a Spokane Indian), and even more for Vine Deloria Jr. (a Lakota), this is unacceptable. It continues the tradition of a long line of whites who claim to either have a kind of creepy closeness with "their people," as blood brothers or wannabe adoptees into the tribe, or to just mystically identify with them. But when you're of the group whose culture is being appropriated or fawned over, it's offensive.

I remember how I felt when an acquaintance once revealed to me that she could understand the horrors my mother had gone through in Aus-chwitz, because in her prior life she had been a Jew at Auschwitz as well. I was too stunned to be angry. Stunned, because she so badly wanted to iden-tify with my mother's ordeal that she concocted this mystical link between them. Stunned, too, at her hubris—that she, a non-Jew from a privileged

Protestant family, would appropriate that Jewish subgenre of oppression involved with pogroms, the Warsaw Ghetto, and death camps. As the son of two Holocaust survivors, I spent my life getting my head around what my family went through, and somehow, she just so effortlessly seemed to get it!

Such hubris must be akin to what Alexie called Frazier out on. Frazier's romanticizing and appropriating of Lakota culture had compromised his work, turning it into a book about his views of the Lakota instead of about their views of themselves. It became a travelogue rather than a work of real insight into the people—his ruminations rather than theirs, stories told not by them but by him *of* them. To keep all this in mind while writing this book was essential.

Lakota often advise outsiders to "walk softly on the earth," which means not only to be careful not to despoil the environment but also to show humility and modesty in the midst of others. I knew this attitude should find expression in the way I conducted my studies as well. As such, research for this book was more exhausting than exhaustive. On my own, I could cover only a portion of the reservation, and as a result, I had to favor certain places over others. Pine Ridge High School, for example, got the majority of my attention. I also had to rely on certain people, and in doing so, I did not get to include others who are every bit as deserving. Going forward, I would like to deepen my understanding of the game by exploring the perspectives of the Red Cloud, Little Wound, and Crazy Horse high schools, all of which have differences of note, but for now, I feel I have made headway in at least getting an outline of the big picture. In any event, long before this book went to print, I gave the people featured in these pages portions of the book to review, along with other observations, so by the time you read this, someone at Pine Ridge may have let me know what I may have gotten right or wrong.

The writings of sport journalists, like Gary Smith, form another well-placed stone. Back in 1991, Smith wrote a remarkable piece on Crow Indian basketball.[9] He's not an anthropologist, but he has an anthropologist's knack for keying into narratives. He's also not a novelist, though he writes captivating prose. More than a few writers feel that to read one of his pieces is to doom oneself to attempting to imitate him. His prose is quite unlike anything in sports journalism (which automatically makes it way better than anything written by sports scholars like me), and not to use him as a model for beautiful and insightful writing would be malfeasance. Gary Smith influenced Larry Colton's engrossing account of a Crow Indian women's basketball team in Harding, Montana.[10] The object of Colton's fascination was Sharon LaForge, a wonderfully talented young woman saddled with a lot of the baggage of reservation youth. In rereading his book, I noted a Gary Smith quote used as an epigraph. It read lyrically, of course, but in my second reading, something didn't sit right; something didn't square with what I'd come to understand about Lakota basketball. The quote read, "Somehow, in the mindless ways that the rivers sculpt valleys and shame shapes history, the Montana Indians' purest howl against a hundred years of repression and pain had become . . . high school basketball."[11] Lovely to read, it rolls easily off of the tongue and rings true in spirit, but it's not quite accurate. Geology and history aren't really mindless. Valleys and history are subject to natural and social laws, fashioned by events and factors we can know and be intentional about. In the case of reservation basketball, history plays an important role, as it was borne out of the intentional effort by the U.S. government to destroy Indian culture via assimilation; in response, Indians hijacked the game, also intentionally, and crafted it into something ennobling, enabling, and uniquely theirs. In other words, while Smith and Colton have the skill to seduce the reader, one has to guard against this literary glibness even while trying to emulate it.

The final stepping-stone I uncovered while writing this book was the idea that I should conduct my work with an eye toward contributing to or participating in the community at some point down the road. Small communities, more than large ones, are riddled with political and social rancor and long memories of slights that are forever threatening to unhinge one's work and one's conversations with its people. By working as though you might want to live there someday or, at least, to be among the community for the foreseeable future, you develop a more refined sense of the treacherous currents of local politics, feel more protective of its people, and become more sensitive to their slights.

Such a perspective may impact one's critical orientation, preventing the hard-hitting stories that uncover all manner of hidden things, but it will immerse one more completely in the local scene. If the academic audience judges me more harshly for taking such an immersive role, so be it. If, on the other hand, the Native audience judges me harshly, they should do so solely on the basis of the book's merit and not on my heart's intent. My goal has been to present just one facet of what it is to be Lakota, and I've tried to do that by allowing Lakota voices to speak as opposed to mine.

The Good, the Bad, the Ugly

In the course of my writing, this book divided itself up into parts that unwittingly borrowed from the title of the old Clint Eastwood Spaghetti Western, *The Good, the Bad, and the Ugly*. Ironic as it is, because it was such a bad rendering of the West, the title somehow fit.

Before part 1 begins, however, chapter 1 provides the ubiquitous overview. As essential as this first chapter is to providing a context for the work, appearing where it does also distances the reader with lots of historical, social, and other kinds of information. So I tried to short-circuit the process by choosing four (among a range of others) social-historical "landmarks" of information affecting Lakota life today: land, school, housing, and family. Through these four areas, I provide a lens to examine all of the other issues raised throughout the book.

Chapters 2 through 5 constitute part 1, *The Good*. Chapters 2 and 3 look at the role of basketball as it aids in the creation and reproduction of traditional culture; the relationships between modernity and tradition that work to benefit the Lakota (and other Native groups) make up the essence of these chapters. Chapters 4 and 5 look at gender and basketball. I've centered these chapters on Laura Big Crow and Jesse Heart, two of the best-known athletes of their generations, but bring a few other players into the conversation as well. The life histories of these women and men are dramatically different, not so much based on gender but on family and vagaries of personality and how that interacts with the social milieu; however, the role of gender plays into the manner in which being male or being female sets the individual on different life paths. In looking at the people in these chapters, we can deepen our understanding of how the game connects with the culture.

The Bad is explored in chapters 6 and 7. Here I deal with the way that the bile of Lakota social life filters through the sport of rez ball. The story of rancorous rivalry between Pine Ridge High and Red Cloud High acts a portal through which we can look at the factionalism that has found expression in a variety of ways since the nineteenth century. Chapter 7 deals with the role of envy in maintaining egalitarian relations when the economic underpinnings for doing so have long since disappeared.

Chapters 8 and 9 deal with *the Ugly*—race relations in South Dakota and the ways that Lakota basketball teams have dealt with it. Chapter 8 looks at race relations within some of the border towns around Pine Ridge. While these towns have traditionally been hostile to native presence (e.g., the town of Winner), I show that the towns of Ohlrichs and White River have evolved and now have workable relations. In chapter 9, I look at how these race relations play out on the court. Whether subtle or dramatic, racism in the game is ubiquitous, and two racial encounters, in particular, have become well known on Pine Ridge. In examining these encounters, I explore the racial mosaic that makes up the game when played between Indians and whites.

The thread that runs through the entire book is that, as much as basketball traditionally conjures up modern urban culture, the Lakota have succeeded in turning the sport into something that evokes their own ways of life, both past and present.

1

Landmarks in Lakota Life

Overviews certainly have their place in books, but do they really belong at the beginning? I mean, that first chapter is so crucial to engaging and retaining the readers' interest; why would we saddle them with reading the background "history of this" or, worse, the "deconstruction of that"? On the other hand, indulging only the most engaging details may be immediately gratifying, but it, too, fails because we risk seduction by myopia, losing the larger sense of meaning. These obtrusive overview chapters matter for the simple reason that background situates readers in time and place; it gives them context. If, for instance, we're interested in the Kennedy assassination on November 22, 1963, then knowing things like the state of U.S.-Soviet relations is crucial. Done well, the delicate interplay of context and detail in an opening chapter builds understanding and appreciation as we proceed through the book. So my hope here is to entice you into my study of Lakota society by looking at basketball: a specific portal opening onto a larger world.

SuAnne Big Crow is a legendary Lakota basketball star from Pine Ridge who amassed 2,541 points as a high school basketball player and still holds the state record for most points scored in a single game (67). That makes her arguably the best woman ever to have played the game in South Dakota. As athletically gifted as she was, SuAnne was more impressive as a powerful young woman who could impact all those around her. South Dakota's charged racial climate has always made sports difficult for Lakota athletes, and SuAnne's knack for diffusing tense situations with her strategic wise-cracking was a boon. Consider an incident, for example, that happened after a game that she and her teammates had played against a white high school. Dana Lone Hill, one of the Pine Ridge cheerleaders at the game, reported witnessing the following:

> The year was 1989, and our high school was still coming off of a buzz from the boys winning state in 1987. We were playing a tough team from Lead-Deadwood. The game was tough, rough, and very competitive. After getting booed, having derogatory remarks shouted at us, and their fans war-hooping, we won in overtime. After we got dressed and went out to our bus, we noticed something. Someone had vandalized the bus. What had once said: PINE RIDGE THORPES had now had two of the letter stickers pulled off the charter bus. It now said: PINE RIDGE HOR ES. That was an instant downer. We all stood around depressed, while our coach called the cops. He was livid. A crowd had formed, due to the cop cars. All of a sudden, out of nowhere, SuAnne yelled "Come on, you whores, let's get on the bus!!" To which we all busted out laughing. As we climbed onto our bus, she started a cheer: "If you're proud to be a whore, clap your hands!" We all continued it in our sing-song way. The righteous parents standing around covered their kids' ears and scurried off. They can let their kids partake in racism, but not hear the word *whore*.[1]

Their laughter in the face of these bigots safely managed the immediate situation, even as the slight built another layer of scar tissue on an already impenetrable barrier of resentment toward whites.

And there you have it: the context for the larger story here, which is the intersection of basketball, racism, and the particular way the Lakota respond to such instances of outrage. This context is what will give the larger story texture and help it to both resonate and inform. And this context will ask questions up front that will inform the rest of the book—questions such as, Where is this racial animosity coming from? How has this racial antipathy continued this long? How does the sport of basketball teach Lakota youth to avoid the worst of the bigotry they sometimes face while rejoicing in their own culture?

To provide this background, I've picked four areas of life at Pine Ridge to cover: land, schools, housing, and family. There are other important social landmarks of Lakota life, of course, but I find these four especially revealing and related to my interests in this book.

The Land

Geography and God

"God created war so that Americans would learn geography," was a tongue-in-cheek, yet all-too-real claim made by Mark Twain. The wars that the Lakota fought in the nineteenth century were certainly about land—and more particularly, about repelling whites who insisted upon trespassing on or taking it. Spotted Tail (a Brule Lakota) summed up the Lakota view of their battling this way: "This war did not spring up on our land, this war was brought upon us by the children of the Great Father who came to take our land [and] do a great many evil things. . . . This war has come from robbery—from the stealing of our land."[2] Geography lesson, indeed. I'll present several instances or "scenes" of this.

Scene I: A Poem in Service of Genocide. Consider the poem, "Sitting Bull is Matched." On August 15, 1889, on the eve of statehood in South Dakota, the *Pierre Free Press* published the poem to commemorate the "freeing up" of Indian land for white settlement. The poem both is giddy in anticipation of white legitimacy and openly applauds the expulsion of the Lakota from their land:

> And so, at last the treaty's signed;
>> Though Sitting Bull has done his best
> To thwart us in our great design,
>> He could not quite control the rest,
> For names enough are now attached,
>> And Sitting Bull for once is matched.[3]

The poem continues:

> It won't be long before
>> Industrious white men till the ground,

Where ages upon ages gone
    The Indians have loafed around;
Nor bettered self nor bettered land,
    Now let the pale face try his hand.

Our many people need the lands,
    And these few Indians worked them not,
They'll never use what they have left;
    But are at best a shiftless lot,
    And blessed, indeed, will be the day,
When every one shall pass away.

This poem represents the victor crowing to his compatriots (since the Lakota wouldn't be reading the newspapers in Pierre). It references the manner in which making the land "white" also made it legitimate, made it a state. In the poem, Indians are derided as too backward to bring the land to fruition, and so they are dismissed as undeserving of any part of the nation's or state's grand plan.

Poetry in service of bigotry seems so at odds with the way we use artistic expression in the twenty-first century. Back then, however, Indian-hating was the norm, and any expression of that attitude was suitable, at times playfully so. The wording in this piece, for instance, has a tone of sports-like trash talking about it, kind of like, "We won. You lost. Get over it." Only here, there's the insinuation of extinction for losers.

Granted, the author of the poem seemed to prefer rhyme and meter to murder, as we see in "And these few Indians worked them not, / They'll never use what they have left; / But are at best a shiftless lot." Still, as lyrical as it strives to be, the poem cannot not be separated from the slaughter of hundreds of Lakota at Wounded Knee by the Seventh Cavalry, which occurred only a year (December 1890) after its publication. In short, it seems South Dakota's whites could joke about genocide in print and then, in short order, go out and actually commit it. Art imitating life, or life imitating art?

Lakota journalist Tim Giago, whose grandmother Sophie lived just a few miles from Wounded Knee, had to water the horses of those same soldiers who had yet to wash all of her people's blood from their hands, literally. He grew up hearing stories from Grandma about the event and has kept the tragedy vividly alive by giving voice to his ancestors and capturing the white racial venom that perpetrated these acts. In one of his lessons of Lakota life and times, Giago wrote that just eight days after the U.S. Cavalry murdered 300 Lakota (mostly women and children), L. Frank Baum, a South Dakota journalist wrote an editorial in the *Aberdeen (SD) Saturday Review*, summing up his views: "Having wronged them before, perhaps we should wrong them one more time and wipe these untamed and untamable creatures from the face of the earth."[4] Baum may have been musing or perhaps wishing. Whatever the case, Baum advocated a dispassionate, clinical geographical genocide. Like the Spanish conquistadores, Baum felt that land was destiny and extermination was the cost of "doing business." Was L. Frank Baum thinking of little Lakota girls trying to run away only to be methodically hunted down and shot, as Giago notes happened at Wounded Knee? Most likely he was; however, Baum would never see complete genocide realized. Instead, he would have to settle for writing a children's classic tale, *The Wizard of Oz*. Thereafter, his impulse to exterminate the Lakota children would be hidden behind the civilized view that someone writing a children's book could never advocate genocide.

Scene II: "Sticks and Stones May Break My Bones, but Names Can Never Hurt Me."

And God blessed them, and God said unto them, "Be fruitful and multiply and replenish the earth, *and subdue it*: and have dominion over the fish of the sea, and over the fowl of the air, and over every living thing that moveth upon the earth." (emphasis mine)
—Genesis 1:28

This selection from the Old Testament could've been penned by the Bureau of Indian Affairs (BIA), which directly oversees all Native matters. Why? The agency that the BIA is housed in is—are you ready?—the Department of the Interior. In other words, Native Americans are categorized as a resource, as if they are woods and ores to be domesticated and extracted—as if they are part of the earth to be subdued. And since Indians "moveth upon the earth," Christians needed to have "dominion" over them. But while the Judeo-Christian God commanded his people to "subdue" the land, it is the devil who is concerned with the details. And, since land is typically spoken for, taking it is often a bloody business, a cultural project involving justifying all manner of atrocities.

Against this Judeo-Christian backdrop, in which one simply works to dominate the land, whites see losing land as cause for outrage and efforts to regain real estate; Natives, however, see losing land as much, much more. To understand the Lakota is not only to understand their loss of land as an outrage; one must also grasp that they are so deeply linked to the land that, a 150 years later, they are still battling for it. Their link to the land is more than a religious connection to nature. It is based on a profound gratitude for the land that has given them their bounty; no one knows better than them that the land can withhold as easily as it can bestow. So they are stewards of the land that they must understand.

The taking of Indian land by whites is an interplay between culture, geography, and brutality. Gaining wealth and seizing land rests on justifying actions that one senses could be construed as immoral. And this justification comes, in part, through a cultural ploy we call the *anthropology of difference*—a zero-sum view of people, in which one group possesses desirable traits to the exact degree that the other does not. One group, then, is deserving to the extent that the other isn't. The result is that almost any act of brutal seizure can be justified without challenging one's morality; outrageous things can be uttered and done.

As such, the settler-colonists were imbued with a religious hubris, which allowed them to pontificate about their fitness for cultivating the "new world" by espousing the lack of fitness of others to cultivate that land. Consider William Byrd, a wealthy and influential tobacco planter in Virginia who, in 1722, voiced this Anglo view of how Indians differ from whites: "Though these Indians dwell among the English, and see in what plenty a little industry enables them to live, yet they choose to continue in their stupid idleness and to suffer all the inconveniences of dirt, cold and want, rather than to disturb their heads with care, or defile their hands with labour."[5] That these native peoples taught Byrd's ancestors how to grow and preserve native crops was lost on Byrd; the Mattaponi and Chickahominy tribes in Virginia apparently lost all semblance of intelligence and industriousness. The zero-sum for Byrd: Indians lack virtue because whites have it in abundance. With this worldview, it would be criminal for whites not to take Indian land, right?

This zero-sum thinking, which created white justification for seizing Indian land, continued into the twentieth century. Take, for instance, Teddy Roosevelt's belief that Indians were too primitive to know how to rationally use land: "The settler and pioneer have at bottom had justice on their side;

this great continent could not have been kept as nothing but a game preserve for squalid savages."[6] By the time of his presidency, Americans had claimed most of the Indian land they wanted, and they had done it with a combination of ruthlessness and legislative action. Twain's geography lessons continue the trajectory of linguistic justification for taking land. It turned out that, depending on whether you were taking land or having land taken, "names can hurt" in different ways. If you had the name "Native," having land taken away embroiled you in a world of racist hate and precarious interracial relations. If you had the name "white," your naked aggression in taking other people's land needed to be sanitized, because acting like a barbarian was not what a civilized Christian did.

Therefore, once their positions were secured, settler-colonists took to reconfiguring their actions as "civilized." And they did it with the language of legitimate occupiers of the land—as "citizens," or representatives of statehood. This was also the legal language of later "settlers" and "homesteaders"— the language of reflected self-satisfaction and a certainty that all that had happened was preordained.

Scene III: Turning the Paha Sapa into the Black Hills. At the same time, the view of those who had their land taken by those taking it became increasingly unkind. Settler-colonists saw themselves as increasingly honorable while seeing those they damaged as increasingly deplorable—in part for letting it happen.

Beginning in the 1870s, white South Dakotans started to demand that the federal government abrogate the treaty it had made with the Lakota in 1868. In that official negotiation between sovereign governments, the United States agreed to form the Great Sioux Reservation, which included all of western South Dakota and swaths of Wyoming, Montana, Nebraska, and Colorado. Subsequently, as whites pushed into these areas, a series of congressional actions and closed-door meetings were enacted to "free up," as the press would characterize it, the heart of the Great Sioux Reservation for white settlement and railroad building: First came the seizure of the Black Hills in 1877. Then came the Allotment Act of 1887. Finally, less well known, was the Sioux Bill of 1889, a strong-arm effort by the superintendent of the Standing Rock Reservation and other government officials to get the Lakota to cede 11 million acres of the Great Sioux Reservation. For this to happen, three-quarters of all adult Lakota males would need to sign the bill (see the first stanza of the "Sitting Bull" poem), a move openly and vociferously opposed by Sitting Bull (which is why he is singled out in the poem) and others. Sitting Bull had fought white encroachment his whole life, and his stature as a hate object for whites had only grown with his role in the destruction of George Armstrong Custer's Seventh Cavalry at Little Big Horn in 1876. Despite his efforts to galvanize Lakota resistance, government threats to halt Lakota annuities worked—the signatures were somehow found or manufactured, and the bill was enacted.

Nothing represents this lesson in land and racial geography more than the *Paha Sapa,* or the Black Hills of South Dakota (home of Mt. Rushmore), which lie just west of Pine Ridge. This area was not just a part of the Lakota's domain; it was their spiritual center and a key resource base until the United States took it from them in 1877. These hills were important enough to be named twice: as *Khé Sapa* and *Paha Sapa*. *Paha Sapa* is the Lakota name used to describe the area as seen from a distance, while *Khé Sapa* represents its spiritual identity, viewed close up. That is, if one is in this place and taking in its ethereal qualities, it's more appropriate to refer to it as *Khé Sapa*. Needless to say, few whites saw it this way.[7]

It's such a physically distinct place—being the highest point (7,240 feet above sea level) between the Rockies to the west and the Swiss Alps to the east. That's right, the Swiss Alps! Even from space, the Black Hills are highly visible, jutting out in the middle of wheat-colored plains country. A 120-mile stretch of granite thrusts out of the earth and is coated with an uplifted island of green-pine-coated mountains. They are the oldest mountains in the United States—older than the Rockies, Appalachians, and Adirondacks. The Black Hills are an environmental oasis in the vast stretches of plains, offering wood, game, and an aesthetic departure from the sameness of the flat grasslands. The formations offer a richness that appealed to the Lakota, feeding their spirituality.

When Ulysses Grant took office, one year after the 1868 treaty with the Lakota, many Americans thought there would be a badly needed stretch of peace in the post-Civil War United States. But by Grant's second term, the country had entered a depression and there grew a restiveness among Americans to find some economic bright spots. One of those hoped-for bright spots came from the Black Hills, where reports of gold had periodically circulated since the early nineteenth century. Grant quickly commissioned a military expedition to explore the Black Hills in July 1874. At the head of a force of 1,000 men, hundreds of wagons and artillery, and invited journalists, engineers, and mining experts leaving Pierre, South Dakota, was Lieutenant

Colonel George Armstrong Custer. While the expedition's miners discovered smaller, not particularly impressive traces of gold in the Black Hills, the journalists in the party (coaxed by Custer) ran with it and exaggerated the claims. That was good enough to set off a stampede, and over the next three years, some 20,000 prospectors trespassed on Indian land, creating towns like Deadwood Gulch in the Paha Sapa. This infestation of whites constituted an occupation, and it wasn't long before they started to clamor for Grant to annex the Black Hills, making it part of what was already being envisioned as a state. Sentiment—by those both within and outside the White House—shifted in that direction, but first they had a treaty with the Lakota that needed breaking. One was crafted.[8]

The Perfidy of Grant and the U.S. Government

Western historians, in combing through the archives at the Library of Congress and the United States Military Academy Library in the 1970s, came across four previously unknown documents. The documents implicated President Grant and several others in a scheme to manipulate the situation in the Dakotas in a way that would enable them to fabricate, out of a false claim that the Lakota were a danger to the public, an ultimatum that Lakota bands couldn't meet. This would allow Grant to seize Lakota land through a justified military intervention and takeover. In these newly discovered documents, President Grant's aide-de-camp, Capt. John Bourke, wrote, "General Crook said that at the council General [President] Grant had decided that the Northern Sioux [i.e., the Lakota] should go upon their reservation or be whipped."[9] The plot to seize Indian land had been hatched. In giving Sitting Bull and others an ultimatum to head to the reservation within sixty days or be considered "hostile," an enemy of the use of U.S. military force had not only been sanctioned, it had been invoked. The act of February 28, 1877 (19 Stat. 254), officially seized the Black Hills from the Lakota.

Outright seizure of Lakota land—such as the taking of the Black Hills described above or the 1942 usurpation of 341,725 acres of Pine Ridge to create the Badlands Bombing Range—is straightforward and transparent. Less so is the insidious tactic involving a Trojan horse called the Allotment Act. In this iteration of land-grab, the federal government promotes a policy or act as benefiting Indians when it actually adversely affects them. Dominicans have a phrase for this, having endured over a century of U.S. intervention, occupation, and control: "Los Americanos dan ala para tomar pechuga. [Americans give a wing, so they can take a breast."][10] Lakota understand this idea as the Allotment Act of 1877. The thinking was that if the government gave Indians a stake in the economic system, they would be economically enriched and more meaningfully integrated into the United States. Depending on whether they farmed or ranched, each male head of household would be "given" 160 acres of reservation land to develop as he saw fit (i.e., "given" land that was already theirs, but now being deeded to individuals rather than to the group). Reasonable, right? By adopting private ownership of land, it was claimed by Congress that the Lakota would prosper. But concealed in that Allotment Act was something pernicious. The allotted lands were less than the total Lakota landholdings. What would happen to the land that was left after individual allotments? For the Lakota, that was millions of acres. The issue was settled when the government took 1 million acres of Pine Ridge and fashioned Bennett County through the Pine Ridge Act of May 27, 1910. This created a new county for white settlement out of Lakota treaty lands. So, in "giving" the Lakota land, they found ways of taking even more of it.

And worse still, the Termination Policy of 1950 actively moved Lakota off the reservation, ostensibly to promote opportunities for them in American cities. In reality, that move ushered in changes in the local economy of Lakota cattle-grazing units. Lakota had grazed their herds in common since the beginning of the reservation era, but as people left Pine Ridge for urban centers, government policy shifted to make grazing units larger and more expensive, further forcing small herders off their land in favor of white ranchers who could afford the price.

In all of these, the Lakota fought back at every level. The largest and longest of these fights—the Lakota attempt to get the Black Hills back—continues today. In 1980, the U.S. Supreme Court agreed with the Lakota that the Black Hills had been wrongfully taken and awarded the tribe $102 million as compensation. Amazingly, considering their poverty, the Lakota refused the settlement, pushing ahead with their demand to have the Hills returned. That settlement now sits in an escrow account, and with its accumulated interest, is valued at over $1.3 billion. The Lakota are still in court, refusing to relinquish the land claim.

Scene IV: Hemp Is the New Buffalo. Whether it's working horses or growing hemp, everything the White Plume family has done or tried to do emanates from the land. It hasn't been easy, because their efforts have been economically hamstrung. Forcing Indians onto reservations assumes that their ability to operate independently has been impaired, their economy shredded. What is offered in place of traditional subsistence is most often dependence and alienation. With hunting no longer practicable, the U.S. government offered them farming or cattle ranching as alternatives to their earlier hunting economy. Plains Indians saw horse and cattle ranching as activities that had cultural traction, and through the first decades of the reservation era, they were actually moderately successful with it. Paul Robertson documents that "cattle raising had become an important part of the reservation economy as early as 1893."[11] President Teddy Roosevelt, while visiting Pine Ridge that year, noted the impressive size of herds. A dozen years later, a government agent noted the same thing.[12] This small Lakota success was undermined however, in a stream of policy abuses by a coalition of mixed-blood (Lakota and white) ranchers who worked to make land available to outside interests—and worked against the interests of smaller Lakota ranchers like Alex White Plume. For this reason, White Plume concludes that "Our own people act like colonizers."[13] Periodically, he's had to sell off stock to make payments on loans. And the vast majority of ranching is now done by a small segment of white individuals; approximately 200 ranchers lease over 1.5 million acres, which makes up 53 percent of the reservation's territory.[14]

Their sovereignty constantly hemmed in and their assets controlled, little is left by way of creating a Lakota economic engine. The original plots of allotted land became, with each generation, divided into ever smaller plots, making them unsuitable for larger ranching endeavors. The Indian Reorganization Act of 1934 took reservation land to be held in trust by the government to prevent further loss of reservation lands by individual Lakota landowners. It was considered a progressive response, but it shackled individuals because it took the only significant collateral Indians have—their land—off the table, in efforts to secure bank loans. All legislation has had the effect of further shackling Native efforts to gain economic independence.

Agriculture has not benefitted Natives either. According to the 2007 USDA (United States Department of Agriculture) Census of Agriculture for American Indian Reservations, the market value of agriculture commodities produced on Pine Ridge totaled $54,541,000. Yet, less than one-third of that income ($17,835,000) went to Lakota producers.[15]

Alex White Plume's commercial efforts to grow hemp hoped to change this trajectory. Following the tribe's vote to legalize hemp in 1998, White Plume set his sights on using the land in a sustainable way while pioneering an economic engine for Pine Ridge. "Our tribe's land base has the perfect soil and climate, where it's easily grown everywhere," he said. "Maybe except for out in the Badlands, it could be grown in every nook, cranny and shady spot on the Rez."[16]

Hemp is sustainable and not abusive of the land. It has scores of commercial uses including rope, clothes, food, paper, textiles, plastics, insulation, and biofuel. And as a ribbon to tie up this economic answer to their prayers, hemp also commands a good price on the market. So when the Oglala voted to allow hemp to be grown, the White Plume family was hopeful—until federal agents swooped down on his ranch in 2000, just as his first crop was maturing, and burned it all. As it turned out, hemp had been banned in 1937 due to its genetic proximity to marijuana—even though industrial hemp doesn't possess the required THC to qualify as a drug and even though it had been extensively used since the founding of the country. White Plume fought it in court for more than a decade, and then the Federal Farm Bill of 2014 passed, legalizing hemp. In February 2017, South Dakota legalized the growing of industrial hemp.

"I'm not really worried about the feds coming in again to take hemp," White Plume said. "If it was marijuana that would be a different story, but it's time that people recognized hemp as a solution to [all] of the issues taking place with our environment. We respected the restraining order and just stood on the sidelines for the last fifteen years. But now it's time to allow us our sovereign rights."[17]

As a traditional Lakota, White Plume relies heavily on kinship, but he's also astute enough to see it as having contemporary functions. "We have the whole clan together, we put all our land together and utilize all resources we have; we don't want to live on the grid, so we got wind power and solar."[18] Now, Alex's daughter, Rosebud, is CEO of his fledgling company and is negotiating outside investments. She intends to use their early crops for medicinal purposes and building products (i.e., particle board-like materials). As a building material, hemp is mold-proof, provides superb insulation, and is virtually fireproof—all attributes that Lakota housing badly needs.

The Schools

Schools are ground zero for understanding race in South Dakota. It is where much of the social drama gets played out. Much larger than hoops, schooling drives right to the heart of being and becoming Lakota, and almost every

Lakota child gets at least minimally scarred by the process. Educating young Lakota can take place both on and off the reservation, in both public and private educational settings, but all forms of education involve these boys and girls learning what it means to be "Indian" in South Dakota—right along with learning math, civics, or earth science.

Fifty years ago, education might have come from what was left of the boarding school era—a century of harsh assimilation policy in which children were subjected to conditions and methods that would be shocking to us today. They were coerced into being "imitation white men," as Henry Pratt, founder of the boarding school system, called them. Children were brought to these intimidating institutions where their culture was repressed—hair shorn, clothes discarded, foods eliminated, language prohibited. For most, it was traumatic, and many never really recovered. Those who did can joke about being "survivors," but they all know others who can't be so jovial about it. The education they received was training to take on menial jobs at the lowest rungs of the workforce.

For Natives today, learning about identity unfortunately still includes a sense of being inferior. It comes in a variety of ways, one of which is when Indian teams compete against white schools. As a fifteen-year-old at Crazy Horse High School, Brianna Bettelyoun traveled regularly to play white teams on the border of Pine Ridge. But each time she entered a white high school, it was as psychologically jarring as it had been on her first visit. There, she encountered all the things that white kids had. "A lot of the schools we went to for basketball tournaments look so fancy," she said. "So much fancy things—fancy floors, new flooring, new design, new curtains. . . . They had technology, they had TVs in the hallway to show the student activities. It makes our school kind of look sad. . . . It's not a good feeling."[19] It could be argued that this is the feeling that is intended: that Indians are poor compared to whites. But intentional or not, schools unarguably reinforce the separation that exists in South Dakota.

On the reservation, schools are most often substandard, places where teaching and learning often come after the fact. Because Bureau of Indian Education (BIE) schools on reservations don't get federal "impact aid" monies that nearby white schools get, their infrastructure often goes long periods before being updated. The American Horse School (K-8) in Allen has 283 students. Like other schools on Pine Ridge, it is dated and overcrowded. Walking through it, one quickly notes the broken asbestos-tile flooring and the absence of the electrical infrastructure needed to support the technology used in up-to-date educational settings. As with so many buildings on Pine Ridge, the school is poorly insulated, resulting in prohibitive heating costs. Former tribal president Bryan Brewer points out that schools are often in a position of choosing between paying for heat and hiring teachers.

Further, the students are fully aware of what outsiders think of them and their schools. "Sometimes when people come here, they think we're trashy and stuff . . . that we're homeless and we starve all the time," said Kristina Looks Twice, an eighth grader at Wounded Knee District School, a K-8 facility in Manderson. "That's what kind of hurts."[20] In these encounters between races, each side has their view of the other reaffirmed. White students can continue to look down their noses at Indians on the basis of their material poverty, while Indian students are made to see the privilege that they don't have. For Indians it's a mixed perception that is generated: they may feel materially challenged and not tolerated, but usually feel more pride in their ways coming off of these encounters

In a "Working Draft Report" to the BIE, released in 2014, it was revealed that three of the four BIE schools on Pine Ridge didn't meet the state's proficiency standards, and one out of three are under restructuring due to chronic academic failure. Additionally, Pine Ridge (BIE) students performed lower on national assessment tests than every other major urban school district except Detroit Public Schools.[21] Clearly, teachers there are not getting the job done, but not for want of trying. The social conditions in schools are so overwhelming that getting students to state proficiency standards are often secondary job goals. Seeing to student's physical needs is both all-consuming and serious—whether it be handling the alarming number of suicide attempts, intervening in gang-related activities, or dealing with developmental challenges that make teaching almost impossible (in some schools, an estimated 20 percent of students have learning and behavioral issues). The result of all of this is a dropout rate of 70 percent and, perhaps more important, a teacher turnover rate eight times the national average.

But then there's Alice Phelps, former principle of Wounded Knee School in Manderson. She entered that district in 2013, when it was not equipped with the essential resources. The school had half the staff needed to run the school and those numbers had been consistent for some time. In her five years there, she secured funding for staff and programs. She got funding for laundry facilities, first-aid, toiletries, and more. (For children as poor as those attending Wounded Knee, keeping clothes clean and getting toothpaste is not a given.) When the school was hit hard by a wave of suicide, she worked hard to boost morale and kept it on track. Her preternatural efforts were beginning to pay dividends when the school board, for reasons that I cannot figure out, opted not to renew her contract for the 2018 year.[22] Phelps is an example of Lakota resilience, just as her eviction is an illustration of the debilitating effects of Lakota political infighting.

Basketball Enters the Picture

Sports has played a big role in the schools, right from the beginning of the boarding school era. For boarding school children, sports and recreation stood in stark contrast to the way they experienced most of their time in schools. It was fun. And white administrators approved of it because it was thought to be filled with white Christian content that would aid in making these Indian children prefer white ways.

Further, basketball and football were discovered to be excellent forms of public relations—a way of promoting the face of the school and well suited to generate donors. Legendary football coach Pop Warner turned the Indian Carlisle football team into a national power and premier fundraiser when his team of Indians repeatedly defeated Harvard, Penn, and others in the early twentieth century.[23] But as sports took root in reservations and schools, Indian children found that it galvanized their tribal identities as well—the very identity that the sport was supposed to take away. Athletic teams in these schools also fostered a "pan-Indian" identity, as kids from an array of tribes forged a common cause as they sought to weather this foreign setting.[24]

In South Dakota, Native sports followed a parallel track. Though sporting teams weren't able to draw on the caliber of players that Haskell or Carlisle could, they still competed well in basketball and running. In Rapid City, when Sharon Mote took over as superintendent of schools in 1925, he tried to bring the Rapid City Indian School into the South Dakota High School Athletic Association. The school competed well, but racial attitudes being what they were, the attempt was rejected with the explanation that Rapid City Indian wasn't a public school. Mote had to settle for independently scheduling basketball games against Indian schools throughout the western part of the state. Notwithstanding, basketball had rooted, and it was well on its way to becoming a key component of reservation communities by the 1920s.[25]

Pine Ridge was among those communities. At Holy Rosary, Bob Clifford started the first boys' team in 1925 and successfully coached at the school for forty years. Information about the game during this time is scanty, but what exists points to a strong community identification with the game. Several factors fueled this: long severe winters, a lack of other diversions, and the affordable nature of the game. Everywhere you go on the reservation, you can find basketball hoops of some type—they may be no more than a bunch of boards and a netless rim, but kids will be using them.

In one of the few basketball recollections, dating back to the 1940s, a Holy Rosary student, Charles Trimble, recalls how widely followed basketball was: "Back in the old days, training for basketball started early in one's school career. In the large playroom where the grade-school boys spent their free time throughout the winter months, the favorite toy was a basketball." Basketball courts were really makeshift, with low ceilings and, at Holy Rosary, actual pillars pockmarking the court. Ohlrichs School, a border town school, had a pot-bellied stove in the middle of their court. Catholic schools played all comers, and Holy Rosary would even take on traveling black teams, like the Harlem Road Kings, or a local team, like the Pine Ridge Red Devils, made up of WWII veterans.[26]

Sports was a pleasant diversion from the harsh reality of boarding school life and from the oppressive school-day regimen, so it doesn't come as a surprise that it was popular. But, it also offered Indian children ways to act out on their own terms without risking punishment. At Pine Ridge, it was no different. And in the difficult racial climate of South Dakota, it offered Indian athletes a canvas on which to paint their feelings and views of things (see chapter 8).

And so today, of all of the sports being played on the reservation, basketball presents the most potent sporting expression of resentment. Combine this reality with the opening anecdote regarding SuAnne Big Crow, where we noted that the interracial meeting ground of schools is most often sports, and the basketball court becomes a natural site to examine.

Education on the Horizon

In August 2016, two dozen girls of the inaugural sixth and seventh grades of the Pine Ridge Girls School entered the small school building that had just opened in Oglala. Like the other schools on Pine Ridge, Pine Ridge Girls School is grounded in Lakota philosophy and practice, but its core is modeled on nationally acclaimed sister schools—the Archer School for Girls in Los Angeles and the Young Women's Leadership Network in New York. The focus is on teaching and preparing young women to go on to college and to do so in a supportive, single-sex environment. The absence of boys, it was felt, would create an added safeguard for young girls in an environment where school-aged girls often become pregnant. Excitement for this experiment has been expressed in all sectors of Pine Ridge, and each year one or two new grades is being introduced to the school.

In another departure from the educational history of the reservation, former tribal president Bryan Brewer has successfully pushed for a new vocational-technical high school to be built on Pine Ridge, to give youth a grounding in the trades. As president of the Oglala County School Board, he has earmarked monies for this, and in 2018, the ground was broken. Together with the already established excellence of Red Cloud School, the tribe is taking giant steps toward reversing a century of high dropout rates, poor test scores, and general underperformance in the schools.

Housing

When interviewed for a story on getting through a Pine Ridge winter, Ronald Robert Red Cloud admitted, "We would have to burn anything—burn clothes, burn shoes, just something to keep warm. There's hardly any wood for us to keep warm. So, we call here and there and see if they can bring us a load of wood, which is good." His survival depends on organizations like One Spirit, which goes out onto the frigid plains to locate and chop up trees, bringing truckloads of firewood back, ready for people to burn.[27] Unfortunately, for too many on Pine Ridge, One Spirit might not be able to get to them on time—or at all.

Poverty dances nonstop with the Lakota. It greets them as they wake up and as they ready for sleep. With unemployment at a level that rivals postwar economic chaos (40 to 80 percent, depending on the figures used), people often have to make decisions between life's essentials. Housing is one of those essentials, and at Pine Ridge there's not enough of it—and what is there is mostly of inferior quality: housing that barely houses.

It has been a chronic problem since the beginning on the reservation. So now, Lakota culture can't be understood apart from a lack of shelter. Former tribal chairman Bryan Brewer told me that during his term, he had to address the state senate about housing needs at Pine Ridge. He didn't have the time to bring the data up to date, so he used older data and added a bit to arrive at the figure of 4,000 houses needed. After he testified and the data actually came in, he was stunned to find that the figure was three times that: 12,000 homes needed. When I pushed him on how the numbers could have been so out of whack, Bryan told me that most estimates don't consider the 10,000 Lakota living in Rapid City, many of whom relocate there because of the housing shortage on the reservations.[28]

The dominant form of housing on the reservation is the trailer, often bundled together into configurations called "cluster housing." These federal-government-issued houses (issued by the Department of Housing and Urban Development [HUD]), are compressed into knots called "cluster housing" that draw together unrelated people, and when combined with unemployment and the availability of drugs and alcohol, life becomes a breeding ground for social dysfunction. Cluster housing represents a rupture from traditional Lakota settlement patterns, which were built on kinship ties and centered throughout out areas of the reservation associated with extended families, or *tiyospayés*. People lived among their own kinsmen, and those ties held the worst disruptions at bay. Cluster housing strips away the family's ability to handle its own. Even so, cluster houses on Pine Ridge are in short supply, tend to be in a woeful state that doesn't allow them to provide adequate shelter, and pose a slew of health risks. When Raquel Rolnik, United Nations special rapporteur on the Right to Adequate Housing, toured the United States in November 2009, Pine Ridge was her only rural visit.[29] She had become aware of the deplorable state of housing among the Lakota even before she arrived in the United States: that it was a situation that could not easily be reversed and one that held deadly consequences. Phil Stevens, founder of Walking Shield, in a letter to his senator wrote,

> The night of January 2 was a truly dreadful night for the Swift Hawk
> family. They had run out of propane to heat their house. They also had no
> wood for their wood stove. . . . The house had only thin plastic sheeting
> covering two large openings where windows were supposed to be. As night
> fell and the temperature plummeted from 16 degrees below zero to
> 45 degrees below zero, Sarah's daughter and her son-in-law put two blankets
> on Sarah in an attempt to keep her warm. The mother then took the other
> two blankets they had and placed them on her six children who were all
> huddled together on the floor where she and her husband would also sleep.
> Since there was only one cot in the house, that bed was given to Sarah who
> was the grandmother in the family. Everyone else in the Swift Hawk family

has to sleep on the floor because the family is too poor to buy any furniture. When the sun came up on Sunday morning, January 3, the daughter got up from the floor to check on her mother, and she found her mother had died during the night, frozen to death as a result of exposure to extreme cold.[30]

While well intentioned, periodic efforts to alleviate these conditions are, as they say, "a day late and a dollar short." They are also poorly thought out. In December 2015, the Oglala Sioux tribal government announced that "214 Oglala Lakota families on Pine Ridge will receive new, permanent homes from FEMA [the Federal Emergency Management Agency]." The previous winter, which was followed by spring storms and flooding, made the already difficult housing situation so much worse that the government stepped in with aid. Public comments by the tribe trumpeted the quality of these houses, "[They are] fourteen-by-sixty-foot manufactured homes. . . . The homes are made to withstand our winter weather."[31]

This was the most current attempt by the federal government to remedy the housing crisis. Selecting the 214 neediest families was a flawed process, based less on need and more on familial connections, and this bred resentment. Joe F., a FEMA supervisor who was building one of the new trailer homes in Oglala for a local Lakota family, found this out when he was confronted by a neighbor to the new home.

The outraged neighbor couldn't believe the injustice. "That guy is a damn drug addict and sells meth to everyone around here! Me, I got kids and I'm sober. I need this house bad."

Joe didn't know what to say, except the obvious, "I'm just sent out to build these. You might wanna take it up with your tribal council." But Joe suspected that the man was right.[32]

Many of the FEMA staff who are on the ground twelve hours a day, every day, have developed a very good sense of the project, based on the product delivered and the need for housing. They've gone into quite a few homes in communities all over the reservation. Anyone with a heart who works closely with these families and sees what they have to struggle with feels they deserve adequate housing. But in a post-Katrina world, where FEMA was criticized because of the kind of housing provided, suspicions abound.

When I asked Joe if the houses were actually permanent and adequate for life on Pine Ridge, he said they were permanent but added that they were very cheaply made: "Plastic pipes, cheapest materials you can find, and we just put them together like tinker toys. They might last ten years if someone really cares for them, but given the way people out here live, they most likely wouldn't last more than five." He sighed and continued. "These houses aren't made for the crowding that most folks here are used to. There might be two women and all their kids and maybe an elderly parent, all in a tiny ten-foot trailer, mold-infested, no windows, and no running water. Why didn't anyone think of running that water line inside? The appliances and furniture (also provided free to new occupants) won't last with that kind of use. The insulation (two to three inches) isn't anywheres near enough for these winters."[33]

But, then again, Joe doesn't know how Lakota understand the concept of *lasting*. Not many people here think long term. Maybe five years is long enough for those most in need, and certainly people take what they have and adapt.

Outside, we were getting clipped by a snowstorm and severe cold, enough so that it was one of the few days that FEMA crews halted work, which prompted me to ask, "How much can you get done in the middle of winter?"

"We tried to tell the tribe that it'd be best to wait till the ground thawed, but they wanted it done right away. Trouble is that when we lay a pad [the cement base on which the house rests] down, the cement won't cure right, and when the thaw hits, these houses will start tilting."[34] Clearly, this conversation didn't leave me feeling that the housing crisis would be answered in any permanent and meaningful way. The new FEMA house would become like the old house, or like the "rez car"—something that gets adapted to as it fails. Windows would be broken and doors would come off their hinges (maybe on their own, maybe helped along by an argument). Walls might separate, floors buckle, cheap plastic plumbing fail—and most don't have the resources to get repairs made, so their use is modified. Duct tape and sheets of vinyl plastic remain one's best friends. Things don't get better; they get covered up: FEMA housing, make work, some new educational program at school—all limp along.

One could at least take solace in thinking that the neediest were gaining some reprieve, but even here, doubt was cast. "Some houses are getting built because someone has a close relative in tribal government," Joe said. "You can tell by the names."[35] He would know, because Joe could tell you in minutes whose house should be replaced on the basis of need. He's seen some people pull up a trailer that's been abandoned for some time and put it up as their habitation. He also cited one housing recipient who had land and cattle on the reservation and who was comparatively better off than others. On one occasion, Joe's crew had just finished the house, hooked up the appliances, and placed the furniture inside, intending to present the recipients with the keys the next morning. That night, thieves or drug addicts (is there ever really much of a difference?) broke in and emptied the place, lending new meaning to "temporary housing" and providing an all-too-frequent reminder to folks here that one person's good fortune is often malevolently viewed by others (see chapter 7). At the very least, these sorts of injustices are kept to a minimum.

Compounding the housing issues, private-sector development that might create new long-term jobs is all too rare. Most work remains U.S.-government-generated (the tribe's biggest employer), estimated at about 20 percent of the total population. That leaves about 80 percent of employable people trying to cobble together an existence. A few entrepreneurs are running small businesses, but they can't hire anywhere near the numbers needed to float the entire boat. So, there is some bitterness toward anyone who succeeds or moves ahead even slightly. Failure builds strong bonds; success exposes schisms.

Thunder Valley Community Development

The Trump Administration's threats to further cut the Department of the Interior's budget will take a situation already in crisis into levels of poverty not seen in a century.

The locally created nonprofit Thunder Valley Community Development (TVCD) will be affected by such cuts, but it also might have the wherewithal to survive because it's built on something different: pragmatism, sustainability, and local empowerment. This Lakota-based nonprofit has generated a bit of optimism on Pine Ridge. It seeks to become and remain autonomous, free from government largesse, and to remain Lakota—two goals that have historically been mutually exclusive.

TVCD is located in the Sharps Corner area of the reservation. Its founder is a young Lakota activist, Nick Tilson (who, after a decade, resigned), whose goal was to build a 34-acre, completely self-contained community, which offers sustainable and affordable housing but also much more: "powwow grounds, a farmer's market, artist live-work spaces, a youth center, a fitness center, a workforce-development training center, and a childcare center."[36]

By being committed to merging tradition and modernity, TVCD also intends to build a workforce—training Lakota in a range of skills related to sustainable practices—and to nurture the arts. It is as committed to developing alternative energy as much as to retaining the Lakota language. Begun in 2007, it has been over a decade in the works and has received funding from the federal government (almost $2 million from the USDA and almost $1 million from HUD), the Doris Duke Charitable Foundation ($1.7 million), the NEA, and the Bush Foundation. Coming from a place of Lakota-empowerment, the Thunder Valley Economic Development Corporation (TVCDC) has also seen fit to partner with outside agencies and businesses that it feels are trustworthy.

During the next decade, thirty single-family homes, forty-eight apartment units, and up to ten artist studios; a market, a geothermal greenhouse, and coops for 400 chickens; and a youth shelter and powwow grounds will be constructed. Foundations have been poured for the first seven houses, and one has a roof. In the summer of 2017, construction began on a 4,000-square-foot community center. They've worked out the costs so that highly motivated residents who get involved via a combination of a manageable down payment and a sweat-equity program will pay monthly mortgages ranging from $546 to $660 on a home that costs $172,500 (building plus land).

The building of houses and other structures involves training a local labor force in sustainable construction—skills that lower the price of homes for owners but also increase employment in that part of the state. Equally important, the houses are constructed, as much as possible, with local materials and built in a way that actually protects its inhabitants and can last for a century or more. For instance, rather than use thick layers of insulation in the walls, they are using straw, which works every bit as well and costs next to nothing.

TVCDC is as committed to reproducing community as it is to economic development. Free-range chickens and traditional ceremonies fit well together in this climate. Concern over teaching the Lakota language is matched by learning guitar licks. Culture is as central a part of the mission here as is job-skill development. Their mission statement: "We believe that positive change on our reservation is not only possible, but that our people working together to create a better future happens every day. Our goal as an organization is to create more opportunities for our people to build their skill sets, work together and take hold of their futures."[37]

The poverty that has plagued the Lakota since the onset of the reservation era will certainly not be resolved anytime soon, but the TVCDC has begun a frontal attack on the issue. They're doing it with integrated planning, youthful vitality, strategic partnerships, and, most importantly, with the Lakota.

Family (*Tiyospayé*)

One of Kathleen Pickering's Lakota interviewees reminisced, "People went visiting by wagon . . . and when they got to your place they'd stay overnight, maybe camp out two or three months at their relatives and then go back to their place. They don't do that anymore. Families aren't close like that. People are always running around here and there."[38]

Lakota kinship is built on an extended family model called the *tiyospayé*. It was these people who visited and stayed, and they were aunties, cousins, grandpas, and others who may or may not have been linked through blood, marriage, or adoption. They were an "affectively" based group built around bonds of kinship. Family and land were bundled, and they dotted the reservation—*tiyospayé* were formed around leaders such as He Dog, Young Man Afraid of His Horses, and others.

While the above quote that Pickering collected laments the passing of this system, it is actually still found among traditional elements at Pine Ridge. Alex White Plume, the elder member of his *tiyospayé*, said, "Within our family we have our own governing system. Our children are also helpers. They help do everything. I am the oldest male and I pulled my whole family together, so I have a governing system."[39] Alex's notion of governance is his way of calling attention to the ability of the *tiyospayé* to respond to any need. Bonds of kinship are still alive and well among the more traditionally minded who, like White Plume, fill their days with activities that call upon kin. Whether it is rounding up horse herds, announcing a "sweat," or calling upon others to help a member who's ill or in need, Lakota find that the *tiyospayé* is the most responsive group.

Even those who are not fully identified with traditionalism have use for the notion. Leisha Goes Bad (not her real name), for instance, is a regular on Facebook. She uses the social media forum, as the rest of us do, to update "friends" with posts and pictures, but she also uses it to ask for assistance or support when needed. And even though she has a large social footprint, it is her *tiyospayé* that is most likely to respond. When the call goes out for "commod(ity) cheese" for that night's chili or a babysitter, the majority of the time, it is her extended family who responds. When thieves stole Jordan A.'s motorcycle, he put the call out on social media, and friends and family made it a point to "steal" it back for him.

Life is too precarious, too filled with issues to be without a support system, and economic deprivation makes pooling resources ever more essential. Social independence and autonomy are simply not workable for most Lakota on Pine Ridge, so rather than shrinking their kinship system, as we tend to do in our contemporary world, they grow it. They do it by extending kinship courtesy to friends who are unrelated (what anthropology has termed "fictive kinship") through the traditional Hunka ceremony or, more informally, through extending familial terms to them. Non-Natives do this as well, such as when we take family friends and call them uncle or aunt, but for the Lakota, the kinship system is more active. Milo Yellow Hair, a well-known traditionalist, explains the kinship as such: "*Tiyospayé* is our first, main way of knowing ourselves and organizing ourselves. . . . It's the oldest way." But also the newest way. "There are three types of *tiyospayé*: the old, big, continuous ones; the re-emerging ones; and the new ones forming."[40]

2

Smudging, Sweating, and Sun Dancing

Dusty LeBeau's Fusion
of Basketball and Tradition

> Basketball connects us to the bigger
> picture. . . . Many things sacred in our
> culture are round: the sun, the medicine
> wheel. Basketball is like that, sacred.
>
> —George Bettelyoun, Lakota

It's not pushing it too far to say that in Lakota Country, Dusty LeBeau is a legend widely celebrated for having won two state championships with two different Pine Ridge teams. He most likely had additional championships taken from him by prejudice, yet he never succumbed to the perfidy he had to deal with. Through it all, he comported himself in a way that conveyed the sense of injustice that he and other Lakota have felt with a steely perseverance. In being voted into the South Dakota Sports Hall of Fame in 2012, for example, Dusty wanted to thank the voting members but wondered aloud in semi-jest, asking, "You're giving me this honor because of the two championships I won, or for the others that were taken from me?"[1]

Despite his acclaim, LeBeau walks softly—proud of what he's done yet, in Lakota fashion, adopting a humble posture. I first caught him in his office at Pine Ridge High School where, in his then new role as athletic director, he was sending emails to reschedule a game that had been snowed out. He moved between screens on his laptop and various papers on his desk with the kind of tech-wariness that older people have, like he's not sure if pressing the wrong key too hard might cost him a fingertip. But LeBeau didn't have that deer-in-the-headlight look either, because he is, as some young players say of him, "chill." Always has been . . . at least on the surface. Like in 2004, in the semifinals game at the state championships. There, against Parker High School, in a tied game with one second on the clock, his player, Christy Webber, got fouled in the act of shooting. LeBeau called time, and then gathering the girls around him, he had them do a collective breathing exercise to calm them.

"Same thing we do in the locker room," he said. "Breathe in and out four times, and on the fourth, let it all out. I knew she was nervous as hell. Nerves stopped."[2] Webber sunk both free throws to win the game, and in the bedlam that followed, he could be seen as calm as a summer sea, with just a faint smile and a twinkle in his eye.

Today, I had come to his office to ask him what smudging meant. He'd used the term in an earlier conversation, indicating that he'd "smudged" the boys on his team.

"I come in every morning and do it," he explained. "I have this cedar [points to a braided twist of it]. There's also sweet grass that we use to put us into that mind[set]." He held one end of the twisted cedar rope and lit the other, and as the smoke curled up, he waved it toward himself, letting it wash over him. "The only time I used to smell this (cedar rather than sweet grass) was when I was a kid. Reminds me of Christmas when those trees were hauled in. And that smell kinda cleanses me and helps me make it through the day. It helps with all the negative stuff."[3] Referring to the unpleasantness, he turned his head toward the door, as if furious phantoms with fists full of demands were trying to knock it down. It must be working.

This contemporary South Dakota Hall of Fame basketball coach juggled twenty-first century tumult—like obstreperous administrators and pushy parents—with the aid of a timeworn Lakota rite of smudging. Tradition intertwined with modernity. And this was not unlike the very sport he coached: after all, basketball, a contemporary white institution, had been retrofitted to serve Lakota purposes.

The irony, however, is that the sport was formerly a weapon in the U.S. government's arsenal to eradicate Lakota culture, but it became co-opted—used by Lakota and by Dusty to strengthen those same cultural foundations once targeted for demolition. In the battle between tradition (Lakota culture) and modernity (Anglo culture), rez ball was the path by which the old guy could bloody his younger, contemporary nemesis to gain some badly needed respect. And if rez ball was the path, Dusty was one of its guides.

This chapter looks at the ways in which tradition and modernity (in this instance, basketball) work in tandem to promote Lakota identity. The result is more than simply presenting traditional elements within a modern setting. Rather, performing tradition within basketball infuses its modernity so that it gains in importance and meanings echoing a quote attributed to Austrian composer Gustav Mahler, "Tradition is not the worship of ashes, but the preservation of fire."

Traditional Lakota Practices

Lakota identity is shaped by beliefs in what it takes to live a fulfilled life, and much of those beliefs revolve around spiritual practices. Lakota spiritual practices are bound into a complex known as the Seven Sacred Rites, or *Wicoh'an Wakan Sakowin*, which were given to the Lakota by White Buffalo Calf Woman, one of their most important deities. These rites foster three broad ends: living a physically and spiritually healthy life, transitioning through life, and fostering relationships both among themselves and with their deities. To discover the relationship between the individual and the creator, in order to gain enlightenment (knowledge), the Lakota perform the following rites:[4]

- **The sweat lodge (*inipi*).** Praying for health and well-being in a mound-shaped structure into which hot stones are placed and water poured on them to release steam and promote sweating and cleansing. Purification is fostered with prayer. "Sweats" is the term the Lakota use for this practice.

- **The Sun Dance** (*wiwanyang wacipi*). An annual summer gathering to celebrate Lakota social identity and to fulfill oaths made during the year that require a sacrifice of flesh. Dancing often involves the skewering of skin and being attached to the Sun Dance tree by leather straps. Praying, dancing, and circling the tree continues until the flesh is torn from the skewer, which then fulfills the oath.
- **Crying for vision** (*hanbleceyapi*). Vision-questing through fasting and isolating oneself in an attempt to secure the aid of a deity.
- **Making relations** (*hunkapi*). An adoption rite that secures ties between people to foster social cohesion and aid.
- **The female puberty rite** (*isnati awicalowanpi*).
- **Keeping the spirit** (*nagi gluhapi*). Related to mourning rituals for loved ones, to usher their dead into the next world.
- **Throwing the ball** (*tapa wankayeyapi*). A rite that seeks to foster the gaining of knowledge through a game. A girl stands in the center and people seeking knowledge cluster at poles in each of the cardinal directions. She throws the ball and people vie to catch it.

While these rites survived in better or worse shape despite missionary and governmental efforts to eradicate them, the only one to whither was the ball game. Perhaps it is significant, then, that a new ball game, a secular one, has emerged in its place—if not from a strict spiritual sense, then at least from a social one.

In addition, other rituals have either been fashioned or have grown in popularity in Lakota ritual life. The *yuwipi*, for instance, was a traditional curing ceremony promoting healing and well-being. Whereas the *yuwipi* had been a secondary ritual in earlier times, it is more prominent now, perhaps signifying an increased need for healing among contemporary Lakota.[5]

Because basketball represents a widely followed contemporary cultural expression in Lakota society, its relationship with tradition would seem, at first glance, incongruous. Yet tradition is found in all manner of basketball contexts on Pine Ridge Reservation. So in looking at basketball on Pine Ridge, I wondered whether we weren't only looking at that segment of Lakota who were more comfortable in white settings. Were remote and more traditional corners of the reservation likely to reject the sport as not Lakota?

Bryan Brewer, who is steeped in sports on Pine Ridge, quickly rejected the notion that traditionalists don't relate to athletics. "Many traditional families are associated with certain sports," he explained. "The Yellow Hairs down by Batesland were into baseball and football. Twiss were football and wrestling. Ten Fingers were basketball and cross country. Dreamers were good in all sports. Good Buffalos were baseball and basketball. Walpamni Lake Community is a very traditional community about twenty-five miles from Pine Ridge, and they have the biggest basketball and softball tournaments throughout the year. Oh, and the Young Dogs were great runners and football. I could go on and on." He definitively put my question to rest.[6]

Done in a low-key manner, it seems sacred and profane hoops work seamlessly. In watching Red Cloud Coach Matt Rama train girls one summer weekend, I was hard-pressed to figure out whether he was running a skills camp or a Lakota language class. The twenty girls attending the basketball clinic were told to form a circle and to smudge with sweet grass. Rama spoke to them further before undertaking a string of ball-handling drills. He then paused the drills to sing a Lakota honoring song. Most significant, however, was that the whole time, Rama was talking to the girls in Lakota! Most of these girls, who typically don't speak Lakota, seemed to find ways of responding to his instructions anyway. When needed, Rama switched to English, such as when he needed to quickly drive home a point. For example, he'd bark, "You're either a warrior, or you're not!" whenever he noticed efforts flagging.[7]

The Lakota Flag Song

Other rituals that have been developed and have grown in importance in the reservation era are also woven into basketball on Pine Ridge. One, performed widely, is the Lakota Flag Song.

The Lakota Flag Song is used to initiate games and is often referred to as the Lakota Anthem. It's a dramatic a cappella song that is reminiscent of an eagle's cry, echoing off of walls, clouds, air . . . anything. The first time I heard it, I was attending my first Pine Ridge Thorpes game. When the teams came out of the locker rooms, the familiarity of seeing young men run into the gym single file and immediately begin warm-up drills—form layup lines, get shots up, stretch to hip-hop music played over the loudspeakers—directly lulled me into hoop hypnosis. I could have been back in Boston watching my son's game for all the similarity. And then the Pine Ridge Color Guard came to center court, signaling the onset of the game. They marched in carrying several flags: the stars and stripes, the South Dakota state flag, and also one I'd never seen before. It was the Oglala Sioux tribal flag: a circle of seven white teepees on a red backdrop. The National Anthem was played while we all stood, and as it ended, I unconsciously began to sit in anticipation of the game. But as I started, one of the Thorpe players, Dusty's grandson Jeff, walked to the scorer's table, picked up a mic, and started singing, a cappella, the Lakota Flag Song. I'd never heard or seen anything like it before, but the Lakota in the gym had waited for it. For them, it appeared to stir their hearts; for whites, however, the song's hauntingly high pitch and unknowable words might make it come off as a bit threatening. The sensation of hearing the song the first few times was odd, in the gym, with basketball players, and so on it was familiar and modern, but the content felt foreign and clearly came from the past—an Indian past, in which the Lakota Flag Song, followed by ululating, draw parallels to war cries.

Indubitably, the song marks the event as Lakota.

"We all do it. It's just us," said Laura Big Crow. "Sometimes we don't even play the National Anthem, but we always sing the Lakota Flag Song."[8]

Today, opening games with it has become essential to the tribe, a way of inscribing the game with the Lakota "mark," but gaining its acceptance could not have been easy in white, culturally conservative South Dakota. Dusty LeBeau can most likely take credit for linking the game with that song.

"I went in front of the board that runs the South Dakota state championship in 1995, and I told them that we wanted to sing our flag song. They were kind of shocked. When my son sang it for the first time, people didn't know what to do. Their eyes opened real wide. 'Holy shit, what's this?' My son Jerome sang, and he's got a beautiful voice."[9]

Whites were shocked into silence, but Indians loved it. "Indians from across the state called and they loved it. One woman called me from Wagner, and she told me she cried when she heard it." LeBeau's claim that the board overseeing the championship was stunned and that those listening "didn't know what to do," in part, attests to his gall in intending to bring Lakota culture to bear on the basketball scene.

The flag song has been around for over a half century, credited to Ellis Chips and Ben Black Elk to honor returning World War II Lakota soldiers.[10] So what LeBeau did by linking the song to the game was to extend warrior status to his players; and by injecting it into white proceedings, he made

Lakota culture that much more visible and audible—no small achievement in South Dakota.

The interpretation given to the lyrics are also somewhat culturally perplexing. In contemporary parlance, the lyrics more or less translate as "The president's flag will stand forever; under it, the people will live; therefore, I do this."[11] At face value, these words openly acknowledge how proud the Lakota are to be American, in having sent generations of their men to fight on behalf of U.S. interests. Some claim the song is a belated expression of gratitude for having been granted U.S. citizenship in 1924.

That the Lakota, who have also suffered so much at the hands of the U.S. military, would so unquestioningly send their men and women to fight for the United States is somewhat bewildering to me, at least. Especially given their willingness to take on the United States in a wide range of areas (e.g., decades of nineteenth-century military conflict followed by hostilities on the reservation, the battle over the Black Hills, the Dakota Access Pipeline), a claim of subservience to the "president's flag" seems even more incongruous.

Two things cut through the seeming contradiction of the Lakota serving in the same military that earlier sought to exterminate them: first is an abiding sense of warrior tradition and second is contemporary masculinity. Lakota Paul Plume, who recorded the flag song, said that the song is "a chance for the Lakota to demonstrate their beliefs . . . that we were a warrior nation," and that, in a way, the Lakota still demonstrate this belief as they continue to fight for their land.[12]

Today's Lakota, most of whom don't speak the language, simply memorize the song and comprehend it as a manly, patriotic paean. They take the song for granted. But the song begs to be examined because of the changes in the way warriors are culturally configured. In addition, while Lakota have internalized their warrior past, no one has sought to expressly link that legacy with either their culture or language. No one, until Maka Clifford, a teacher at Red Cloud High School, who saw the flag song as a direct ancestor of something much older. In a brilliant little deconstruction, he repatriated the song into Lakota history.[13]

The tradition of honoring returning warriors goes back to at least the nineteenth century, when the Lakota were expanding their territory and considered one of the most feared societies on the Plains. It reflected the core features of masculinity, and the warrior role included an elaborate stratified ranking of war deeds called "coups," in which the act of striking an enemy was called "counting coup." Warrior status was also linked to political stature through the *akicitas,* or warrior fraternities that defended the people against attack and governed parts of everyday camp life.

This responsibility bridged the gap between war and daily life; it fused combat with altruism. Lakota Richard Charging Eagle notes that same idea while expressing his contemporary view of veterans: "There's no such thing as a retired veteran. When you are a veteran you have a lifelong responsibility of taking care of the people. . . . We never forget where we come from." The reminder to care for the community links nineteenth-century ways to Lakota soldiers returning from Afghanistan.[14]

Clifford has astutely linked those serving the U.S. military with warriors such as Red Cloud, Crazy Horse, or Gall who fought the United States in the nineteenth century. His interest was with contextualizing Lakota service in the U.S. military within the traditional warrior societies, particularly the *Sotká Yuhá,* or Lance-Owners Society. This military fraternity was composed, according to Clifford, "of men that were particularly brave, strong and loyal, and therefore suited to a defensive role in their community. . . . During particularly dangerous raids or battles, the role of the *Sotká Yuhá* was to stand as a final defense."[15] Forming a ring around the unprotected women and children, they planted their staffs or lances into the ground and committed themselves never to yield to the enemy. They both faced the enemy and protected the people.

It is with this understanding of pre-reservation male Lakota bravery that Clifford has interpreted the modern flag song. As a scholar of Lakota language, he knows that words understood to mean one thing in modern parlance might have had a different meaning for the "old school" Lakota. Hence, *thawápaha,* which is often translated as "flag" had a different meaning to earlier Lakota, who didn't have flags. That word, according to Clifford, would more likely mean "lance" or "staff." And the word *thuŋkášila* (grandfather), understood in modern parlance to refer to the U.S. president, was, back in the day, closely identified as with a word more akin to "god" or "creator." In this way, Clifford reinterpreted the flag song lyrics "Iyóhlateya oyáte kiŋháŋ wičhíčhaǧiŋ kta čha, léchamuŋ weló" not as "The president's flag will stand forever; under it, the people will live," but as, "Because of the staff, the people shall live and flourish."[16] For Clifford, the song doesn't derive its meaning from the politically diminished Lakota of the reservation era; instead, it draws on the Lakota's exalted warrior past. To this end, basketball players function as warriors protecting their "house," acting in some capacity along the lines of George Orwell's dictum that "sport is war minus the shooting." After all, winning a team game is very much about vanquishing someone.

The Lakota Flag Song is just one instance of modernity being scripted by tradition via basketball. The actual song isn't very old at all (mid-twentieth century), but it "plays" old, in large part because it seizes on the pre-reservation rituals performed for returning war parties. British historian E. J. Hobsbawm referred to new rituals that feel old as "invented traditions."[17] They foster a common identity in places and times in need of one, and people respond because they feel tradition as a comforting shawl used by those who precede them. Using tradition in basketball games has the same effect.

More recently, Dusty's son Lyle LeBeau, who coaches girls' basketball at Little Wound High School, has expanded the singing of Lakota songs at games by incorporating the Crazy Horse Song into their pre-game rituals. The Oglala are Crazy Horse's people, and this was his song. LeBeau and his girls had sung it in their locker room before, but as he related it, "There was a game up north and we were on the court getting ready to sing the Lakota Flag Song, but Miracle (Spotted Bear, one of his star players and identified with traditionalists) wanted to sing the Crazy Horse Song. She was lookin' at me—" (he glanced sideways as if she were secretly asking his permission). "I said, 'Go for it.' So, she sang it. The Lakota there went crazy."[18]

Many of the whites in attendance had likely become accustomed to hearing Lakota songs being sung and couldn't tell one from another, but according to LeBeau the Lakota in the gym appeared to immediately identify it as Crazy Horse's, and a loud round of war hoops and shouts followed its conclusion. It was as if the song were being sung only for Lakota ears.

James Scott would have called this a "secret transcript," a hidden discourse between members of a subordinate group in the midst of the dominant group.[19] The whites there may have felt uneasy at the end of the song, when the Lakota reacted so forcefully, but then they seemed to let it go because they had no real sense of what it was. Traditions like this—a Lakota song in the context of a contemporary game between cultural groups that do not particularly trust each other—do more than just bolster Lakota identity. There, in a "white" arena, with whites watching and listening with implicit judgement about Indians and their incomprehensible music, the Little Wound girls sang a song in defiance of the "white gaze."

The Sun Dance

By comparison to the recent origin of the Lakota Flag Song, the Sun Dance is ancient, the most important of the seven major rites of the Lakota. A four- to eight-day ritual occurring in the full moon of late June or July, it marks both a time of tribal renewal and of personal sacrifice in fulfillment of vows made in the previous year. Historically, a number of Lakota bands gathered into a very large camp, at the heart of which they erected a massive cotton-wood tree surrounded by an arbor. Dancers and others had to be instructed and purified. The final day of a string of preliminary rituals brought out the dancers and those making sacrifices. Skewers were pushed through a nar-row fold of skin over the pectoral muscle, sometimes the back, and attached to long leather thongs that were, in turn, attached to the large Sun Dance tree. The music and singing directed the dancers to lean back against the strap and dance clockwise around the pole, all the while gazing at the sun and blowing on eagle-bone whistles. They did this until they broke free from this restraint, "released," their obligation fulfilled.

Because it was essential to their cultural identity, and because it had a bloody sacrificial component, U.S. government officials and missionaries in the nineteenth century had the Sun Dance outlawed as pagan and backward. From that point on, it was haphazardly, almost secretly performed. The American Indian Freedom of Religion Act of 1978 reversed this. Today, the Sun Dance has experienced a resurgence of interest in Lakota Country. There's no longer only one per year. Rather, dozens of Sun Dances are held throughout the summer. And changes have been made. In some cases, they depart quite a bit from orthodoxy, such as including women in the dance; and some even allow whites to take part.

The growing nontraditional parts of the dance concerned traditionalists enough that in 1993, they convened a meeting and drafted a manifesto ban-ning whites: "Whereas sacrilegious "Sundance's" for non-Indians are being conducted by charlatans and cult leaders who promote abominable and obscene imitations of our sacred Lakota Sundance rites; We hereby and henceforth declare war against all persons who persist in exploiting, abus-ing, and misrepresenting the sacred traditions and spiritual practices of the Lakota, Dakota and Nakota people."[20] Despite this condemnation, rendi-tions of Sun Dances have continued.

Perhaps more importantly, the drift away from orthodoxy has allowed Lakota without strong traditional roots to take part in these rites. Certainly, the inclusiveness of contemporary rituals has made it easier for basketball players with little or no link to traditions to experience them through the link to male camaraderie: "On that court nothing else matters, it's you and nine other guys going to battle," concludes Austin "Coop" Kirkie (a rare native whose playing has gone on into a second decade), "It's the only other place besides *inipi* [the sweat lodge] and Sun Dance that I feel at home. It's a brotherhood."[21] Sweats and Sun Dances promote community identity, and connecting those rites to what happens on the court serves the same purpose but in a more secular fashion.

Dusty LeBeau's Thunder Valley Sun Dance has been part of this resurgence, and though he was a bit surprised that it became so popular, he also knew why: "It's one of the hardest."[22] Vine Deloria called Thunder Valley "the Boot Camp of all Sun Dances"[23] referring to the conditions endured and the length of the dancing. Dusty pointed out, "We do ours [Sun Dance] on the twenty-fifth of June, because that's the day of the Battle of Little Big Horn. That's a tough day to dance."[24] The psychological symbolism of that day is known to all Lakota.

The Little Big Horn River in Montana was the site of the annihilation of General George Armstrong Custer's command on June 25, 1876 by a combined force of Lakota, Cheyenne, and Arapaho. But late June also marks the onset of the hottest part of the summer, making the singing and fasting all the more demanding.

LeBeau said, "See, a lot of them dancers go a half an hour and then they take a break. We dance anywhere from two-and-a-half to three hours straight! Constant. And everyone has to blow their [eagle bone] whistles. Ours is so tough."[25]

For such a quiet man, being at the center of a well-attended Sun Dance was certainly not the goal. So how did it get to be so large?

"A friend of mine started a Sun Dance," LeBeau said. "He's a Two Dogs, and I was with him. There were only four of us, but it grew big. Me, I didn't wanna be with a whole bunch of people. This is between me and the creator. And then my son had a "tree" to do his own thing. So, it got to be just me and my sons, kinda like by ourselves, our own shade [arbor]. When we started, there was just three or four of us, and now it's grown to be one of the biggest. We have over a hundred dancers now. It's so beautiful! This is what me and my wife talked about. We wanted people to leave our place with that love."

Thankfully, his wife Theresa saw his dance become widely praised before she died, and now his sons have taken the helm.

"All my kids dance. We got the one who's a spiritual leader. Another one sings. My boys run it now. They said that I don't have to run it anymore. I'm the oldest now, so I can be the boss and help with stuff."[26]

The Traditional Warrior

Lakota masculinity is primarily defined in terms of a warrior ideal. Certainly, by the early nineteenth century, when the Lakota had reinvented themselves as horse-riding Plains hunters, their life was built on gaining access to prize herds of horses and buffalo, a calling that required territorial expansion against other tribes. Warfare, in the form of horse-raiding, retaliation, or taking territory, was unquestioningly brutal. In a previously lost autobiography of Red Cloud, gathered in 1893 but not published until 1997, we see the famous Lakota chief detail the viciousness of Lakota warfare.[27] Anyone killed instantly was lucky, because if taken alive, all manner of torture and mutilation was inevitable.

In wartime, the skill set necessary to vanquish an enemy (strength, marksmanship, speed, ferocity, and daring) was the same as that needed for success in hunting or stealing horses. And the masculine ideal was centered in this trifecta of killing enemies, hunting, and stealing—attributes that were light years more developed than those possessed by the Lakota in the Eastern Woodlands.

The near extermination of the buffalo herds in the latter part of the century, along with the Indian Wars, forced the reluctant settlement of the Plains tribes on reservations. This collapse of traditional economy and the loss of most tribal land eviscerated male privilege by removing the ability to practice their role effectively. If people regarded Red Cloud, Sitting Bull, or Crazy Horse as leaders of their people, it was in large part because they were accomplished warriors and horse raiders. Once confined to reservations, warrior status frayed badly. Thereafter, Lakota men seeking ways to express their warrior ways joined the U.S. Armed Forces, which they have since done at a rate higher than the national rate for the U.S. population. Bryan Brewer, a veteran, claimed that there were 3,500 veterans on Pine Ridge in 2018.

But for those serving in the military they would spend their time far from Pine Ridge. Basketball emerged as a way to claim warrior status while staying on the reservation. Earlier, I noted Ben Pease, a Crow elder, recounting how, in his tribe, basketball came to be a focal point for young men who wanted to achieve the warrior ideal. And this connection between the sport and the ideal is now clearly understood among Plains Indians in general.

Lindy Waters Jr., a Kiowa from Oklahoma who played collegiate ball in the 1980s, made this connection between hoops and masculinity when he said, "When I played, it was like I was a warrior." His son, Lindy Waters III, who would go on to play for Oklahoma State, internalized this link as well, characterizing basketball as "the last battlefield for Indians. We could show our manhood and show that we were warriors."[28]

Former Little Wound High School's basketball coach, Dave Archambault, likened playing ball to the traditional Lakota twin pillars of manhood: war and hunting. "It's the modern way of counting coup,"[29] he said once, and then later said, "Back when we were a great nation roaming the plains, people didn't make it unless they had physical ability. You had to be strong enough to guide a horse into a buffalo herd using just your legs, so your arms were free to shoot a bow and arrow. Nowadays, there's nothing else on a reservation that comes as close to that physicality as basketball."[30]

Brandon Ecoffey, who played at Red Cloud and Pine Ridge high schools a generation later, echoed this link between traditional masculinity and the modern game of basketball: "We know, as Lakota, that back in the day you had to prove yourself—that you had to steal horses and count coup, but these days there isn't that outlet to find praise except through basketball."[31]

A victory for any Pine Ridge team over a rival, and especially against a white team, is savored as a victory for the community, for the tribe over an enemy. It's more than shallow, because in victory, those young players have experienced what it was to "strike an enemy"—an age-old notion of manhood—and with that experience, each one bolstered a flagging sense of self.

LeBeau: An Unlikely Championship Coach

"I used to drink. People used to say I was crazy. I'd be drunk and have fun, but I quit when I started goin' to sweats and Sun Dance."[32] Dusty's past is one shared by many Lakota—a slippery slope made up of little to no structure in one's life and the omnipresence of alcohol. Tradition and spiritualism broke the fall for LeBeau as it did for many others. While he feels that

Lakota spiritual life saved him, however, he has never pushed it on others in a heavy-handed way. An avuncular vibe is what he was able to convey in dealing with his players; but an effective balance of respect, player account-ability, and calming protection was always the hallmark of Dusty's teams. LeBeau always knew full well that, just outside the gym doors, was a world waiting to swallow up many of his players. If they failed or relapsed, he never judged them, and they, in turn, trusted him. When he had to discipline, however, he did, and they took it in the spirit it was intended: "I'll chew them out, but I always build em up."

The boys and girls who played for him, as often as not, didn't have that connection to old-time spiritual practices. Their frequently fractured family relations tended to cause them to lose any connection to spiritualism. "I really never paid it [traditional practices] no mind," he said. "None of my peeps did."[33] LeBeau just wanted something positive to help his players navigate the frequent turbulence that came into their young lives—a very secular-feeling traditional ritual. He explains, "All the basketball players know that that's what I do. I show 'em a different way. I take 'em to the sweats, and kids get to pray. It doesn't have to be my kind of praying, just pray from the heart. . . . We smudge to cleanse the mind. We do it all the time."[34]

The players that stay with the Thorpes do so in part because the team gives them a semblance of normalcy through belonging to a cohesive group, and LeBeau's attempts to link the game to spirituality is part of that effort.

"Their parents know I run a Sun Dance," he said. "Good or bad, it's talked about. Every year I used to take the kids, but it was optional. I tell 'em, 'You might not be interested now, but later you might need this.'"[35]

Dusty also introduces life lessons, though less as religious proselytizing than as soft parables. He sits with the team after practices or between games and, in his soft, peddled way, teaches them about being a good person: "Whatever you do in life, be the best," he says. "If you're gonna be a doctor, be the best doctor. If you're gonna be a drunk, be the best drunk." When, in response to his latter comment, one player laughed and asked, "You mean like those people at White Clay [a liquor-buying destination just off of the reservation]?" He answered, "You know, we put those people down, but they have something inside of them that makes them worthwhile in God's eyes. They just have a weakness. Those winos have their jugs, but they pass it around and share it. And they put their mark on that jug to where they're gonna drink, and they only drink to that mark then they share the rest."[36]

As such, he taught them to look at the virtuosity in a drunk's life to see the respect that lurks even in those who are downtrodden and easily dismissed. How's that for a life lesson?

For the Lakota, basketball, sweats, and Sun Dance work together. And the circularity of events and rituals is lost on no one. George Bettelyoun pointed this out, "Basketball connects us to the bigger picture. . . . Many things sacred in our culture are round. The sun. The medicine wheel. Basketball is like that: sacred."[37] This sense that the game offers egress to a grounded sense found in spiritualism is something that LeBeau's players are exposed to. The Lakota are fully aware of how easily young lives are lost to the seamy underbelly of rez life. Most think basketball should be just enough to allow an Indian kid coming off the rez to get by in a threatening white world, but as we see too often, it isn't. Family and religion often go the extra distance necessary to helping young people make the transition.

But Pine Ridge has Dusty LeBeau, who offers a path to kids who get such opportunities to move into the foreignness of a white world or who are tempted by the dysfunction all around them: "All the basketball players know that that's what I do. And they see me not drinkin'. There's some coaches who drink in front of their kids. I show them a different way. I say, 'Come on, let's go sweat.' And the majority of them come. We would sweat before the basketball season starts."

Some Lakota misread this practice, saying that LeBeau would sweat and smudge for wins. "Not really," said Dusty, a bit peeved at the charge. "People think that we go to ceremonies for wins. That's not what you do."[38] Conversely, just as prayer is used throughout the sports world, Lakota spiritual traditions are used in basketball on Pine Ridge.

Gary Smith, writing about Jonathan Takes Enemy, related how his family gave a shaman a cigarette (tobacco) to light, to offer up a prayer before big games. Other players tuck small medicine bundles inside their socks or tie them to their jerseys; this is no different than Christian players who light candles or kiss their crucifixes at crucial sports moments—except that, for those who have survived outside attempts to crush their culture, the ability to openly express themselves culturally, and especially in front of those who once sought to expunge them, is important. Being able to sing their songs and smudge in public is meaningful. And in South Dakota, with its long and ongoing history of white intolerance, singing or performing pieces from Lakota culture is important.

Case in point: in 2013, Indian students in the border town of Chamberlain, South Dakota signed a petition asking the school to allow the Lakota Honoring Song to be sung at graduation, to honor all graduates. Indian students constitute about 35 percent of the student body and bring thousands of dollars into the system by virtue of federal funds for schools that take in Indian children. The Honoring Song request was denied. Rather than the community taking pride in their Indian students, they voted the request down, and it wasn't the first time. The following year, family members of the Lakota graduates gathered across the street from the hall where graduation took place and "honored" all of the Chamberlain class with the song—across the street, in the space provided for those not allowed to express their pride. Thankfully, this separation did not go uncommented upon. Nick Estes, a member of the Lower Brule Sioux adjacent to Chamberlain, wrote, "How does it feel to be a problem?" W.E.B. Du Bois famously asked in 1903 on the question of race. Estes extrapolates on that question, "Exactly, how does it feel? Growing up in Chamberlain, I asked myself that question a lot. When you transgress these boundaries, these borders, you feel it. You disrupt and upset the boundaries. You upset people's emotions and expectations. You feel out of place. You are out of place. You are reminded, if not shown, you are out of place. You are made to feel a stranger."

Chamberlain's rejection of the Honoring Song request was still in place in 2018 and goes to the heart of a longstanding relationship between races in South Dakota, in which expression of Lakota culture in any context is potentially a battleground.[39]

Better Basketball through Sweating

The link between players and spirituality isn't automatic; it needs to be coupled by a person who not only lives in both worlds but also has the ability to bring them together. For the Pine Ridge High basketball team, Dusty LeBeau is such a person.

His style of leadership might be described in a way that is similar to how Boris Pasternak described good literature: as "the art of discovering something extraordinary about ordinary people, and saying with ordinary words something extraordinary." Watching the way he coaches basketball or runs a Sun Dance is like watching someone braid the remarkable and unassuming into a single plait. In the brassy world of coaching, it would normally be easy to overlook the unassuming LeBeau, but his highly successful track record, which includes two state championships, makes you sit up and take notice. Whether he's coaching the team with the game on the line or sweeping the court alone after everyone's gone home, he does it with few words, a soft voice, and a patient visage, embodying humility and dignity in the way that the Lakota value.

But he can clown around as well. While coaching boys' basketball at Pine Ridge High in 2013, a video was shot in which the team was gathered watching him diagram a play. With his back to the boys, he was writing on the board when suddenly Lakota drumming began. After a few seconds, Dusty started moving his body, dancelike, with the traditional music. He then turned and egged on the boys to join him. On cue, they jumped up and, for a moment, the locker room scene was straight-up powwow. They were laughing, shouting, and dancing under the direction of their trickster coach.

Though his family more or less identifies with traditional Lakota, Dusty LeBeau's early life was lived far from the world of sweats and smudging. "I learned [spirituality] later in life," he explained. "It was by accident. I used to drink. I was twenty-one, and I had some friends who took me to a sweat. I didn't know what it was, and after I got out, I was like, "Holy smoke! This is a natural high!"[40] At that point in his life, "natural high" was the only way Dusty could contextualize the experience. The desire to get high, which was so widespread in America in the 1970s, was, in Dusty's youth, considered a congenital condition. Alcoholism, rural poverty, and, later on, drugs had afflicted Indian reservations since the beginning. So initially for Dusty, the sweat lodge was just another way to get high—but with a difference: "I seen different things, but I didn't take anything [any drugs] to do that. It made me feel so good." To boot, the euphoria he felt through Lakota spiritualism was not like that of his other highs—directionless, requiring only more highs to offset the periods between highs. Rather, going to sweats informed life, gave it meaning.

LeBeau stopped his self-destructive ways and got some timely mentoring that worked to encourage this new path. "This old medicine man who was runnin' that first sweat I went to said, 'The spirits want you to come back.' I felt so good I learned from him, and after a time I picked up the [prayer] pipe."[41]

The disconnect between being able to play the game at a higher level and to successfully coach it is about as clear in Dusty's case as it can be. He never really played the game, and coached only a handful of truly remarkable players during his twenty-six years in the game, but he's always known how to bring the most out of the talent he has, and, more important, he has understood that the whole is greater than the sum of its parts. For him, "just being with kids and getting them to believe in themselves, that they can win" drove him as a coach. But after I probed a bit, Dusty also said that getting players to believe they can win meant "they can compete with those white schools." Race just creeps into everything in South Dakota.

Between 1987 and 2015, Dusty led teams from three different Pine Ridge Reservation high schools to state tournaments a total of nineteen times. He did it with both boys and girls, and he did it in different decades. "I'd notice that our [Red Cloud] kids were happy playing, but I'd notice the kids at Little Wound and Pine Ridge were sad. I told my wife, 'I wanna go share this with the other schools." He started coaching at Little Wound, but while there, he was approached by members of the Pine Ridge team who wanted Dusty to coach them. The principle was on board, and they quickly made it worthwhile by giving him a full-time job in the school, as opposed to only coaching.

What was his secret? He had no special background in the game as a player. "I started coaching late—thirtysomething. I was married, and I'd watch basketball, but I was a cowboy." He filled out his sporting resume: "I rode bulls. I'd go to Arizona with my brother, the rodeos down there. My older brother was a champion bull rider, but I won too. I wouldn't a done it if I didn't win money. My younger brother and my dad rode too."[42]

While Dusty has an interest in the game as most Lakota do, he's definitely not an "*X*'s and *O*'s" kind of coach. He's a motivator who has just the right blend of caring and drive. What he does with his teams looks like magic. I watched him coaching late in a crucial game, with his Pine Ridge team down by one. Calling for a time-out, LeBeau brought his boys around him. I was just out of earshot but could see him speak in his typical calm, halting way. No chalkboard plays, no pulsating commands for this or that, no high-blood-pressured face with bulging eyes. Dusty LeBeau just gently filled their collective cups with basketball sense and *esprit de corps*, and they drank it all in. His boys looked directly at him. There was no player dazing off, thinking about what *he* would do. Instead, they listened and nodded with respect and, after just a few words, the boys executed to perfection. Though folks are impressed with Dusty's record as a coach, his championships, and his selection to the South Dakota Sports Hall of Fame, the looks on the faces of those boys said so much more.

"He shows these young guys that it is not about basketball; it's about life," said Casey Means about his uncle who he coaches with. "He still helps his ex-players, he helps us coaches, things we struggle with. The kids, he's always been there. If they ever need anything, he's right there. His words, everything about him, is awesome."[43]

Nevertheless, there's bound to be both players and situations that come along from time to time that test him. In those situations, Dusty continues to exact discipline, even though he knows that the conditions these kids face when off the court are often so dire that hoops are their only haven.

> They know that when I get a certain look that I mean business. They do. You want the kids to listen to you and so you try to be a good role model. I don't do drugs or drink. I tell them, "You stay away from this and specially when we're playing." But then, they go home and it could be a different thing. One year, I had a kid and he came in and apologized to me. He said, "Dusty, I was home, and it was New Year's and my dad said, 'Have a beer!' And I said, 'No,' and my dad was gonna beat me up. He said, 'What are you? Too good to drink with me?' So, I didn't wanna get an ass-kicking." This kid got drunk with his dad. I didn't punish him of course.[44]

He claimed only one player deliberately violated his ban on drugs and drink. "I had one boy on a trip to the LNI [Lakota Nation Invitational] come back to his room drunk. But even then, I didn't wanna throw him to the streets." LeBeau convinced the school board to suspend the boy for five games and to get him alcohol counseling. Weighing compassion and justice, Dusty takes a page from King Solomon of the Old Testament.

After he assumed the position of athletic director at Pine Ridge High, I asked him what he didn't like about coaching, and without pausing, he tersely declared, "Parents." This is a familiar refrain in school sports just about anywhere:

> They say the hardest thing to do here is to be tribal president and Pine Ridge head coach. The people know here that I'm the boss. This is what I tell the kids: "I'm the coach, and I don't care what Mom or Dad or Grampa says. I'm the boss and you're gonna do it my way." They say, "How come my kid was a star in grade school and he's not playing?" I tell them, "All these kids

were stars, but when you get up here, the competition is tougher and the other kids are better than yours.[45]

Once he quells the outraged parents who insist on their kids playing, the pressure to win takes hold of everyone's senses, especially since he's already been successful. "They want you to win, 'cause of the tradition," asserted LeBeau. "They're just never satisfied. I win one championship, and they want more," he laments. It's as if the crowds are telling him that nineteen appearances at state is only a drop in the bucket.

No one, however, doubts his ability to forge winning teams. He's earned respect in Indian Country; still, his pride is a quiet one, so sometimes educators who don't particularly value sports and don't know how well-regarded he is act dismissively toward him. When that happens, LeBeau can get prickly. Like the time a Pine Ridge school board member questioned whether he could do the job.

"Coming back to Pine Ridge High School, I told the school board, 'You give me the job, I'll get you to the tournament the first year.' This lady sittin' over there laughed and said, 'We heard that before.' I told 'em, 'If I don't make it to states my first year here, I'll give you your money back.' We made it to the states."[46]

What strikes me right away is that though he'd been so connected to it, coming back to Pine Ridge High School posed an unpleasantness, or at least a dissatisfaction, for him. It wasn't the kids though. He lives for them. It was the institutional environment, the extraneous demands, and the politics of small-town sports that hounded him.

So, he purifies his office through lighting these grasses and lets the smoke do its job. Here's where Dusty LeBeau sits between two worlds: the world of modern pressurized high school basketball and the traditional spiritual ways of the Lakota.

He laughed when he saw me looking at the smoke curling its way to the ceiling. "See that fire alarm there? It went off the other night at a game, 'cause I was smudging [lighting these grasses]. I tell the kids to pray anyway they know how. Doesn't have to be my kind of praying; just do it from the heart. And, then we smudge 'em off [let them cleanse], and we go play. Well, the smoke set off the fire alarms, and the principle got mad." He went on. "Last time, I went to the state tournament, I did the sweet grass at Sioux Falls. They wouldn't let us, but I did it anyway."[47] He gave a slight smile.

Using the Past to Save You in the Present

For Dusty LeBeau and certain others, traditional religious practice is part of the haven he tries to build into what is, too often, a heartless world. They have found that sweats, smudging, and sun dances can help keep kids away from alcohol and drugs as much as being in the gym playing basketball can. It may seem that hoops, both the sacred and profane parts, are done for their own separate reasons, but both are part of a larger project, which is to protect and heal a lot of very vulnerable young people. Suicide, abuse, and privation are all too close to the daily lives of many of these kids. Although many Lakota continue their age-old sense of *tiyospayé*, which includes protecting their young, in the twenty-first century, it seems they must expand the sense of caring and protection to include anyone that comes into their world.

This is what Dusty has always done. Now that he's no longer coaching, however, Dusty thinks less about bridging the world between hoops and spirituality; instead, his "work" has become increasingly about his ceremonial life, which he believes will make his transition to retirement smoother. When I wondered aloud what his kids did for a living, he answered in terms of their ceremonial work as well, but with the comment that they rarely see payment for it. "They're all workin, but as far as really making something. . . ." For LeBeau, work is making money to live on; but ceremonial work is labor that really counts.

Together with his wife Theresa, who died in 2006 after a battle with cancer, Dusty raised eight kids. He coached them all—four boys and four girls. He even coached his grandson in 2014. LeBeau's family is never very far away. It's the Lakota *tiyospayé* hallmark—those tight kinship bonds. "We got the one son who's the spiritual leader round here," he explained. "Another one sings. For a while, we were building sweats almost every night. . . . Oh yeah, I'd be doing other things like basketball, but that [ceremonies] is real important to me." Dusty said he felt like he's at a point in life where he's no longer balancing these two areas, but rather intentionally choosing one over the other. "I said that I'd walk away if you try to tell me that I can't do this or tell me how to live my life. 'Cause that [spirituality] is my family, my health. Our family helped a lot of people."[48]

In summary, to understand how basketball acts as a conductor for Lakota traditional culture, one must look at Dusty LeBeau. He isn't just an amalgam of coach and spiritualist; in taking the role of coach to include mentoring, nurturing, and protecting, Dusty has also fused the desire to win state championships with the long-established Lakota virtues of parenting and teaching. Making sure that a player is fed and has a secure place to sleep is the foundation to teaching that kid to be a better basketball player. Giving them the psychological wherewithal to deal with adversity and avoid bad choices makes them better players; and teaching them humility and reverence for all things makes them better Lakota. Good coaches in Lakota Country are good Lakota in coaching country.

3

The Lakota
Nation Invitational

Bryan Brewer's
"Invented Tradition"

Like the nearby Badlands buttes, Bryan Brewer can look different depending on the angle of the sun and time of day. With his glasses on and listening, he can look like a professor. In profile, with his long, graying hair, he might look like an aging warrior. And with his grin, he can look like a classic trickster. On this day, however, he looked piqued. The easy smile and engaged voice that makes Bryan Brewer so well known in Lakota Country would occasionally slip away, but then he'd quickly rebound with a joke.

"Alan, you know who Dave Strain is, right?" he asked me in one such instance, then went on before I could answer. "He's well liked in Indian Country because he played our boys when other white coaches wouldn't. One time, he had a reporter keep asking him what his offensive strategy was, and Dave was getting tired of it, so he just said, 'I use a 3-2 offense.' The reporter looked at him and asked him if he meant a 3-2 defense [there is no offense called 3-2]. 'Nope,' said Dave. 'What's a 3-2 offense?' the reporter asked. Dave said, 'Three Lakota and two Chippewa [another tribe].'"[1] The gleam in Bryan's eyes reemerged.

Bryan should have been taking it easy, as he was only three weeks past a heart attack, but for forty-two years now, mid-December has been his "shine time"—the Lakota Nation Invitational (LNI)—and with it always came the pressure to rise to the occasion.

"I'll take it easy after it's over," he promised. No one really believed him.

The most comprehensive cultural basketball fair in the region, the LNI requires oversight by a team of experts, but Bryan who created the LNI runs it as if it were a kiosk. It's exhausting even to watch. As I walked through the Rapid City Civic Center with him, he got stopped every minute by some well-wisher whom he greeted personally and respectfully. His cell rang nearly nonstop as people called him with logistical questions about events two days out. And then with the phone still to his ear, he stopped a bunch of kids who were getting rowdy, bouncing small basketballs around in a reckless manner.

"Come here!" he pointed to one of the boys. "Let me see that ball. You can't be bouncing this off of the walls. This isn't a gym. Where'd you buy this?" After being told, Bryan made a mental note to himself out loud to talk with the vender about overinflating the balls for sale. "We had to pay eleven hundred dollars in fees last year for broken lights and other things," he explained to me. Talk about attention to detail![2]

In Lakota Country, the Brewers are a well-known family (his branch of the Brewers are part of the Thunder Hawk *tiyospayé*). In his seventy years, he's worn almost every hat I can think of at Pine Ridge—from tribal president to teacher, coach, and spokesperson for veterans—but his most remarkable role was in building the LNI. Few ever get to claim that they created an enduring cultural institution acknowledged both among one's people and by outsiders. In contrast to the hardships that haunt Lakota Country, the LNI radiates excitement, community spirit, and pride. Bryan Brewer did that with two cofounders, but mostly by himself, carefully, respectfully, and well.

Each year, for four days in mid-December, the heart and soul of the tribe is transplanted from reservations all over the Dakotas to Rapid City's Rushmore Convention Center for the LNI. In this cavernous building, thousands of Lakota gather to watch the premier basketball tournament of the region and to celebrate their identity through a massive cultural fair. Lakota and Dakota high schools from all nine reservations in the state send their boys and girls to compete for the bragging rights of being the best in the nation. Other tribes are also selected to compete, as is the white team from Custer, South Dakota (ironically named). Only at the state championship tournament does the caliber of basketball played exceed that at the LNI. And a blinding array of Lakota nonsporting events has also grown up around the tournament, sharing its space, amplifying the sense that this event is about much more than sports: it's about Lakota celebrating who they are.

The "contest" is the dominant theme of this cultural fair, whether it's in basketball, traditional dancing, one-act plays, Lakota language, or any of the dozens of other events. An equally important theme is the blend of tradition and modernity. Over its four decades, the LNI has sought to incrementally add traditional Lakota events, which has not been a simple task, but the result has been a seamless integration into contemporary life. LNI attendees seem to flow easily between contemporary expressions of Lakota life and old-time enactments. So, for instance, center court at halftime during basketball games is an occasion to enact tradition by lauding the winners with an Olowan Song Fest or holding a somber Wiping of Tears ceremony. On the other hand, traditional events that take place have a sense of being contemporary. When the timeworn hand game is played, for example, participants display high-fives and even a touch of trash talk rather than performing as if they are involved in a static museum re-creation. Basketball, on the other hand, feels as though it's been part of Lakota culture since the buffalo-hunting days.

Origins

As the face of the LNI, Bryan has crafted an event by, at various times, thinking like a Lakota, a coach, a disciplinarian, and a marketing guru. Originally, in 1975, in an era of turmoil when normal basketball competitions were judged to be too dangerous, he and fellow coach Dave Archambault at Little Wound High School began brainstorming ways to get their teams involved in quality games. Red Cloud School Superintendent Chuck Cuny joined in on these discussions. In short order, Brewer, Cuny, and Archambault created the foundation of the LNI; the latter two would move on to other things, leaving Bryan to tend to the event. For over forty years now, Bryan has nurtured it, training it to grow into something substantial, mature, and a bit different than what he and his colleagues initially envisioned.

You really couldn't find three better prepared men to get this going in the thicket that is reservation politics and pettiness. Normally, lack of vision, a legacy of failure, and ineptitude threaten to derail any proposal. But basketball is something that Pine Ridgers need to see played, so there's a social impetus working to see it continue, regardless of the obstacles. Bryan was well suited to meet the challenge as well. He bucked one trend prevalent at Pine Ridge when he got an education, first at Holy Rosary, then at Pine Ridge High School. Two and a half tours of duty in Vietnam as a Navy Seabee disciplined him further, plus gave him a sense of how he, as a Lakota, fit into global patterns. So, when he finally returned in 1976 and completed a degree at Black Hills State University, he was primed to return to Pine Ridge as an educator. Having played varsity basketball, Brewer would also take on the role of coach. Brewer was teaching in Montana when his wife's father took ill, so they returned to South Dakota, where he quickly got a job at Red Cloud School. While he appreciated what people were trying to do at the school, he was a Pine Ridge Thorpe at heart, so as soon as an opportunity presented itself, he jumped over and had a long career there. As coach, he was responsible for putting together each year's basketball schedule, a chore made nearly impossible in the early 1970s.

Fast-forward to December 2018. As I watched the quarter-finals being played in 2018, the announcer used a time-out to broadcast to the crowded arena: "Folks, I'm happy to let you all know that NBA legend Bill Russell has just come into the house." The crowd roared approval. Former WNBA star of the Sacramento Monarchs, Ruthie Bolton, was also attending, as was a delegation traveling all the way from Russia. To anyone unfamiliar with the event, these kinds of visitors would validate a sense of long-lived success for the LNI.

Its roots, however, are much more modest. In the aftermath of the upheaval caused by the 1973 AIM takeover of the town of Wounded Knee at Pine Ridge, a civil war wracked the reservation, causing most normal activities to cease or be altered—including basketball, recalls Bryan. "The community split between those who supported AIM and those who didn't. No one wanted to play any of our schools because of the violence. We couldn't get a full schedule. None of us on the reservation could."[3] Bryan Brewer, then teaching and coaching at Pine Ridge High School, together with Little Wound's Archambault and Red Cloud's Cuny, responded by creating the All Indian Tournament in 1977 with eight teams. It worked—bringing in teams from outside Pine Ridge and slowly getting people elsewhere to think of the event as being stable enough to play at.

What was going on at Pine Ridge was also being felt among some of the state's white leadership, primarily Governor George Speaker Mickelson, who pushed for racial reconciliation during his term of office (1989–1993). Though the olive branch offered by Brewer and Cuny to white South Dakota was tentatively taken, most whites remained dubious. Public sentiment held that Pine Ridge was the most dangerous place in the state and should be avoided, but that sentiment merely masked a deeper, century-old racial hostility toward Indians. Crossing that divide, however, was basketball coach Larry Luitjens, at all-white Custer High School, and Dave Strain, at Rapid City Central High—the first white coaches to sign on. Luitjens showed no hesitation at all in accepting the invitation to have his kids play.

"Indian people will always appreciate that about Larry," says Brewer. "They have a great deal of respect for him and his teams."[4] Luitjens recalls how it all happened:

> Chuck Cuny and Bryan Brewer called and said they were short a team in the All Indian Tournament. That's what they called it at the time. And they said, "Would you like to come?" And I said, "Yeah, that would work out really well in our schedule." And so, we started. And, uh, were the kids a little nervous the first time we went over there? Probably were. We didn't talk about it. I just said, "Hey, you'll get in a situation where you probably won't have a lot of people in the stands cheering for you. You know, it'll be good for you." But they really grew to respect the kids, and the kids grew to respect the Natives. And I think, eventually, it was a great deal for the Custer kids, to get a chance to get down there and see, "Hey, these are basketball players. They're not Natives and whites playing. These are basketball players, and if you don't strap it up, you're going to be in trouble."[5]

Whites like Larry Luitjens are all too rare in South Dakota. His racial views were the product of having lived around Indian people in the Sisseton Sioux area and having parents who pushed a more tolerant view of folks than most. For him, it was always about "strapping it up," because if you didn't play against the best, you wouldn't be among the best. So, bringing in Custer to the tournament was good for all concerned. Brewer and Luitjens both knew this.

"Bryan and I have talked about it a lot of times," says Luitjens. "And Bryan says, 'Well, I didn't do this for reconciliation.' He said he did it for basketball. We feel the same way. And Bryan and I are really good friends."[6]

Eventually, Brewer and Cuny decided to abandon the all-Indian identity of the tournament and go for something more inclusive. One reason was because they recognized that resistance to having a mixed-race tournament wasn't all white. There were those on Pine Ridge who also resented having a white presence in what they felt was their tournament. Bryan recalled, "So Chuck said, 'Why don't we call it the Lakota Nation Invitational, and we can invite white teams?' End of story."[7] And it was the beginning of the most successful cultural event in the state.

What's the Tournament Mean?

Everyone I met in the Lakota basketball universe insisted I go to the LNI. "It's amazing—not like anything you've seen," insisted Laura Big Crow in a sentiment echoed by all. Jesse Heart told me that if I went to only one basketball event, it should be the LNI. As a result, when I finally went for the first time in 2016, I expected to see a tournament filled with top college prospects and Division 1 coaches. When I walked inside, I had to reorient myself. The tournament had more than a few good players, some of them worthy of Division 1 interest, but the LNI was more about Indian basketball: primarily by and for Native people. I quickly realized what makes the LNI incomparable: unlike elite Nike or Adidas league teams that draw players from all over the country to staff their teams, LNI teams are reservation-based high school teams built on a base of small tribal enrollments in an underpopulated state. It's Lakota focused.

Talented teams and individuals could be found there, but a high skill level would reflect particular years when good cohorts existed. In 1987, the Boys Class A state champions were from Pine Ridge High School. In 2016, the Winnebago tribe's team, and Lakota teams from Little Wound and Red Cloud were very good.

There were more than a few really skilled players as well back in 2016. Winnebago's senior, Dave Wingett, and a fifteen-year-old from Pine Ridge High School, Corey Brown, were a pleasure to watch. At six foot and seven inches, Wingett dominated the tournament, scoring from any place on the court. Averaging 29 points per game in 2015, Wingett was just too talented to be stopped, and later he would go on to be recruited by University of Memphis. At six foot two, Brown was such a package of strength and skill that he could play in the post, both scoring with a beautiful fade away and out rebounding guys considerably taller than he.

From the girls' teams, Janay Jumping Eagle, a senior guard at Little Wound High School, was one hardnosed player. She, too, could score in a range of ways, but she played a physically punishing defense as well. The girls at Little Wound won it all with a balanced team that could rebound, handle the ball, and shoot. In other years, one might find D1 basketball supernovas such as SuAnne Big Crow or Jesse Heart.

And almost each year, new girls and boys surge to the surface of our attention with breathtaking performances. In 2018, a young girl from White River, Caelyn Valandra-Prue, was mesmerizing to watch. Even White River's quarter-final loss in a hard-fought contest showcased Caelyn's performance. Having played varsity basketball since she was in eighth grade, Caelyn had a preternatural feel for the game. Her passing and court vision were mature beyond her years. She could score in a variety of ways, and she was hardnosed, willing to dive into the stands, if necessary, to get the ball. She is also one of the most accomplished runners in the state.

In the LNI, while the athleticism was there, the size and length were not. Aside from Wingett, no one was going to elite programs like Kentucky or even to mid-major college programs. A good number of players could, however, be successful at the D2 and D3 levels. Regardless, skill level is a poor way to measure the LNI. The LNI is about pitting the best Lakota teams against each other for local bragging rights. It draws its fire and excitement from its tribal-boundedness in the same way that other local rivalries do. In Boston collegiate hockey, for instance, Boston University, Harvard, Boston College, and Northeastern University meet each February for the Beanpot Tournament. These are good hockey teams, but with the exception of Boston University, none of them is expected to vie for a national championship. Indeed, at Beanpot time, national championships fade from view as local college fans focus all of their attention on the two Mondays when these games are played. Beanpot, like the LNI, is not looking "outward," seeking approval from D1 coaches or even a national audience; rather, it is about looking "inward" to generate competitive zeal and a common sense that they are all Boston institutions. Likewise, the LNI is a closed universe. In short, the basketball being played at the LNI is solid, but what makes it pop is the local meaning—the stories and legends and classic games being played that resonate among the six Lakota reservations in the state.

Facing Outward

Despite being crafted, performed, and consumed primarily by and for Lakota, the LNI does have an outward-looking face. In South Dakota, in some way, it seems whites are forever watching and judging Lakota, always ready to have their least generous views of Indians confirmed. Former McLaughlin High coach, Hank Taken Alive, contends that the LNI has a job to do in this, saying, "Our battle is to beat the stereotype of the drunken Indian and to be recognized and treated as equal citizens of this country."[8]

Taking place in Rapid City, the LNI becomes a cultural satellite—one hundred miles from the rez, smack dab in the middle of a white city. LNI's footprint makes it impossible for non-Indians to ignore, but this conspicuousness is understood in many places as semi-intrusion. Indian-white relations in South Dakota being what they are, the geniality presently enjoyed between the city council, business community, and the Lakota remains a bit too formal—perhaps even contrived—due in large part to the history between the races.

What has paved the way for Rapid City's acceptance of Lakota is the economic boom that comes with LNI's thousands of visitors. Lakota journalist Tim Giago noted this when he wrote about the LNI, saying, "But the *ka-ching* of the cash registers in the restaurants, theaters, retail stores, and shopping malls in Rapid City bring that Christmas cheer to the local businesses and that alone can put a smile on the face of the grumpiest store owner."[9] The thousands of visitors coming in are frequenting local businesses and doing so at a time when the city's economy needs it most. During the summer, tourism is what drives Rapid City economics, but by December, merchants are desperate to find sales. The LNI is the antidote to these out-of-season economic woes, and this means that white attitudes toward the Indian presence there has to change.

White reluctance to genuinely accept the LNI, particularly by the police, was echoed in Bryan Brewer's quip about the difference in how police treated Pine Ridgers. "When we first started coming to Rapid City, we used to have to sneak in," Brewer said. "It was hard coming, and we had to break down barriers. We used to have the police escort us out of town, but now they escort us into town."[10]

What this tournament means to the city is an annual revenue stream in excess of $6 million, resulting in a willingness of sorts to work against racial slights. In the 2005 LNI tournament, a racist incident occurred that illustrated this newfound Indian respectability. Brewer related the incident as follows:

> Jessie Mendoza, the coach over at Eagle Butte went into a restaurant with his boys and they refused him service. He called me up: "Bryan, they won't serve us here!" I called the mayor immediately. He came racing to the Civic Center with his staff members, picked me up, and went right to that restaurant. He was boiling, and we've never had a problem since. But if that incident had happened ten years earlier, nothing would have been done about it.[11]

And the revenue LNI brings to local businesses translates into influence. Even problems endemic to Indian Country involving law enforcement have played out differently because of such influence. "We had problems with the highway patrol and especially during the LNI," Brewer said. "So, we had a big meeting in Rapid City, and it stopped. Same with the sheriff's department. They were coming into the LNI looking for people with warrants on them. They don't do that at Sturgis Motorcycle Classic [the biggest motorcycle gathering in the country at Sturgis, South Dakota], and you'd find plenty of warrants there. So, we raised hell about that, and they stopped that too!"[12]

"More and more, doors are opening to us with non-Indians. We do have some power because of our money," Brewer concludes. At a breakfast held by the LNI board for Rapid City's chamber of commerce, a spokesperson for the mayor's office gushed about what an important event this was for the region, saying, "and let's not forget, it's always about the kids." And in what seemed to be a spirit of long-needed reconciliation, the spokesman mentioned Bryan Brewer's story about having to sneak into the city back when he'd first started the LNI, ending the anecdote by saying they are now feted. Among the Lakota in the room, there was an invisible raising of the eyebrows at the disingenuous sense that this breakfast attested to anything more than the beginning of real healing for the state's race relations.[13]

Facing Inward

By the third year of the LNI's existence, the numbers of people it was drawing in proved too much for the Pine Ridge gym. "We had the fire marshal out threatening to shut us down," Brewer recalled.[14] In 1979, they moved their venue to Rapid City's newly opened Rushmore Civic Center. Both of its sport arenas, as well as most of its smaller breakout venues, are used for the many competitions that now comprise the LNI. "The Rushmore," as it is locally referred to, is an unimaginative structure that was built in 1978 with function foremost in mind. There's a wide interior square corridor connecting everything. This boulevard contains a food court and wide swaths along which one may place venders of all kinds, and the LNI fills the spaces. There are artists and agencies offering products and services of interest to Indians, ranging from "land buy-back" programs to military recruiters; from disability-awareness programs to Lakota language-proficiency lessons; and from nutrition-promotion services to alcohol treatment programs. Kitty-corner to each other are the two main arenas: the ice arena and Rushmore Hall, the concert venue arena. Both are used for LNI basketball events.

More recently, in the wake of the incident in Rapid City, in which a group of Lakota children were racially harassed while attending a hockey game, many Lakota urged Bryan Brewer to begin thinking about moving the tournament away. It was by no means a simple thing to consider, as LeBeau pointed out: "You know, to me the LNI is everything to the kids playing in it and even the little ones watching. Bryan talked about movin' that tournament 'cause of 'the incident.' My grandson said, 'Grandpa, don't move it. I wanna play at the Civic Center.'" How many dreams would we destroy if we moved it to a place like Sioux Falls? All these kids are gonna lose out 'cause of some white men?"[15]

Lakota Spaces

Before getting to Rushmore Civic Center, I wondered whether the Lakota could make the soul-less convention center their own. The notion of cultural space, which is so central to the Lakota, takes much of its meaning from their connection to their land, and this connection not only frames major rituals like the Sun Dance; it inscribes them. So, how would the dancing, singing, and drumming in the *wacipi* ever come off as authentic in a large, characterless event room two-thirds the size of a football field? The cinder-block walls were painted some nondescript color, and the light—so important and breathtaking on Pine Ridge—was replaced with rectangular panels of hideous florescent yellow. There were two stands facing each other, adding to the confusion of what was supposed to happen in this place. What a soul-crushing place for a cultural event of any kind!

Yet it was the B-side, the nonsporting side, of the LNI that both transfixed me and not only kept the Lakota spirit intact throughout the event but also helped that spirit shine through the physical spaces of the center. Though there was a spatial divide—with hoops on the courts and everything else in the center's broad boulevards—altogether, this was a renaissance-like fair of everything that the Lakota were proud of and concerned about. It was at various times gripping, thought-provoking, informative, and jovial. Sometimes it was a feast for the eyes. Basketball may have been the centerpiece of the four-day celebration, but by this time, the LNI had grown to include wrestling, chess, and the traditional Lakota hand game as well. It also included a healthy dose of academic events, including a "knowledge bowl," a science contest, Lakota business plans, traditional Lakota language contests, and plays.

Walking around, people could stop and chat with those manning the tables about all manner of things related to rez life. There were vendors trying to get Lakota back into school and some recruiting tribal police. There were organizations touting services for everything from addiction to elder care. You could stop by the table selling Lakota language courses on tape and have a conversation about teaching Lakota language to schoolchildren. There was a table selling Lakota-themed reproduction postcards from the 1930s, where I talked with a woman who claimed that her return to a traditional buffalo-based diet had helped her with a myriad of health problems. She insisted I sample some of her *wasna* (dried buffalo, pounded with fat and chokecherries), and others quickly joined me in the taste-testing.

In addition, Lakota art, both traditional and modern, was on display. Artists and T-shirt vendors infused the dimly lit corridors with color, whether from clothing, crafts, or paintings for sale. An array of arts and crafts by tribes like the Lower Brulé Sioux and Diné provided wonderful splashes of color. T-shirts representing the various LNI schools were being printed and sold, and it seemed that everyone around was sporting their team's colors. One Pine Ridge artist, Quincy Maldonado, had latched on to a traditional Lakota artform called "ledger art," giving it a modern interpretation. When first settling on reservations in the late nineteenth century, the Lakota no longer had access to the buffalo robes that they had always used as canvases for their paintings. All they were able to get were pages from ledgers in stores; and so, they painted their pictures over the distinctive backdrop of dates, figures, and other entries. Now, Quincy paints on them as well, but he uses modern themes, such as a memorial of the Wounded Knee massacre or the LNI logo. While trying to make a living as an artist, he also sees himself as an educator of sorts. "A lot of people don't know our history—even our own people—so I can teach them through my drawings."[16]

A large room brimming with drumming, excitement, and high-fives was the site of the traditional hand game (a kind of ancient ice-breaker gambling game that trading partners engage in), and it seemed that as many kids were competing here as in the basketball tournament. In this game, high school teams of six would face off, and one person at a time would come forth, hiding a marked bone in one hand, and a clear one in the other. Then, in a version of the street hustler's shell game, in which the hand is quicker than the eye, this person would try to throw off the competition, deftly disguising hand moves while their teammates attempted to distract the opponents with songs and hand moves of their own. Each team had sixteen sticks and with every correct guess the correct guessing team claimed one of the opponent's sticks. The game ends when you have all of your opponent's sticks. (When he first introduced this contest at LNI, Bryan had to have older adults sing the songs because the kids didn't know them, but as its popularity grew, so did the young people's desire to learn the songs, and eventually the kids were singing on their own.)

And then there was dancing. Even before I walked into the Rushmore Civic Center, I was met by the haunting sounds of Lakota drumming and singing seeping out into the cavernous corridors. Once inside, I stood along the back wall just in time to hear the announcer say it was time for the "Jingle Dress Competition." Jingle dresses are formal and exceptionally beautiful, made up of a seemingly limitless combination of materials (satins, beads, sequins, leathers), and the women who design them are fiercely committed to putting together explosions of color and patterns. But the hallmark of these dresses is the curled, tubular 1- to 2-inch pieces of metal (which used to be the tops of snuff cans) sewn across swathes of the dress. They are sewn close enough to each other that when the woman dances, the dress jingles.

The dozen women dancing were competing for honors, and as they entered the center of the floor, families and friends cheered and ululated in the way that generations of Lakota women have egged on their champions. The dresses were luminescent—a perfect antidote to the dull walls of the room—and the women capped off both ends of their dresses, with gorgeous beaded moccasins and leggings underneath, and eagle-feather fans in their hands, which they waved above their heads in lovely flight-like motions.

Round 1 commenced when one of the five different drum groups began their other-worldly beat. Five to six men sitting in a circle around a large base drum covered with hide were pounding in slow, four-beat rhythmic sequence that seemed to overtake you with its baseline. Then one of the drummers changed the cadence to be between the beats, elevating the effect into a baseline at once eternal and unexpected. Next, singers entered suddenly and dramatically, with surprisingly high-pitched vocals that intersected with the low tones of the drums. This seemed to quicken the pulse in both listeners and dancers, and it was at this point that the women began to dance with short, quick foot movements. Legs are de-emphasized in this dance, where all the motion is from the knees down, almost like a Lakota version of River Dance.

Almost all of the women were young, displaying that boundless energy that seems to strain against the confines of this kind of dance. Because of these short hopping motions, their dresses bounced slightly, and in so doing the jingles . . . jingled.

It was a wonderful display of Lakota beauty and elegance, but one dancer particularly captured my attention. Her dress was blue sateen—less visually complex than the others, but she wore it well—it fit like a glove without pandering to her femininity. The jingles were sewn in regular rows, and she wore her hair pulled back in a braided ponytail. Two eagle feathers rose straight at the back of her beaded headband. But it was her dancing that mesmerized me. Her steps were staccato and precise but intricate at the same time, as if she had added a half step or two to the conventional moves. Then she raised her eagle feather fan and, as she gracefully swooped it, her body flowed in sync with the fan. It was like watching a flock of birds simultaneously changing direction—at once fluid and precise—and I couldn't think of a more alluring performance of Lakota womanhood: dignified, understated, yet dazzling.

Those attending gathered, talked, ate, and enjoyed their time in this setting, rich with Lakota culture. Older guys argued whether Jesse Heart or Willy White was the best Lakota baller ever. Friends who hadn't seen each other in some time met over lunch. Without this infusion of Lakota social and cultural content, the thousands of attendees would be standing around between events, perhaps even leaving early. As such, these vendors were a kind of social scaffolding, holding things in place between basketball competitions. But they were also integrated into the games, as event winners were publicly lauded during halftimes, where the largest crowds would be found. Little Wound star Janay Jumping Eagle was honored there, being voted South Dakota Athlete of the Week for scoring her one thousandth point and for displaying commitment to her community and school. A star quilt was draped over her shoulders, which is a traditional sign of respect for one's accomplishments.

All in all, the transformation of space from bleached, nondescript aesthetics into an arresting, vibrant Lakota spectacle was the part of the LNI that impressed upon me the most. Certainly, the fortieth annual event had matured into a wonderful blend of athletics, academics, and games, with a whole that was greater than the sum of its parts. It was a masterful and compelling cultural statement, as the arena effortlessly breathed Lakota life.

Performing Hoops

High school basketball and the LNI version of it stand as the apex for many on the reservation. Lakota coach Dusty LeBeau said it the best: "This is kinda like their career. We had some kids who went on to college and played, but for the majority of kids around here, high school ball is like their Final Four, their big thing."[17]

Where a talented white player might enjoy his or her high school career but envision greater playing days ahead, Indian high school ballers typically don't. Their "glory days" occur as teens. They peak at eighteen, and then what follows is too often disappointment. Against this contrast, the LNI, and high school basketball in general, appear to shine even more brightly. For instance, you'll see spectators walking around the LNI wearing sweatshirts proclaiming what they were once a part of: "Thorpes—1987 Champions—26-0." And they never moved beyond that accomplishment. They didn't have to because they were valorized forever.

As a result, games can feel more like performances. The five hundred players and coaches from the thirty-two teams at the event are, in essence, playing not only against each other but also in front of each other, making it all that more important to give a good performance. And the accompanying cultural festival and rituals make an even more striking pageant, drawing a large number and broad range of Lakota to watch.

Further, in some sense, a player's performance might extend beyond the court. Modern Indian hoopsters, who draw their influences from the NBA and the world of hip-hop, often wear oversized shorts resplendent with color and tribal markings, along with tats and lineups. And all the while, hip-hop is blaring on the loudspeakers as a kind-of soundtrack to the event.

Despite appropriating a black style of basketball, however, there's a distinctly Lakota (or Indian) edge to the way the game is played. Indian Country has adapted this sport to what life is like on reservations across the country. As such, "rez ball" has become a uniquely Indian style of play, known for its speed and constant movement up and down the court. The high degree of athleticism in this approach may tempt one to think that Indians are mimicking the black game, but there are differences. First, the tempo at which they play is beyond upbeat. The only speed is all-out run-and-gun. This differs considerably from the black game in that Indians racing down court seem to have an uncanny peripheral view of the game that allows the ball to move around at warp speed. Second, for Lakotas, there is no ghetto "iso-ball"—(*iso* standing for isolation), which focuses on one person's effort to score past his defender. Rather, the emphasis is team play: pass first, find the open player, crush the defense, and do so all at a top speed.

Nothing Says Lovin' Like the Grand Entrance

Nowhere was Lakota pageantry more visually commanding than the Grand Entrance. Evoking comparisons to the Olympics, each team's contingent of athletes in school uniforms, along with tribal leaders, snaked onto the court to the sound of drums. The idea for the grand entrance started as a casual suggestion, Brewer recalled. "So, someone said, 'Let's have a grand entrance just like the powwow,' and two dancers from St. Francis (a school on Rosebud Reservation) asked to lead it. I said, 'Sure,' and that was the first cultural part of the LNI."[18]

The lights are dimmed at the main arena at the Rushmore, and a spotlight shines on the corner of the court where people will enter. It's a bluish-white light, kind of specter-like, creating a feeling of being part of something large made more real by the drums' four-beat syncopation. The procession might begin with a traditionally garbed Lakota dancer, with color guards, or with a senior LNI official, eagle-feather staff in hand, but whoever was leading was doing the slow, two-step shuffling that the drums demanded. Then singers started singing and more leaders entered, some dressed traditionally and wearing full headdresses. Next up might be LNI officials, who, on occasion, wore traditional outfits, but who usually preferred their LNI sport jackets. After them, the honored guests for the year came in. (In 2018, guests included basketball Hall of Famer Bill Russell, WNBA star Ruthie Bolton, and a Russian delegation involved in indigenous affairs in that country.)

The profusion of national, state, tribal, and military flags held by the color guard offered an interesting juxtaposition of Lakota feathers and shiny military helmets or fatigues. The dancers entered in their Lakota dresses, as did more traditionally dressed men. While most shuffled along to the drums, the younger girl dancers picked up the pace, dancing right to the edge of traditional notions of what is appropriate. The procession circled the outside of the basketball court, curling back in toward center as they completed a circuit, and then the teams began entering the arena. At that point, drums, loud and singing, filled the arena as the announcer called out each contingent: "Ladies and gentlemen, welcome the Crow Creek Chieftains!" Shouts, clapping, and ululation filled the air as each team in the tourney entered: Pine Ridge, Little Wound, St. Francis, Crazy Horse, and others. It was an impressive assembly.

There may be variations in the entry procession from year to year. In 2016, in the spot-lit corner where they all entered, a girl seemed to greet all of the entering athletes. I looked closer and saw her holding lit sweet grass. Those entering faced her briefly and then, with both hands, palms up, waved the smoke from the sweet grass toward their chest, their head, and then over their head. It was a smudging, meant to cleanse a person of any thoughts other than good ones. These ballers sauntered onto the court, all too cool, but then dropped their pretenses and embraced the act of smudging.

Finally, after the last team entered, the court was filled with players, old and young, Indian and white, Lakota and non-Lakota, in a sea of uniforms in wonderful blues, reds, greens, and other hues.

Before the opening tip-off, the LNI announcers joked with the crowd, often using Lakota expressions like, "*Hoka hey* [let's go], everybody!" (This was a traditional battle cry). The flag song was then sung, as was the national anthem. But the latter doesn't matter, just as the U.S. senator from South Dakota doesn't matter, and just as I don't matter. This was Lakota performing for themselves.

Wiping of the Tears

Finding opponents to play was behind the creation of the LNI, but Bryan Brewer and those close to him operated as if the even were an empty canvas—experimenting with various things and operating loosely.

"We're exposing our culture not only to non-Indians, but also to our own people. . . . A lot of our students aren't aware of our culture. When we had the first Wiping of the Tears [a centuries-old ritual], for many of the Lakota people, that was the first time they ever saw that ceremony."[19]

However educational the Wiping of Tears ceremony may have been, it was not accepted without criticism. A family experiencing the death of a loved one traditionally mourned for a year, during which time they assumed that the spirit of their loved one was not quite ready to move on to the Milky Way, or the afterlife. That period was called Ghost Keeping. At the end of that period, a formal ceremony occurred—the Wiping of the Tears—marking the end of the period of grief and sadness, allowing both the spirit of the deceased and those on earth to move on.

Brewer elaborated. "We started honoring Indian ball players that died. We talked to the families, and I was gonna have a little picture in the program commemorating them. Eddy Young Man Afraid of His Horses thought it'd be nice if we could have a Wiping of the Tears for players who died. It was odd, but that year we had a white player from Custer that got killed in a car wreck. So, we had a Wiping of the Tears for him and his family. They all came to it. It was nice."[20]

But, then the criticism began. Eddy Young Man Afraid of His Horses had become the *de facto* spiritual leader of the LNI and thereby the point man in these matters. When critics claimed, "The Wiping of the Tears is a private thing. We don't do it in public," Eddy would broker the cultural divide between critic-purists and the LNI version. "We explained to them that when all the teams come together, we are one family. When we have that ceremony, it's our *tiyospaye*. Everyone said, 'Yes, you're right.' So, that stopped the critics."[21]

In 2018, the family being celebrated was brought to center court to be seated while a holy man got ready to chant in Lakota. Before he started, he asked people (in English) to refrain from using their cameras out of respect for the mourners and to send their thoughts to the mourners to help them "move forward" following their period of grieving. The crowd was then directed to move in unison to the four directions. With so many people supporting the family, it couldn't help but heal.

A Great Coming Together

A Lakota man who was working one of the tables along the boulevard called the LNI "a great coming together." That analogy stayed with me. Historically, the only times the Lakota regularly gathered in large numbers across bands was for the annual Sun Dance or, more haphazardly, for war. Even then it was rare that more than a few of the seven council fires (as the distinct Lakota bands were referred to) would get together. At the Sun Dance, it was generally only two or three bands that gathered. Now, however, there were so many Sun Dances that congregating across tribal bands didn't really happen. The LNI, it was becoming clear to me, was the contemporary manifestation of this tribal-wide gathering—not religious, but still serving the same social function.

The traditional Sun Dance gathering was a complex logistical undertaking. There had to be an economic underpinning for people to gather in such large numbers. There had to be a place that could handle the crush of people and their horse herds. In the mid-nineteenth century, there were approximately 15,000 Lakota with horse herds of tens of thousands. An assembly of that size put a lot of stress on the land to support it.

Most importantly, it was the specific migratory patterns of the buffalo that restricted the list of possible places for these Sun Dance gatherings to occur. In later June to early July, the many herds began forming larger masses of animals in preparation for the rutting season, and since Plains Indians lived off of them, they too started gathering in larger numbers. The Sun Dance was the social testimony of Lakota as a unified people as well as a religious ceremony for all to take part in. Following the gathering of this mammoth body of people and herds, which might last for days, things turned solemn. Medicine men convened at the center of the gathering, and sun dancers with oaths to fulfill prepared for their ordeals. It was during this time that the most sacred rituals of the nation were celebrated. There were just too many Lakota to congregate in their entirety, but they did gather as aggregates of two or three bands, with numbers between three to five thousand. So, there might have been two or three Sun Dances total per year. Other than war, these were the widest expressions of Lakota social identity and cohesion.

By the 1880s, however, the buffalo were almost completely wiped out. Their economic base gone, and decades of warfare having taken a toll on life as they knew it, even the most reluctant bands were being forced onto reservations. To add to the social and cultural turmoil, Christian missionaries were pressing them to abandon their spiritual ways. Most of this effort was directed at Lakota children, who were herded into Indian boarding schools where they were prevented from carrying on their culture. It was the Sun Dance, with its bloody piercings, that came under the most criticism. White missionaries interpreted the ritual as pagan self-mutilation and argued that it should be repressed. By the late 1950s, practicing the Sun Dance had so dwindled that its future was at risk; but then came the 1960s era of social activism. In Indian Country, a newfound pride and refusal to tolerate social injustice was embodied in the American Indian Movement (AIM). As part of this movement, primarily made up of young urban Indians in need of connecting with their roots, AIM activists sought out the most traditional people on reservations. They wanted to know about sweat lodges and Sun Dances. On Pine Ridge, the Sun Dance not only resurfaced; it proliferated. Spiritual leaders arose with differing interpretations of the dance and other ancient rituals, so there might be fifty or more Sun Dances held throughout the summer. Some were sticklers for traditional practices: ceremonial objects, prayers, piercing. Others might allow whites to dance. Dusty LeBeau and his sons run a Sun Dance that discourages white attendance: "Round here people know it. It's called Thunder Valley. It's also one of the hardest. 'Boot camp of all Sun Dances' is what Vine Deloria [the Lakota author] called it."[22]

From a social capacity to once represent all Lakota, the Sun Dance has splintered into many events. It would be easy to argue that the LNI has stepped into that void, that it is *the* "great coming together." From a simple response to a problem of finding basketball teams to compete against, the LNI has matured to become a force in the cultural landscape of South Dakota. It might be tempting to argue that such is the power of sports, that it can impact life beyond the playing field, but that would be a vast overstatement. It might also be tempting to attribute all of this achievement to Bryan Brewer, but that too would more than is warranted. However, it isn't hyperbole to say that both the game of basketball and Bryan Brewer have presented the Lakota with a lasting cultural gift. Brewer and Cuny nurtured this tournament into its present form; and over forty years with an array of others who bolstered him, Brewer grew the event. This is too much of a task for any one man, and even though his prints are all over the LNI, Bryan would be the first to admit that. The growth of the LNI was the outcome of the joy that the Lakota everywhere felt by gleefully coming to it, competing in it, and sharing of it. And, it is grander than Bryan or anyone could have imagined. It is a great gathering, a social expression for all of the Lakota. That's how it succeeded.

It would be sacrilegious to argue that the LNI is equivalent of the Sun Dance. It is a powerful collective and individual religious rite that is the essence of their world. The LNI merely fills the role of being the largest, most complete social and cultural expression of Lakota culture that annually occurs. Every society needs something in its calendrical system that expresses its most collective persona, its sense of nation. Every society needs its holidays, and origin myths to give themselves a collective story of who they are. Currently split among six reservations, competing jurisdictions, and divided by the daily struggles, it is hard to come together as a people in one place at one time.

Even though the Lakota number only around 60,000—a fairly small population as entire societies go—Lakota Nation, like any nation, needs a cultural center to hold this population together. While there are kinship and marriage ties between different bands of Lakota, too few opportunities to connect exist, and those that are used are often short circuited by finances (e.g., broken-down cars, no gas money) or personal situations (poor health, being pulled in different directions), or factional dispute. There are no longer cross-cutting ties by *akicitas* (military fraternities) weaving together the whole of Lakota society. What usually binds people who don't really know each other together is what Benedict Anderson called, an "imagined community": cultural constructs (e.g., newspapers, society-wide rituals and holidays) designed to forge a common identity.[23] Regularly occurring major sporting events, and this tournament can be thought of in this regard. But it is Eric Hobsbawm's "invented tradition," that captures the LNI best- rituals and performances that look ancient but are of recent vintage.[24] Such events sear a common identity into its practitioners and devotees because they foster the feel that one is engaging in an age-old event that countless generations have also shared. These two constructions forge collective identities among people who might not know each other or are too spatially separate to be an easily viable grouping. That's what the LNI has been able to do for the Lakota. As Brandon Ecoffey reminds us, "Although it seems strange that our people have accepted the notion that a basketball tournament could, in fact, serve as the backdrop to one of our most vivid expressions of culture, identity, and sovereignty, an examination of the event is all that is needed to justify why it has come to encompass so much for us as Lakota people."[25] And, I should add that there is no other Lakota gathering as likely to attract to it dignitaries from Russia or the annals of NBA history. This event that started as a sporting endeavor, has evolved into something much greater, more satisfying to Lakota Nation. It is the "Great Coming Together," the pantheon of cultural expression both to the tribe as well as to the outside world. This is what I meant when I said Bryan Brewer accomplished something remarkable and rare. Not bad for a teen runaway from Holy Rosary Mission School.

4

Jesse Heart

Modern Lakota Warrior

When he played for Little Wound High School, Jesse Heart was the "anointed one." No Lakota athlete of his generation was more anticipated, expected, and awaited than he was. All over the reservation, people were certain that Jesse would be an impact player in D1 collegiate basketball and maybe even beyond. Bryan Brewer, captured the aura around Heart when he said, "He had a following. He'd get fans of other teams to applaud him—young white kids would come to watch him play. He was so charismatic that the girls would go crazy over him, players were in awe of him. Good-looking, tall and lean, he looked like the ultimate ball player. And, boy, could he play!"[1]

Yet, for all his promise, Jesse Heart managed only brief stints in junior college ball and never came close to earning a degree or playing in the biggest arenas. And when he failed to live up to the expectations of some of his fellow Oglala, coaches and opponents dismissed him as yet another Indian phenom who had disappointed. I'm going to argue that Jesse Heart of Potato Creek, South Dakota was actually a basketball success—that he was one of a few Indian ballers to have crafted a high-level playing career for twenty years. The key to my argument lies in Jesse Heart's willingness to pursue the game off the reservation and develop a life outside of Pine Ridge.

The reservation may be home, but it can also be one's prison. Leaving it has proven difficult for Jesse and most other Lakota, because the reservation doesn't easily relinquish its hold on you. It wants to continually pull you back. And as Heart's departure shows, any escape simultaneously rewards and punishes. In that it failed to make an impact in college, Jesse's hoops career was typical of that experienced by other rez ball players, but his career was also studded both with super exploits on the court and a high-handed disregard off of it. In an effort to grasp a context for comparison, I take a glimpse at basketball in the lives of two other men who played ball on Pine Ridge, Corey Shangreau, and Brandon Ecoffey, and additionally refer to others. While by no means an exhaustive study of men and basketball at Pine Ridge, this chapter does look closely at three Lakota men whom the game guided toward adulthood.

Jesse Heart

At thirty-eight, Jesse looks like a more filled-out version of the player he was in Little Wound High School in the late 1990s. Because he trains maniacally, the ravages of time and hard living haven't been visited on him. Jesse's six-foot-four, square-shouldered frame provides him with the perfect shooter's body, and he takes those "threes" as quickly and dangerously as a rattlesnake strike—except, unlike the snake, he can do it all day long. When Jesse is talking about something that excites him, he can get a slightly impish gleam in his eye. The mythic Lakota figure of Iktomé the trickster comes to mind. Iktomé is a deity who can alternately hurt and humor people, and though I've never seen any representations of the trickster, in watching Heart I feel he bears a kinship with him—playful yet a bit dangerous.

By the time he graduated Little Wound in 1999, Jesse Heart had lit up the South Dakota basketball firmament as one of the brightest stars of his generation. "His fluidity was unbelievable, and he had the ability to know where he was on the floor," said Fred Paulsen, coach of rival Custer High School. "I've seen a lot of basketball, but it seemed he played with a passion that was unbelievable."[2]

In the semifinal game of the state tournament his senior year, Heart scored 48 points before fouling out in overtime in a losing effort against De Smet

High. Even his fouling out of the game became the stuff of legend, with most Lakota claiming that the referees stole "yet another" game from this Indian team. Those 48 points were a tournament record at the time. All-State and All-Tournament honors followed, along with designation as a finalist in the state's most coveted honor: Mr. Basketball. His season's averages of 30 points, 12 rebounds, and 6 assists were outstanding enough to get him an honorable mention as a *USA Today* All-American.

He was lionized throughout the state, attracting the attention of D1 coaches who were generally wary of signing players off of the reservation.

Coaches whose teams competed against Jesse at Little Wound High School and others who once watched him play now shake their heads in disbelief. "I've talked to several coaches who think Jesse Heart was big-time," said one. "If Jesse had played four years of college basketball, he'd probably be known as one of the top five players who ever played in South Dakota," said another—a college coach who had tried to tap Heart's potential.[3]

Glass Ceiling on D1 Indian Prospects

Younger rez ball fans are probably familiar with the splash made in 2017 by University of Wisconsin standout Bronson Koenig, a member of Ho Chunk Nation who, in the summer of that year signed with the Milwaukee Bucks of the NBA—a first in Native basketball. What they may not know is how completely unlikely that was; even more, they probably don't know how problematic it has been to get D1 college coaches to seriously offer scholarships to top Indian talent—and for some time. Looking at NCAA data (which doesn't include tribal colleges), we see that Indian players too often transition to college poorly, and the best ones often not at all. Two of the most famous basketball players to ever play in Montana high school history (both Crow Indians), Elvis Old Bull and Jonathan Takes Enemy, typify this. Both were super novae, playing at different ends of the 1980s, and both should have played with high-level D1 teams. Both, however, succumbed to the psychological suffocation typically associated with a cultural cocktail that consists of the following: cultural myopia (discomfort in white settings); academic underpreparedness for college; and asphyxia born of both the close-knit Native family unit, which supports but holds on to you, and the mentality of the wider community, which desperately wants its own to succeed and fail at the same time.

Takes Enemy was a standout, able to do just about anything with a ball. He was a State Class-A MVP, All-State, Converse Basketball All-American. "He was as good a Native American player as I've ever seen," declared Kelvin Sampson a Lumbee Indian who coached basketball at the University of Houston. "But at seventeen, he had three kids and a drinking problem."[4]

He, and later Jesse Heart, were supposed to be the ones who made it. "That's what Native American kids needed; they needed him to make it," said Sampson of Takes Enemy.[5]

BYU brought Jonathan to campus, but the whiteness of the place and the size of the program unnerved the Crow. He just wanted to drop out and flee the pressure to succeed. A few days before the school year was to begin, one of his coaches at home talked him into entering Sheridan College, one of the most highly touted jucos (junior colleges) in the country. He lasted six games before quitting.

Elvis Old Bull, also a Crow from Montana, was a three-time All-State selection in the late 1980s. He scored 1,948 points, holds 16 school records (including 22 assists in one game, lest one think he's a selfish shooter), and took his team to three straight state championships—and he managed to do all of that while drinking heavily. At the end of his final championship run, he just stopped competing (except for in local games).

"He leads his team to the third state title, wins his third tournament MVP trophy, then simply stops going to school, wrote Gary Smith. "He watches his classmates graduate through eyes swollen from a car wreck from another night's drinking."[6]

Stories like these abound on just about every Plains Indian reservation. As a result, coaches tend to shy away from risking scholarships in these situations. "Well, I tried to work with Indians," said Herb Klindt, who coached at Rocky Mountain College from the 1930s through the 1960s, "I tried to keep them in college. But I got to a point where I just threw up my hands in disgust and gave up, and most of the other coaches did too."[7]

It's hard to get coaches to talk openly about why they neglect Indian talent, but in a *New York Times* article, Montana State University's former head basketball coach, Mick Durham, who recruited talent on the reservations, opined, "It seems like the reservation is their comfort zone more than it would be for an inner-city kid. To me, I just think they get the government checks, and they stay. I don't know. I guess it's the way they're raised." For his inappropriate candor, he was publicly rebuked and had to apologize to the Indian citizens of Montana. Still, in talking about comfort zones, Durham did address something valid: the psychological centeredness of being among one's own is something that many people seek to reclaim, but among Indians it is magnified by a stronger kinship system and by the guardedness they feel in being among whites.[8]

Comfort and reluctance to leave their families and friends is a push/pull phenomenon keeping many young people on the reservation. Protected at home, they are also kept at home. Durham noted, "With the inner-city kid, you hear it all the time: 'I want to get out of here.' You don't hear a Native American kid ever say that."

Coach Rick Sanchez, who played and coached at Alchesay High School on the Apache Reservation, noted another reason for the reticence Indian players had for leaving the rez: "It's sad. Instead of helping someone get out and make a name for themselves, we just pull them back in. It's like crabs in a bucket. They're trying to crawl out, but the one right behind it is pulling it down."[9]

Jesse Heart's Collegiate Days

Despite this, coaches just couldn't stop looking at Jesse Heart. After watching his game videos, Kansas State University visited Jesse with the intent of offering him a scholarship. They came to talk to the family and local coach but then examined his academic eligibility, and that's where talks stalled. To say that Jesse was a lackluster student would be kind. As a senior, he struggled in the classroom; that is, when he bothered to show up at all. It's a well-known strategy everywhere in sports that too many schools, communities, and families find it easier to take the path of "greased resistance"— to pay lip service to academic efforts while disproportionately rewarding athleticism.

Central Community College Coach Jack Gutierrez, though, was not deterred and came after Jesse. "When we recruited him, it was a nip-and-tuck whether he was even going to graduate. He didn't attend high school on a regular basis. But he was such a quality basketball player, they let him do whatever he wanted and that carried over to college."[10]

Even though, according to NCAA regulations, Jesse was academically ineligible for D1, wormholes exist. Theoretically, junior colleges are remote holding tanks where an athlete can be cached and prove himself academically worthy of transferring to the four-year school interested in claiming him. In reality, he can spend a year honing his athletic skills while paying scant attention to academic remediation—yet his GPA somehow invariably rises. So, in 2000, Jesse packed off to Platte, Nebraska to play with Central Community College. Jucos offer some of the country's best collegiate players who, often, are either academically ineligible for D1 or have been in D1, run afoul of their programs, and are looking for another chance (e.g., "Last Chance U" is a remarkable documentary series that looks at this same path by players of collegiate football). The epitome of such a student, Heart shone on the court against some of the top players in the country. He had 42 points in a game against Mid-Plains Community College and, at the end of the season, he scored 46 points (including 9 threes) in a game against Northeast Community College. In a qualifying game against United Tribes, his prodigious scoring (33 points) led his team to the National Junior College Athletic Association Tournament. Jesse exploded at the national tournament, setting a record with 10 threes one night, and following it up the next night with 11 threes against Baltimore County (Maryland) Community College, who went on to win the national championship. He was an All-Conference and All-Region selection after averaging over 20 points per game and hitting over 100 threes during the season for Central Community College. There was no doubt that Heart had the talent to play a high level of D1 basketball.

If all you get is the final line of his college experience at Central Community College, however, you'll read or hear that, after this breakout season, Jesse inexplicably just walked away. The team finished fourth in the national tournament—a powerful showing. It didn't have much of an impact on Jesse though. When they returned to Nebraska, it was just in time for spring break.

"Everyone went home for spring break, and then we didn't see him the rest of the semester," recalled Coach Gutierrez. "I'd call him up at home, and he'd say, 'Oh I don't have a ride.' He would have been a junior college All-American," the coach laments.[11]

Heart had his reasons—he had a girlfriend and new baby back at Pine Ridge. And after having the summer off to think about it, he decided to give college ball another try, this time at Northeast Community College in Norfolk, Nebraska (after he and a friend were offered scholarship support). That stay was even shorter, and if you get the short version, Jesse Heart quit while having to sit out his first semester because of his grades. In reality, however, he met another Lakota woman; and perhaps without basketball central to his mind, Jesse and his new sweetheart quickly got pregnant, and school receded from view. Second attempt; second failure.

In 2002, he tried once again to head to college, this time to Huron University, which had just been bought by the Cheyenne River Sioux Tribe and renamed Si Tanka (after the famous chief) University. The school would make national news when one of the basketball players contracted the HIV virus and knowingly passed it on to his girlfriend. In short order, three other students became infected, and the player was convicted and sentenced.

Jesse's decision to join was purely basketball-related, but again he couldn't quite motivate himself to meet the institution halfway—by just attending classes. One person closely associated with the school characterized Heart's attitude as, "Oh, I'm not going to do it [attend class]. I don't care how good I am or how good you think I am or what you think I can become."[12] Still, he might have squeaked through, as so many athletes do. This time, however, Jesse's departure was triggered by a preseason confrontation:

"We were down there chillin', gettin ready to start the season. I got into it with one of the captains of the team. We were in the middle of practice, and he made us run, and I wasn't running hard and not making time. And he's actin' like he's my father! He was gettin' mad and jumped in my face. I told him, 'You need to run too. What kind of 'leader' just stands there?"

It derailed his career right there. Either that team captain overstepped his authority or he didn't know how to deal with Indians from the reservation, but Jesse wasn't going to be motivated by that kind of approach. Being older than the other players and having a younger player confront him set off Jesse's street impulses.

"So, he got in my face," Jesse continued. "He shoulder-checked me, and I swung on him and tackled his ass. We got into it on the court. I went outside and waited for him. Coach came outside and said he ain't lettin' him come out and told me to go to my room. I went to sleep. Next morning, he kicked me out of school. Yeah, like that. And, I just went home."[13]

Writing about this incident, Stu Whitney of the *Argus-Leader* quoted Heart as saying, "I was doing pretty good there . . ." while at the same time admitting, "Me and the coach and my teammates weren't really getting along, so I just decided to quit."[14]

It is in this contradiction—his admitting to me that he'd been booted out of school but telling the reporter that he'd quit—that we should try to understand the very conflicted young man that Jesse Heart was. He was booted out of the school, but in a social and psychological sense, he'd also "quit." Whenever Heart said he was "bored," or "didn't get along," or wanted to "be around more Indians," those are all genuine feelings. The fact was, Jesse Heart wasn't really ready to attend college, and for two serious reasons: first, he wasn't ready to live off of the reservation; and second, though he's smart, he had neither the interest in nor the skills associated with formal education. The pressure weighed on him.

"When you become a senior, they just start pounding you like, 'Where are you going to college?'" he said. "They don't prepare you for the stuff you'll go through in college, so that made it a lot harder. I never felt like I was ready."[15]

He was ready for playing, however. Sadly, for him, a career in basketball involved only brief but successful stays in college. The European pro leagues, so popular with good players today, were not known to Jesse.

The Plainzmen

Jesse Heart played at the "next level," and he played for a length of time that would constitute "a career." Following his failed collegiate attempts, Heart briefly signed a contract with the XBA Rookie All-Star Team, comprised mostly of NCAA D1 and D2 players. They competed against Midwest universities like University of North Dakota and Minnesota State at Moorhead. Heart stayed only briefly, but there too he shone—for instance, scoring 12 points in nine minutes against North Dakota. What is clear is that Jesse Heart had the ability to play basketball at almost any level.

After a year, he left for "the circuit"—a network of all-Indian tournaments that pays out cash prizes and attracts the best Indian players in the country. Jesse has continued to play for the circuit ever since; he has been with the Plainzmen for years. Most reservation high school players are lucky to have played regularly on the varsity team, and a precious few go on to a bit of D3 college ball. But for a player of Jesse's caliber, although his collegiate "career" crashed and burned on takeoff, there were always other opportunities.

The Cattaraugus Community Center located in western New York is the social hub of the Seneca Nation. It's on par with modern, fully equipped community centers around the country, and early in November the center hosted the annual Basil Williams Memorial Tournament. The Plainzmen were one of the "ringer" teams that always came to this All Indian Tournament, and as such, they were expected to compete for the championship. Along with several other nationally competitive teams, the Plainzmen roam the country, usually playing each other in the final round.

Today, coming onto the court sporting lime-green uniforms (one of several they have), with their team name emblazoned over a feathered headdress, they moved with "swag." This was a seasoned kinesiology of players who had logged a lot of miles and minutes, both together and alone. In basketball age, they were "getting long in the tooth." Ranging from their late twenties to mid-thirties, the Plainzmen had put on some heft since their college-playing days, and since they no longer practiced and conditioned as they once did in school, they were a step slower. Their basic skills had not eroded, however, and they could shoot, dunk, play a tough defense, and pass with the best of them. Leave Jesse Heart or Austin Kirkie undefended, and it was, as they say, "a wrap."

Malcolm Moore was more of a presence down low than he had been as a college kid. Jim Archambault could find the open man as well as ever. And should an opposing team have younger and more lean players, the Plainzmen would "body" them—or physically push them out of the way.

Jesse Heart did some of this in their first game. Playing the aggressive defense that's a hallmark of rez ball, he knocked the ball out of the opponent's hand and sprinted to the basket on a steal. The step or two he initially had on the defender disappeared, and sensing that, Jesse stopped on a dime at the three-point line, shooting the ball in a perfect arc for the basket. Embarrassed, the man who had the ball stolen from him sprinted hard, determined to stop the dunk.

"He caught me just past mid-court." Jesse smiled. "But I hit the [three-point] line, and it was over."

After the Plainzmen made short work of this team, everyone—the players, wives, girlfriends, and children of Plainzmen Nation—was happy and heading to a local restaurant for a "feed." Round Two would take place later that afternoon.

Meeting the Plainzmen. The Plainzmen play in "All Indian" tournaments, a label that was confusing to me. Looking at the men on the court, I found it hard to visually identify some as Indian. Players looked black, white, and Latino, as well as Indian, and really, they looked like racial mixtures of all sorts. I soon discovered these teams rely on tribal identity cards—proof that you were an enrolled member of a tribe.

As much as poverty sets groups apart from each other, poverty also proves to conjoin members of different groups. Tribal identity cards are require because, certainly, here in the eastern part of the United States, Native people mingled easily with other poor folk in cities and towns, making judgment on looks alone hard. And, when prize money is at stake, it could be tempting to bring in a non-Native who could win it for you.

What constitutes citizenship from one tribe to the next differs, however. Eligibility for citizenship is all about blood quantum—the percentage of Indian DNA a person must have in order to be traced back to original reservation tribal rolls. The qualifying percentage is determined by a federal government edict created to help govern reservation Indian tribes, and the approach is not at all the way indigenous people determined membership prior to reservations. While most tribes require a 25 percent blood quantum for citizenship, meaning one of your grandparents had to be of that tribe at the time the reservation was formed, a few, like the Chippewa and Cree, demand 50 percent quantum, and some have as little as a one-sixteenth quantum. That's why you get teams made up of ballers looking like a Colors of Benetton commercial for the disenfranchised.

In their first game, while players were busy lacing up their shoes at courtside, I asked some of the Plainzmen about this. "What's with that team over there? They look like they're mostly 'brothers' (African-American)." Jesse Heart winked. "Oh them? They're from the Blackfoot tribe."[16]

Jesse Heart was the only player I knew here and the reason I had come to the tournament. He wasn't the only Lakota on the team though. Casey MacKenzie was also from Pine Ridge. He had played at Red Cloud High School before going on to play at South Dakota State University. Jim Archambault was from Standing Rock Sioux Reservation, north of Pine Ridge. He played for Standing Rock Sioux High School, graduating to play for United Tribes Technical College. Austin Kirkie, known as Coop, was Dakota from the closely related Sisseton tribe in North Dakota. He played at Crow Creek High School and then at Sisseton Wahpeton Tribal College. Brothers Malcolm and Jerel Moore are Mesqwaki from Iowa. Malcolm played at University of Texas-El Paso and University of Wisconsin at Milwaukee, while Jerel played at the junior college level, as did Heart. The Plainzmen shapeshifted, picking up additional pieces depending on where they played. Others did as well. There were seven of them in this tournament along with an array of wives, girlfriends, and children.

How do we think of Plainzmen? Basketball is the most played sport in Indian Country. And, in South Dakota, where almost 10 percent of the state's population is Native American, only 1.2 percent of the athletes in South Dakota's three largest colleges are Indian. The Plainzmen all played college ball; but with the exception of Malcolm Moore, who played D1, the others played at local D3 schools, mostly tribal colleges. It could easily be argued that their skills should have translated into playing at a higher level and that, when it didn't, they disappointed people back on the rez. Still, given the paucity of Indian players in college generally, the fact that they all played college ball in itself constitutes an accomplishment of sorts.

If you buy the argument that all of the Plainzmen, for a variety of reasons, played hoops below their potential, then they did convincingly well off the court. Three of them earned college degrees: Casey MacKenzie graduated from South Dakota State University with a degree in education; Malcolm Moore got an interdisciplinary degree from University of Texas-El Paso; and Jim Archambault earned a degree at Florida International University in information technology. Again, relative to the low numbers of reservation males going on to college and earning degrees, this constitutes an impressive showing.

Most of these Indian tournaments award small cash payouts. By contrast, the biggest cash tournament in the world, simply called the Basketball Tournament, has a $2 million payout for the winning team and draws the best non-NBA talent in the country. Nothing like this exists for Native players in their circuit. Ho Chunk Nation (Winnebago) sponsors a "March Madness" tournament with a first prize of $10,000. This is about as big a pot as there is in Indian Country. There are dozens of others that award between $1,000 and $5,000, and many more in which players win jackets and trophies and other symbolic gear—but all in all, this is no way to really earn a living.

"You could win $10,000 in a year if you win most of them," Jesse said in a hardly convincing voice.

The hard, economic truth is that unless you have a nice-paying job, the average guy can't afford more than a tournament, because the expenses for each range between $800 to $1,500. You need benefactors: a wife, relative, girlfriend, or tribe. Elite teams have these patrons.

Heart had joined the Plainzmen after a stint kicking around with other teams on the circuit, a stint that was interrupted with periods of going back to Pine Ridge. In the Plainzmen, several other Lakota had already formed a core. "I started playing with Jimmy (Archambault) in 2010. . . . Before I left Pine Ridge, I was workin' and coachin', not playing too much ball. Just raising my two babies there. I left Pine Ridge for a tournament in Florida and lived with one of my friends. Then I went back and played again and met Mercedes (his partner)."[17]

For Jesse, this relationship was life changing in a number of ways: in one move, he left Pine Ridge, found happiness, and could afford to play. Coop commented on how difficult it was playing on the tournament circuit before the Plainzmen patrons showed up. "I remember when I first got started, and I had to either save up money all the time or approach the tribe and ask them for $200. Sometimes they would give us that, and we would get together some food stamps and we would travel on that."[18]

Coop also noted that having sponsorship was much more than having a distant business relationship; Plainzmen sponsors had become extended family. "The thing about our sponsors is that they are really good-hearted people, who do this because they like to see us play and they like to spend family time together with us. It isn't like if we play a bad game that this is going to stop. It isn't about that, and it feels good playing with no pressure and being with family."[19]

Where does this kind of competition fit into the world of competitive basketball? Most athletes I've come into contact with relish the thought of playing against the best competition, so I had to ask Jesse whether he didn't regret not playing in tournaments against urban players. He had a ready answer: "Every Indian kid likes to play against the best Indians. Everyone knows who's who. I go home and try to pick up guys to play in tournaments with me. I show 'em that these are the best players around." I pushed him, reminding him that the best players in the country would be in the big-city tournaments. "I played against black kids. All "iso" [one-on-one basketball]. That kind of team, we shut 'em down. It's something I learned from my dad at a young age. I played against 'hood' [black urban] teams. 'They're so good,' (is what people say). Well, I think maybe not."[20]

Jesse Heart: Success or Failure?

Understanding Jesse Heart as a Lakota and as a man is as nuanced as understanding him as a basketball player. Everyone who knows him finds it easiest to see Jesse as baller. Coaches coveted his talents, opposing teams feared him, and teammates welcomed him. He had the ability to play professionally and certainly in Europe for top-division teams in the elite basketball countries like Spain or Italy. Because of this, there is a tendency to think of him only in basketball terms, a perception made stronger because it mirrors Jesse's self-perception.

As noted, public expectations that he would go far mixed with the prophetic fear that he'd self-destruct. Jesse's father said, "Just because he didn't make it to the D1 school, didn't get drafted to the NBA, some people think he's a bust." Regardless, Jesse takes the high road. "Coming from here [Pine Ridge], I try to never run my mouth about what I've done. I let it show on the court, but I know people thrive on the shit talk."[21]

For himself, Jesse always tried to "keep it real." It was simple: he loved his home, he didn't like school, and he very much wanted to play ball. That they were asymmetrically linked was something he had to grapple with. Fortunately, schools made it easy for Jesse by allowing him to regularly miss class without penalty. And Little Wound High School gave him a great coach and teammates along with a supportive world to star in.

The Cultural Cocoon. Jesse has always been candid about his time in higher education. "I felt out of place in college," he told me. His father Narcisse Heart explained it like this: "When you're on the reservation, you're surrounded by that Indian atmosphere. There are Natives all over, and so when you go into the outside world, it's a culture shock. Kids have that link to the reservation that they can't get rid of."[22] And they don't want to either.

In reflecting on his alienation at these schools, Jesse was clear about the discomfort he felt. "They just didn't have enough Indian kids there. It's tough to explain, but I just like being around my family and the people I've been with my whole life."[23] Such a preternaturally strong bond between the person and his or her culture is one we see relatively little of outside of these insular communities.

Comfort is almost always associated with a place nestled into the core of our memory and identity. Jesse was waiting for me in Kyle, in the empty parking lot of his old school, Little Wound High. Standing there, holding Braxton, his little one-year old, both of them smiling, he seemed so at ease. The other places he and I had met, by comparison, seemed . . . maybe not alien, but definitely different—a tad more guarded. Here, he seemed the same color as everything around him.

We walked across the road to his uncle's house to wait for his aunt, who was loaning him her car. She pulled up in a classic rez car—the Indian version of Havana's 1950s cars—only the Pine Ridge version runs as badly as it looks. When she got there, "Aunty" got a big hug and kiss from Jesse. He asked about a lengthy list of relatives he hadn't seen in a long while and got an equally long list of people with ailments and in various stages of disrepair (diabetes, cancer, etc.). Her instructions about how to start and operate the car lasted a good minute and a half and included directions on everything from starting it in the heat to popping the trunk. Through it all, Jesse made gentle jokes with her, showering her with care and tenderness. This was a man in the buxom of his family—acting unguarded, feeling safe, enjoying the warmth of *tiyospayé*. You couldn't find this at college, in Florida, or at any tournament.

I followed him in my car for 15 miles past Kyle to Potato Creek—a little clump of houses in a cul-de-sac. "Cluster housing" is what they call it, and it's often reviled for concentrating a lot of dysfunctional behavior. Not this one, however. We walked into a perfectly serviceable tract HUD house, in relatively good condition and kempt. Unlike many other homes at Pine Ridge that I'd entered, this one had windows and doors hinged and caulked, with a small but tidy interior. Jesse's dad, Narcisse, was busy at the kitchen table making a drum using buffalo hide that he had painted beautifully. With a warm handshake and handsome smile, Narcisse, a self-taught artist, brought out the ubiquitous pot of hot coffee. He had been quite a ball player back in his time at Haskell Indian School, and at six-foot-three and lean, he looked like he could still play. Narcisse was very much enjoying having his son and grandson from Florida visit.

During his time on the rez, Jesse was moving in a family circuit, shifting between houses of cousins, brothers, and uncles, with everyone "chillin" or just coming and going. He also engaged in workouts in his uncle's home-made gym and, of course, played some hoops. Seeing him here made it clear why the pull of the rez was so strong. The dynamic here made life so easy in comparison to the demands that felt so onerous on the outside. There weren't tons of options for things to do and see, but in just hanging around, you somehow slowed down to Potato Creek time and found an appreciation for it (though it drove Jesse's Seminole girlfriend crazy, so she opted to stay in Rapid City with Jesse's sister). Here, for Jesse, it was about his family, friends, ball, and "chillin." Good luck to the college coaches to match that comfort level.

But for all of Jesse's fondness about being home, there was an ambivalence here. As a sporting hero, "He's like an NBA star around here.... People see him, and they want his autograph," his dad said.[24] Conversely, most people on the rez knew the path had been made easier for Jesse than for others. In the beginning, people were more than willing to overlook his unwillingness to work at academic eligibility, and when all he could do is go to the juco, they thought it only a temporary setback. But when he repeatedly failed to stay in school, those same people all too easily expressed criticism, as if they'd been waiting all along to dish out their opinion that "You know, I just think Jesse was too lackadaisical about too much. If he would have had somebody making him take care of things both on and off the court a little more, I think he probably could have played in the NBA."[25] His coach at Central Community College lamented that Heart's failure to finish his first year "was a travesty, because he's as good a talent as we've ever had here."[26]

Jesse knows he disappointed many. "I think most people have written me off, except those around me."

I wondered how he processed not playing at the elevated level that everyone thought he should.

"Did it bother you that you didn't play D1 basketball?" I asked.

"My dad asked that too: 'Did it bother you not playin' at Kansas State?' No, it didn't." He took decisive tone. "I went in playing right away. If I'da gone bigger [to higher D1 schools] and not played, it would've really bothered me. But I went to junior college and played. I didn't care that it was a juco 'cause I had the ball in my hands. I'm the point guard. I was good. Puttin' up numbers. National tournament. I was good with it."[27] And with that statement, Jesse Heart had made it crystal clear what mattered to him most: having the ball in his hands.

Now, eighteen years later, claiming that he will play "till the wheels fall off," he knows his days are numbered. But he also knows that for twenty years, he's had the ball in his hands—that he's had a career. "Players gotta play," as they say, and Jesse is a player. For more than nineteen years after graduating high school, he played ball in college and on the Indian circuit, starring at every level.

And Heart defined success in his own terms: "Everyone likes playing against the top Indians. Everyone knows who's who."

But, while Jesse Heart was one of the few Indian athletes to have kept his sport central to his life and to have played it at the highest level available to an elite athlete, it came at a price.

He bristled a bit at some of the things people said about him. "I'm one of those guys that don't give a shit 'bout what you say 'cause you never left the rez." And with this statement, the pleasantness of being at home temporarily left his face.[28]

Heart or Heartless. The only thing other than balling that mattered to Jesse was being a father. "I love playin' basketball," he told me, "but I'm a dad too."[29]

Heart's sudden departure from Central Community College was seen by non-Indians as cavalier—an immature response by a young Indian who was given an opportunity to escape his background. But unlike most college freshmen, Jesse Heart had to do more than buy textbooks and find the right courses—he had a daughter and a girlfriend to care for back at Pine Ridge. It weighed on him while he was isolated out in Nebraska. "My high school girlfriend and I had a baby, so I was playing on the team but going back and forth (to Pine Ridge)," he said. "So toward the end of the season, I wasn't even gonna show up at the national tournament. . . . Then, after that [national tournament] ended, I went right home to be with the baby."[30]

But though his priorities took him away from basketball and back to the reservation, like so many young people who have children too early, his relationship faltered, then failed. Too often, the scenario ends with a single mother and a father who orbits, whether that be near or far or not at all. And Jesse's scenario was no different.

Some people attacked Jesse Heart for his lack of involvement in the lives of his children and for not contributing to child support. (To be clear, I am talking about the two children he fathered with two women, not including his current relationship and child with Mercedes.) Understandably Jesse got defensive about this.

"People say stuff to me about it, but they don't know shit," he said. "People hit me up for child support. They know I don't make money, but they think I'm makin' money playing ball. I barely get by."[31]

He said most of the vitriol was coming from his two former girlfriends, who were the mothers of his children, as well as the girlfriends' families. This is almost always framed as mutual recrimination between families, but what gets concealed, and what is at the core of the conflict is staying on the rez or leaving it. Not to help support the mothers and his children is seen as abandonment. Leaving Pine Ridge to play adds betrayal to the mix.

When I met him in 2014, he was living on Pine Ridge and working. He talked a lot about training his little ones, laughing when he recalled his kids trying to do the physical exercises he put together. Clearly involved in his children's lives, he might have stayed that way, except that he was Pine Ridge's best baller. He was courted to play in the All Indian circuit and, in short order, met Mercedes in Florida. This path gave him a crash course in what was expected of him back home: help your kids, but if not, stick around.

Had Jesse stopped playing in high school, it's likely that he would be solidly ensconced on the reservation. Statistics indicate that he probably would not have stayed with his high school flame or even been in a position to support them, but he would likely still be around and distantly involved in his children's lives. After all, the trope of poor, young high schoolers having children is certainly alive in Pine Ridge. Out of one dozen tribes studied in 1995, Pine Ridge had the lowest percentage of children residing with two parents: 35.2 percent. Almost two-thirds of all children resided with only one—mostly the mother. Pine Ridge also topped the list of tribes in the percentage of women over fifteen years who never married.[32]

Jesse was made to choose between being a baller and possibly being a marginal figure in his children's lives. The choice he made was based on the reality that his identity and life had been built around basketball and around avoiding the dysfunction found on the rez. It was a decision that, while somewhat successful, came at a price.

Because of basketball, he avoided drinking, drugs, criminal activity, and hypermasculine violence toward women. But, in doing so, he ran headlong into that unfortunate characteristic of Lakota life—the one that resembles a sinkhole, sucking anything down that tries to get away. In this instance, that characteristic was played out by the women with whom he had children and by those girlfriends' families, as they sought to tether him to Pine Ridge. Their demands that he "grow up" and take responsibility for his part in their families is certainly not to be argued against. Jesse, however, had a different take on the situation—one worthy of argument.

Jesse did *not* see the situation as a contradiction between playing ball and having a family. "She knew that having a baby with me is still about basketball, and knowing this, how can she try to change me?" he rhetorically asked. Was he being self-centered, or was he being committed and focused? Was there a way to have both? If he would have substituted practicing medicine for playing ball, would his objection to their demands carry any less weight? Yet, in typical fashion for a would-be Lakota baller, Jesse's determination to realize his dream led to serious problems in his relationships with women.

"And that's what it comes down to with my girlfriends that I had kids with—they try to pull me away from basketball. 'Oh, you got a baby now, so you gotta . . .'"[33]

For Jesse, choosing between his life's passion and his family was a false choice:

> To me, playing and bringing my kid [and his mother] with me is showing them how much I put into basketball. You want your kid to see how hard you work. It's that her mom don't wanna make a change that's good for both of us. What you gonna do? You gonna stay on the rez and be ugly together? Stay here? Stay for my family? Give up the dream? Is that really right? So, you gonna judge me for leaving? That's what makes me a bad father? I never dogged out my baby's mama about any of this. I told her, "Let's move together!" She said, "No, I can't leave." What's the difference between us?[34]

Great question. In Jesse Heart's mind, the refusal of his girlfriends to compromise and sustain his commitment to play made these women and their families just as culpable as he was in their eyes. He felt that it wasn't him leaving that was the problem; the problem, rather, was their refusal to break free of rez confines. But because most Lakota had never been in his position, they saw his decision as heartless.

This impasse was reached in his relationship with the mother of his second child, which happened in the summer of his second year at junior college. Both he and his new girlfriend had quit school and ended up living in a trailer right next to her parents. He was beginning his career in the circuit when ". . . her mom started in on me about things I shouldn't be doin' in my life. I was working and playing and working at basketball, traveling to all these tournaments, and they were trying to make me change my life!"

Importantly, Jesse Heart was defending his decision to commit to his game as work—as a career that was being relentlessly attacked by what he considered provincial rez thinking. Again, he offered a different way of living life as a family: "You guys are acting like I'm leaving you, when we could all go to these tournaments! There's money in those tournaments! We could make a living from it."

The girlfriend and her parents dug in and refused, leaving Jesse a choice: stay on the rez or leave. "They're sayin', 'We don't want this. If you're not gonna be here for your daughter, we don't need you.' Me, being a young kid, twenty-one, I got all defensive. 'All right, whatever.' They never contacted me again."[35]

Because he had talent and drive and the support of his family, Jesse persisted at his dream. In his own way, he had the same singularity of purpose that often blends elements of success and callousness. Still, a part of Jesse now feels an undeniable loss in having missed out on his children.

"I do miss my kids, and I would see them every day if I could. Some people say I'm a bad father, but I can't see them 'cause they [the mother of his first child and her parents] keep them from me. My oldest son, eighteen, he comes around all the time when I'm here." He held no bitterness toward his second partner. "I don't judge them. They're doin' a good job with Caelyn, if you ask me."[36]

It's important to keep in mind that in urging his partner to come along and share in his basketball life, and expose their child to it as well, Jesse was trying to redefine expectations of what families are supposed to do. What makes this novel is the rarity of this opportunity for most men on the reservation. In this regard, his third and current relationship is what Jesse was striving for. While at a tournament in Florida, he met and subsequently fell in love with Mercedes Osceola, a Seminole woman who shared his vision.

"Mercedes is the first girl I ever met that lets me do what I love: hoops. She brings along our son, and she lets me bring him to visit my dad. These other girls wouldn't let me visit my dad, and they lived right here on the rez!"[37] As noted earlier, the Plainzmen often travel as a collective of family units, and the children and wives and girlfriends all validate this basketball lifestyle. It's a reality that people on Pine Ridge are unaware of.

Midway through 2018, Jesse and Mercedes decided to split for various reasons. At that point, Jesse had only one place to go—back to Potato Creek, South Dakota; back to the rez. He was lucky enough to be able to both escape from it and, ironically, to return to it. He returned without baby Braxton, however, and that weighed very heavily on him. Too heavily. By summer's end, Jesse went back to Florida and his family.

It wasn't an easy decision. At home in Potato Creek, he had unquestioned support. On Pine Ridge, he could consider taking courses at Oglala Lakota College and clown around with his "boys," cracking wise about living on the rez: "Oooh, it's bad out here," he said, laughing. "Terrible. We live like this—with a big-ass TV. And this is my recliner. Ha-ha! All I need."[38] And in South Dakota, where he is a legend of sorts, he heard talk of being offered a coaching job at an Indian school. In Florida, on the other hand, he had a turbulent relationship, but he also had his child—and he had the Plainzmen close by. And he opted not only to return to his newly created family but also to extend his career. "This season in ball, gonna try to 'get 'em all' one last time," he said. Heart's relationship with Mercedes remains on-again, off-again, but it is anchored by his tie with baby Braxton. It must be noted that Jesse risked a lot to return to Florida, and his commitment to fatherhood overrode all else.

So, Jesse Heart is clearly not the norm—for a ball player, a family man, or a father; but neither is he especially different. Atypically, he managed to forge a path outside of Pine Ridge conventions and expectations, and his talent is what fueled that. It allowed him to escape the rez and, in so doing, to forge a basketball career. But Jesse Heart's personality was also well suited to buck convention: his pride in his game, his defiance, and his willingness to articulate both gave him the steely resolve to leave.

Corey Shangreau

At six foot two and about 235 pounds, with a shaved head, tatted-up skin, and impassive dark eyes, Corey Shangreau can seem a bit intimidating. His deep voice and short sentences enhance this menacing exterior. But then one of his little children scampers up his back, throwing tiny arms around his muscled neck as thoughtlessly as if he were a jungle gym, and his eyes turn soft and a smile appears out of nowhere. The secret's out: Corey Shangreau is a mush. Not so much on the court though.

When he was head coach at Pine Ridge High School, Shangreau expertly knew how much rope to give his players before he pulled it taut. He ran practices in a way that blended the disciplinary approach his coach Dusty LeBeau had used with him at Little Wound in 1999 and 2000 with the looser, player-friendly style that today's coaches understand. He put players through no-nonsense drills with little barking—just a staccato of deep vocal imperatives. And each practice was bracketed by a Coach Shangreau who always welcomed his players to talk with him. With his quiet vibe, players felt safe with him, not judged. They talked with him about all the things that really mattered to them.

His looks and demeanor also belied an edgy sense of humor, as evidenced by a Facebook post his partner, Laura, made in 2017: "Corey jumped out of bed this morning about 5:30 A.M. He went into the bathroom, I don't know what he was doing but he came back into the room and said, 'Yes, I'm still Indian.' Then laid back down and went to sleep. Makes me wonder what kind of dreams he has."[39]

Corey played on the powerhouse Little Wound team that was dominated by Jesse Heart. Everyone played a secondary role to Heart, but Shangreau would shine as well, becoming an All-State selection in 2000. The two men contrast markedly, though they share one thing—the game of basketball was instrumental in putting them on, and keeping them on, a life path that spared them the experiences that swallows so many others. Corey, like Jesse, fathered a child while still in high school, and his relationship also failed. They differed in ways. Where Jesse had no interest in school beyond providing a venue to play, Corey actually did well in school. "When I graduated [high school] my girlfriend got into SDSU (South Dakota State University), and I applied and got in." Corey wasn't your typical freshman, though, nor was he a courted athlete as was Heart. "We both (girlfriend and he) went to school and our son went to daycare. I would go to work from 4 P.M. to midnight. I played basketball at noon, though. Got to play with the college players. I don't know; they weren't that good."[40] Corey and his girlfriend split sometime in their second year at college, but he continued to go to school.

In his third year, Corey's world shattered when his dad died. He headed back to Pine Ridge. "I had a little brother, and my mom wasn't around. She was drinkin' a lot—hitting that point where you had kids all your life, and it was your turn to be young and go party. So my sister started to take care of him, and I went to help out but wasn't too much I could do." School was the furthest thing from his mind, and the pain of losing his father derailed Corey. "I started getting into trouble. Started drinking and became a dumbass, just 'cause I missed my dad. I wanted to hurt myself 'cause I didn't have anyone to talk to. No father figure there. The only one I wanted to prove myself to was him, and he was gone. I didn't know what else to do. I guess that's what happens on the rez."[41] Shangreau concluded almost matter-of-factly that, on the reservation, family tragedy normally leads to alcoholism, just as alcoholism leads to family tragedy.

At this point in the interview, Corey turned to me and said that it was a dream that straightened him out. "I can't tell you about it except that in it, my dad told me to stop or I was gonna get killed." Lakota don't reveal their significant dreams or visions, but clearly his father reached him from the "other side." This was also about the time Laura Big Crow walked into his life. Her extroverted and upbeat personality was just what he needed, and he had the sense to know it. "I met Laura, and we moved to North Dakota [where she went to college] and I been sober ever since."[42] He made it sound easy. Of course, it was anything but. The social world of rez drinking is womb-like, in that it offers a complete and welcoming environment. There are no shortcomings in that world. Instead of strangers, one is surrounded by childhood friends and family, so that getting drunk is as comfortable and warm as your favorite jacket. "I stopped drinking. It was hard. All my friends were drinkin'. "Come drink with us. We'll pick you up." Corey rightly points to the power of peers in poverty when he says it was hard to stop. Former University of Minnesota Lakota player Russ Archambault noted how early that starts when he admitted to "huffing gas" (inhaling gasoline fumes) with friends at age twelve.

Corey and Laura were both hired at Pine Ridge High School when they returned. He has worked as a teacher's aide, coached football and, until 2018, basketball. What lies at the core of Shangreau's purpose at Pine Ridge High School is a commitment to the kids themselves. "My dad's dying taught me a lot, so when I see these kids going through the same things, I help them." His efforts have been to create a safe, welcoming environment— one separate from both school and home, where they often struggle to survive. "It kinda takes a while to get to them, but after a while they come around. We shoot around the gym together, and pretty soon they start talkin'. [I] help out, I guess. I wanted this gym to be a place where they could come, shoot around, lift weights. Nobody ever did that for us, so if I can open the gym for these boys, I'll do it. Nothin' wrong with that. Sit here for a few hours."[43]

And Corey has made a difference in the lives of some of these kids with nothing more than a willingness to listen and not judge and by using the sport of basketball to help them through difficulties. "There's some boys I'm close with. One is Sun Dancing now. When I first started working here eight years ago, he was a little guy with a little chubby face. I'd wrestle with these kids. One day he looked sad and said he didn't wanna go to class. [I said,] 'What's wrong? You know you gotta get to class.'

"'I don't wanna come to school.'

"'Why?'

"'Cause my dad's there.'

"I said, 'It's better to be here than at home then.'"

"No, he's at home and he's gonna hit my mom."

From that time on, I always talked with him. Now he's a senior here and been Sun Dancing. Good kid. He lifts [weights]. He got bigger and stronger."[44]

Corey and his gym were that haven that a little boy needed in a heartless world. It wasn't the high school that helped him deal with the abuse his mother would face; it was Corey and lifting weights and playing football that helped him cope. And in the case of this particular youngster, traditional spirituality also played a role. Stories like this are all too common, and sport plays such an important role in aiding these kids, whether they're in the hard-pressed inner cities or on reservations. By drawing on his own life on the rez, Corey was a vital conduit in helping such young ones weather these tempests.

Clearly, Heart was as outgoing as Shangreau was introverted, but each, in his own way, carved out a path of salvation from the minefield that threatens most men on the rez. Jesse may have left Pine Ridge, while Corey came back, but both were able to establish families and pursue their passions. And as quiet as Corey was, he had remarkable depth, which he could articulate. His satisfaction with life, for instance, is something he could present with such simple elegance: "I got all I need and then some. My kids are amazing and hyperactive. I have the perfect lady and the best job. Don't need nothin' else. Don't need money. And don't need attention from anyone else. I'm changed. I'm different and will always put children first before I listen to bullshit adults. And I just 'cooked out,' so if anybody's hungry, you better hustle and get here."[45] He had reduced all of life's vagaries and pitfalls to their essences.

Corey was also aware that his fortune can create spitefulness in others and said he turns his back on that, though he admits it's hard. In 2018, after coaching for two years, he left his position, fed up with parental politics in high school sports. The rez can, at times, be a petty place.

Fatherhood

As a doting father of three, a devoted partner, and a hardworking employee at Pine Ridge High School, Corey, more than Jesse, better fits most people's idea of being a family man, in large part because he's there. Unfortunately, no one at Pine Ridge can make a case for Jesse, because it's his absence that speaks loudest. No one, for example, can see that Jesse is a caring father to his son Braxton (and to Mercedes' other children) in Florida. In one of her Facebook posts in 2017, however, Mercedes wrote, "Happy Father's Day to Braxton's Dad. Our son lives for his father. Follows him around the house, watching his every movement. In a perfect world, all fathers and sons would have that special relationship. I thank the Creator every day for my partner in life. He walked into our lives when we were so broken after losing our baby

Chooshke ♥. He gave us Braxton, and the sun began to shine again. Happy fathers day jess."[46]

The similarity between Corey and Jesse, then, is that both worked their way through early failed relationships that produced children and learned from them. Pine Ridge families too often suffer as the result of the failure of men to find work and assume economic responsibility. In different ways, Jesse and Corey both used sports to overcome such failure and suffering.

Brandon Ecoffey

Having a college degree from Dartmouth College makes Brandon Ecoffey stand apart from others at Pine Ridge, but within his family, he was merely meeting family expectations. In many regards, the Ecoffey family is quite middle class, probably more likely to live in a tasteful suburb than in Pine Ridge. Brandon readily admits that in his family—two parents and a sister, all with college degrees—one was expected to be a good student and make something of oneself. His college education, and most recently his tenure as journalist and editor of the *Lakota Country Times*, would bear testimony to Brandon's efforts. On the surface, then, Brandon Ecoffey seems light years away from the world of Jesse Heart or Corey Shangreau. But then just below that surface, we see that what brings Brandon back into the conversation here is basketball: "I think basketball was everything. As a kid on the rez, the greatest thing you can accomplish in the community is basketball."

And, that's exactly where his energies were invested. The legends in the community were those who starred for their teams or played on the 1987 State Championship team from Pine Ridge, and every kid was reared on their stories and their victories. Every kid "was raised to admire Brent Brewer and Willie White and all those guys on the Pine Ridge team that went undefeated. That was the highest point you could achieve in reservation society." Trying to gain access to any measure of social standing, Brandon got into the game early and with the kind of focus that smart players cultivate.

"I was always trying to play better. That was my driving force. I didn't have a girlfriend 'cause I wanted to be on-point. I did my work in school so that I'd be eligible."[47] Boys like Corey Shangreau and Jesse Heart had natural talent that allowed them immediate standing, but if you had just enough talent to play high school ball, and you were smart, you could find the needed edge. Corey and Jesse just played. Brandon played hard and smart. Heart and Shangreau had girlfriends and even children in high school. Brandon's family groomed their children for life beyond high school.

But Brandon was, despite these differences, also like any kid at Pine Ridge. How, I wondered, did he avoid the stigma of being a "smart kid" in an environment that didn't really encourage that? In chapter 6, I discuss the antipathy toward "smart" kids that exists in many quarters of the reservation, and Ecoffey might have fallen prey to that were it not for this binary view of himself: "Basketball was always the leveler. Whether you grew up as a gang member from East Ridge or from the district of Oglala, once you got on the court, it didn't matter. What happened at home last night didn't matter. You were gonna play until you lost, and then you got off the court." In addition, whether it was at school or on the streets, Brandon made it a point to fit into the flow. "I wasn't one of those 'smart kids' who was better than everyone," he said. "I was a smart kid that ran with the ballers and stoners."[48]

Brandon's story took an odd turn, however—not while he was on the rez, but when he left to go to college at Dartmouth. While Dartmouth was his mother's wish for him, he fell for the beauty that is Hanover, New Hampshire. Once he got to Dartmouth, however, he entered an overwhelmingly privileged white world, one guaranteed to make him feel like "the other."

"It was tough, but I survived it" was how he characterized the experience. This seems like an odd way for a rez dweller to talk about an Ivy League college, but Brandon was referring to a contrast of a very different nature. Of course, he hung with other Native students at Dartmouth, where about 4 percent of the enrolled students (approximately 175 students) are Native Americans. But what seemed to irritate Ecoffey as much as anything was that most of the Native students there were what he termed "Check-the-Box Indians."

"There were lots of kids that checked the box saying they're Native," he explained, "but there were only a few of us who were connected to our communities. We were a minority within the minority Native community."[49]

He and the few other reservation kids grew resentful of what they saw as the somewhat unethical way that these Check-the-Box Indians commanded resources. "There were kids from reservations who didn't have the extra money for necessities or help, because resources were going to all these other people who were pretending to be Indian," he said. Compounding the alienation he felt was the knowledge that he was at odds with these other Native students. In response to the negative experiences, he donned the mantel of an activist, hard-partying, and aggressive student. "We were looking for ways to survive in such a horrid place," he explained.[50]

Following graduation, Ecoffey returned to Pine Ridge as a success story. He worked for the Chamber of Commerce and coached basketball, settling back into life at home; but he also reconnected with old friends, some of whom had drifted into the world of drug sales. In 2009, Ecoffey and eight others were convicted of drug conspiracy charges. Brandon was sentenced to sixty months, but in large part because of his family's standing, he served only forty-two. Chastened, he rebounded and, in short order, moved into his chosen profession of journalism, winning awards and serving as editor of the *Lakota Country Times*.

Oddly, it might have been because Brandon ran afoul of the law and was made to pay the consequences that his reentry into Pine Ridge went so smoothly. He thought that the perspective he gained from doing time and the articles he published in that area were well received in a community that has a disproportionate number of its people incarcerated. Most recently, he started a media consulting firm called Bad Face, and he is positioning himself to succeed in a new venture in Indian Country.

Basketball continues to loom large in his life. It has to, because he's Lakota. He engages it as part-time player or coach or astute observer. At the 2017 LNI, for instance, Brandon grew frustrated with the long-running practice of refs calling fouls on Indian teams—often resulting in losses—among other racist behaviors by security. Lakota talk about this all the time, but with his ire triggered, he confronted the South Dakota Activities Association in a post. That post got 70,000 views, and in its aftermath, it was discovered that the three refs at the tournament that were most identified with excessive foul-calling were from Sioux Falls (the part of the state most culturally distinct from the western reservation-heavy area of South Dakota). But whether it's through playing, coaching, or reporting, Brandon Ecoffey, like most Lakota, is never far from the game.

"Manning Up" on Pine Ridge

What do these three young Lakota men represent in regard to Lakota ideals of manhood? Have their backgrounds as ballers affected their decisions and pathways into adulthood? What links to the past can be found in their histories?

White Buffalo Calf Woman, the Lakota deity who presented them their moral compass, did so in the form of gifting seven sacred ceremonies and their sacred ceremonial pipe. She also passed along seven core values: prayer, respect, compassion, honesty, generosity, humility, and wisdom.[51] Lofty as these are, they don't include the values that came to be central for Plains Indian men from the nineteenth century onward—values heavily related to expanding and protecting territory.

Participating in warfare, raiding for horses, and hunting buffalo were the three activities that increasingly defined warriors' and men's work, and all were based on a set of physical skills related to aggression and combat. The emphasis placed on these skills inflated the value of bravery and the warrior ideal.

Meanwhile, the other, more noble and peaceful values noted above pertained to the softer side of a man's status, and while lauded, by themselves, they wouldn't garner the highest respect for men as the golden era of warfare grew. You could be a holy man, a transgendered person, or a powerful healer and still be esteemed, but the most unassailable status went first to warriors who could show at least a touch of affinity for the less martial side of manhood (community, diplomacy).

Was there a tension between the man of the people and the warrior ideal? Was there room in Lakota society for men who did not identify with the bellicosity of the warrior? Lakota masculinity allowed for a relatively wide range of behavior, but by the mid-nineteenth century, the warrior ideal had triumphed, ranking as more valued than all others. Sociologist R. W. Connell would call such a value system "hegemonic masculinity."[52]

Thinking of this kind of hypermasculinity in recently colonized egalitarian societies undergoing change, presents wrinkles in how to conceive of the ideal male. In Plains Indian societies of the nineteenth century, it seems gender roles had grown more heavily bifurcated and male dominant than at any time before.[53] Warfare, horse raiding, and buffalo hunting were essential for survival, so naturally, gender roles became increasingly governed by a concern for martial performance.[54] As such, training for these skills began early, and young men were encouraged to beseech the deities for help, forging a dominant cultural link between masculinity and religion. And because fighting was horribly bloody—enemies were frequently mutilated while still living, and in the most gruesome ways—this lent status to those able to excel in it, meaning war honors were glorified.

Yet, while men may have linked status to inflicting pain and killing enemies, being cold-blooded (to outsiders) and caring for one's own were accorded different social values. So to be truly respected they also had to take care of their families, not to mention the weak and needy. Protecting the vulnerable and being generous to a fault factored into the ideal forms of manhood—certainly among the Lakota they did—and, as such, the ability to protect and provide was paramount to being among the most influential men. Other masculine roles were respected as well (e.g., healers and transgender [or *winkte*] individuals) but not nearly as much as the role of warrior chief.[55]

The shift to reservation life wreaked havoc on these traditional means to achieving manhood. Just as the reservation became a physically and economically diminished version a tribe's original domain, so did masculinity. Reservations functioned as holding tanks, ghettos, and prisons that held all the Lakota on vastly reduced tribal lands, and doubly so for men furloughed from status and privilege. On Lakota reservations, traditionally oriented men found it difficult to protect and meet the needs of their families and to offer their sons a viable male path for the future. Further, proving oneself on the field of battle was completely gutted. The warrior was furloughed; replaced by increasing numbers of idle men with no traditional way to "claim" status.

At that point, for those men still clinging to atavistic forms of hypermasculinity, the search for warrior ferocity took a U-turn inward, ultimately manifesting into what scholars of masculinity have called "protest masculinity."[56] Like an amputee who thinks he can still feel his leg, a man who manifests protest masculinity will continue to act out aggressively but with no functional avenue of egress. In Lakota society, this hypermasculine behavior and the look of ferocity is too often expressed internally against other Lakota (especially women and children). Mary Crow Dog,[57] Bea Medicine,[58] and Kathleen Pickering[59] all discuss this as a problem that continues to the present.

I use "manning up" to refer to today's Lakota warrior ideals because it valorizes masculinity as a marker for status. But which warrior ideals were being summoned up? Is it the warrior ideal of Sitting Bull and Crazy Horse in defense of Lakota land from white incursion? Or was it the atrocity-riddled warrior for whom dismemberment and humiliating enemies is synonymous with victory on the field of battle? To us, separated from Plains warfare by more than a century and a culture, these behaviors invoke differing notions of warrior.

Basketball has become an arena for performing these anachronistic warrior manifestations (see chapter 2). Rez ballers seem to effortlessly translate competition into surrogate warfare; "going to battle," "counting coup," and being "a warrior" are regularly called-on linguistic analogies on the court, where a sense of toughness, aggression, and skill, along with a view of opponents as enemies, mimics the battlefield.

George Orwell's quote linking sports and war has particular resonance for this phenomenon in Plains Indian culture. He said, "Serious sport has nothing to do with fair play. It is bound up with hatred, jealousy, boastfulness, disregard of all rules and sadistic pleasure in witnessing violence: in other words, it is war minus the shooting."[60] We can dismiss some of the vituperative tone of this quote by noting that Orwell simply hated sports and never played them. In this, he's like a lot of "haters." But by linking athletics with war, he put his finger on the social psychology of sports that we now see playing out in Lakota basketball.

The Cultural Underpinnings of Rez Ball

Much of the contemporary game of basketball, including rez ball, draws on a particular cultural style centered in the urban world of African Americans. The game that we see in the NBA and even in college has been influenced by the aggressive and flamboyant style of play and meta-combat of inner-city ballers; and it is compounded by crowds that extol the displays of trash talk and the extravagantly athletic plays designed to anger and humiliate opponents who are momentarily dominated. The sense of masculinity infused in the style of play is in line with the hypermasculinity of much hip-hop music and some of the "thug-ish" elements of the hip-hop scene.

For the Lakota, however, the display of masculinity on the court comes from a different place. It is symbolic of a former greatness that was ruthlessly wrenched away and razed. In some sense, the baller may be a wannabe warrior that seeks to recapture a bloodstained and valorized time—not out of a sense of nostalgia but out of a desire to bring back honor to Pine Ridge and to continue their resistance to whites. As such, when Indian teams play white schools, this resentful and angered warrior is readily called upon. At times, that may mean Indian players come perilously close to tapping into the mindset of warriors who would eviscerate and humiliate.

In the history of rez ball, however, while players may have come close to true enmity, they generally haven't reached it. And, more important, it seems rez ball has become a healthy outlet for that feeling of protest masculinity that many Lakota males experience—which translates into male ballers who are better equipped to stop the abusive behavior that their thwarted manhood has visited upon women, children, and each other.

Jesse Heart Counts Coup

The most revered act of war, the mark of an accomplished warrior, was the "coup." Killing the enemy, while revered, was secondary to showing bravery by weathering an enemy's attempts to kill you while you struck him; in this act, considered the bravest of all coups, one was showing both bravery and contempt. There were many variations of coup, but whenever a man performed one, he kept track, often with eagle feathers, which he accumulated and wore in his hair or elsewhere.

There are times when the Lakota ballers have to don the bellicose personae of warriors of old—when heading toward the opponent's gym is uncomfortably close to riding into a hated enemy's territory, for example.

In chapter 8, there is a detailed account of Jesse Heart's silencing of a hostile crowd in Winner, South Dakota. The history of Winner's prejudice toward Lakota is well established, and on this night the disrespect the Winner crowd showed to the Pine Ridge players was especially bad. Coming onto the court, Lakota players were spat on as they passed in front of the white crowd. The act understandably riled many of the Lakota, but none more than Heart, who took it upon himself to vanquish the crowd with a dazzling display of scoring. His true outrage was revealed in the manner in which he engaged with the white crowd. "I liked it. They'd boo me, talk shit, call me racist names; and I'd look at 'em, light it up, and watch those ugly white faces."[61] Then he went much further. After silencing the crowd, he taunted them by motioning for them to start their heckling again; and when they did, he put his index finger to his lips commanding them to be quiet. By himself, in full view of these hostile fans, Jesse Heart toyed with them, controlled them.

After the win, Heart and his teammates ran off the court, waving their spat-upon jackets as though they were bloody trophies. While no one was killed or mutilated, the psychological fury felt by both sides had to rival that between enemies on the field of battle—just raw hatred. It was certainly on the face of Jesse Heart as he recounted that night. And it was in Corey Shangreau's face when he waved the warm-up jacket that spectators had spat upon.

The social history of the groups involved in that game informed much of the behavior of the fans and players; and what was clearly in evidence was a Lakota demonstration of basketball skill combined with social animus. As part of this demonstration, Jesse Heart came as close to the embodiment of the traditional warrior as anyone in recent memory. He had "manned up."

5

Laura Big Crow

Come Back to Pass It Forward

Laura is a Big Crow. The Big Crows are a large *tiyospayé* on Pine Ridge, and Laura's related to the best-known Big Crow of modern time—SuAnne. It might have been the second time I was meeting Laura; I walked into the Pine Ridge High School gym during the Lady Thorpes team practice, and there, at half court, was a very pregnant Laura Big Crow, launching basketballs some 42 feet. She went 2 for 4 from that distance. She's a large-boned woman at about five foot eleven and was groomed to play the center position in high school and college. Recollections by some who saw her play at Pine Ridge High between 2000 and 2004 centered on Laura's being dominant: large, strong, unmovable, and gifted with a deft touch. So, she was most comfortable in the paint—in the trenches of basketball combat near the basket, where she could best use her gifts to get rebounds and put up shots. But shooting from out there at half court—the hinterlands of the basketball world? And running a step and a half before shooting that distance, with a large round baby bouncing inside? Strong and skilled indeed . . . and a wee bit funny. (Let's just say that continues to be a very enduring visual I have of her.)

Laura and the other women that I look at in this chapter have used basketball as an oasis—a haven in what was often a troubled world. For these Lakota girls, playing for their high school teams eased their tribulations by offering an antidote to places that troubled them. The sport has also given them a base from which to find a meaningful adulthood.

Is there something distinctly female about this? Yes and no. All Lakota athletes derive an extra measure of security and status from being on a varsity team. But, as I point out below, Lakota girls are especially vulnerable, and so being a Lady Thorpe or Lady Mustang or Lady Crusader is more than appreciated: it can be downright lifesaving.

Passing It Forward

Those girl ballers who went on to college have been able to draw on the focus and discipline that playing hoops in high school gave them, and a goodly number of those young women managed to earn degrees. In turn, some have come back to Pine Ridge, committed to give back to the community. *Oyaté*, meaning "the people," is the Lakota word for the community; Lakota athletes often internalize this ideal of taking care of the community.

Like Doni DeCory, who may well have been one of the best all-around female athletes to ever have come out of South Dakota. She starred in basketball and track at Pine Ridge High School before going on to play D1 hoops at Brigham Young University (1990–1991) and then at University of Southern Utah (1992–1993), where she earned her degree. She came back and set to work, directing programs that aided young people on the reservation.

Though she left Pine Ridge, Sunshine Archambault Carlow is another example. A 1998 graduate of Red Cloud High, where she was an all-conference selection in basketball, cross country, and track, Sunshine went on to play one year in the Ivy Leagues at Penn before returning to the Dakotas and Si Tanka College, graduating with her degree in 2003. Sunshine now heads up a successful program at Standing Rock Sioux Reservation that is teaching Lakota language to those who haven't had the opportunity to learn it at home.

Of course, men have done this as well. As mentioned in the previous chapter, Bryan Brewer played at Pine Ridge in the 1970s, then went on to college, returning to teach, coach, and hold office on the rez. Likewise, Christian

McGhee played at Red Cloud and then at Chadron State, after which he went back to his alma mater as a coach and athletic director. But among all the Lakota who have returned to contribute back to the reservation, none could look more impressive than Laura, especially in that moment when she was eight months pregnant and shooting at half-court.

Every female basketball player in Lakota Nation gets measured against the standard of excellence created by SuAnne Big Crow. And to date, no one has ever matched either her record of 67 points in a single game or her average of 39.2 points per game (a record she set her senior year). In fact, no one comes close.

But the bar is set much higher, and the comparison much harsher, if your name is also Big Crow. Laura Big Crow knows this, and though she hasn't broken or even met her namesakes' records, she can still most definitely "play some," and as I'll show Laura has made original contributions. As a player, she controlled the paint, using her strength and toughness to do it. Like most girl hoopsters who excel, she credited this ability to playing around boys. In her case, she said, "My older brother showed me no mercy, and he's probably the reason why I can handle so much. I mean, he would block me, push me down. I would get so mad at him." She laughed. "He'd say, 'If you wanna get good, get up.' He taught me the intimidating part of the game."[1] Her dad didn't coddle her either. As a freshman, trying out for the Lady Thorpes High School team, Laura was tagged as "large" girl, and Coach Dusty LeBeau wanted her in playing shape, agile and long. In an effort to get her slimmed down, he had her running up and back on the court, wearing a heavy-duty garbage bag. When she told me the story, she laughed. "Everyone just heard the squishing sound the bag made on me. I went home and complained to my dad that Dusty thought I was "big." All he said was, "So what?" And he wouldn't let me feel sorry for myself."[2] Everyone in the room laughed heartily at the story, but it was that story that made her the dominating player she had become.

In her senior year, the Lady Thorpes had a lackluster season, barely making the state tournament as a low seed. At states, however, they surprised everyone, beating their opponents in the first two rounds to send themselves to the 2004 final. For a good chunk of the time, she carried her team in the post-season run. In the three games played in the state tournament, she dominated, scoring 23, 27, and 30 points (the last of which was in a losing effort in the finals), which went along with 16, 16, and 8 rebounds respectively. Based on that capstone performance, along with a season average of

23.5 points and 15 rebounds per game, Laura won the prestigious Spirit of Su Award, given annually to the top Native athlete.

She went on to play impressively in college as well. At Williston State, she was MVP of the Mon-Dak Tournament in 2006, before going on to showcase her talent at Mayville State University in North Dakota. In her senior year, 2008, she averaged 17.4 points and 7.8 rebounds per game and received All-Conference honors.

Because she was one of the most decorated players in Pine Ridge history, it was natural that, when she returned to the rez, she'd go on to serve as head coach of the Lady Thorpes. She quickly became the heart of girls' basketball on Pine Ridge. As a student athlete and coach who earned a college degree and excelled at every level she played, Laura is unique. And because SuAnne Big Crow died before she could impact the college scene, Laura emerged as one of the most successful women on the basketball scene. She was equally proud, however, to have landed a position as an elementary school teacher in Pine Ridge. Now, ten years into that job, she is as ready to meet the challenge of teaching second grade as ever.

That she is also brimming with self-confidence and optimism makes her even more unusual. Not many people in Pine Ridge would easily declare, "I love meeting new people. I was always a social butterfly." Laura explained that, in high school, "I just got along with everybody. I was student council president, I won homecoming queen. I was the kid who walked down the hallways and knew everybody."[3] Self-confident, friendly, and easygoing is a great personality cocktail, and I have to think that a big part of hers came from her family. That's what Sir Arthur Conan Doyle would argue: "A dog reflects the family life. Whoever saw a frisky dog in a gloomy family, or a sad dog in a happy one? Snarling people have snarling dogs, dangerous people have dangerous ones."[4] And Laura's folks had confident kids.

I don't know how strong the bonds among Big Crows are at the larger level, but Laura's immediate family was tight indeed. They were centered in Wolf Creek, a few miles east of the town of Pine Ridge. Wolf Creek has an elementary school and is presently constructing a new technical high school (the first public school on the reservation), but it was pretty small when Laura was growing up. The Big Crow family formed a kind of critical mass in the town the way old-time Lakota families did. "My older brother lives and works at Wolf Creek (School) and has a house next to the school. My mom lives 200 feet away from him. My sis works at the school and lives out there. My mom and dad have three kids together, and then I have an older brother and sister from my mom, and then I have two older brothers and an older sister from my dad's previous marriage. These were my friends growing up. We lived next to the school and had access to the gym. On weekends, we were at the gym. On snow days, we were at the gym. We were there all the time."[5]

When I listened to Laura describe this concentrated family, I found myself wondering how often this kind of tight-knit, loving world happens. It certainly wasn't anything I'd seen in my family; nor was it common at Pine Ridge. But for her, the people she grew up with "were my family, *and* they were my friends. If I could move my family into a house somewhere, I would. I just loved being around my mom and dad and brothers and sisters."[6] What to do with such an unequivocal statement of love? I think it speaks for itself. And if it doesn't explain the reason behind Laura Big Crow's enthusiasm, then it certainly is another illustration of it.

She got to travel at age fourteen to play in tournaments far from home, and she didn't shrink from those opportunities. "We traveled with the Youth Opportunity Program from the Boys and Girls Club all the way to New York to play. It was a little after 9/11, and we were afraid to go." She laughed. "Five days of doing nothing, just exploring and looking around."[7] For some reason that Laura can't explain, they even went up into Harlem and ended up playing at the famous Rucker Park, before heading off to play in Boston.

If anything set her off from her family and others on the rez, it was Laura's college experience—not just the opportunity to go but the capacity to last it out and graduate. This was no mean achievement.

Of course in high school, as a standout on the Lady Thorpes, Laura was on the minds of several college players and coaches. One of them was a slightly older friend of Laura's: "She was two years older and playing at Williston State College [in North Dakota]. Coach was looking for players, and my friend gave him my name. He saw me play at the LNI and kept in touch. In my senior year, he made me an offer. My dad said, 'Yup. She's going.' I was unsure, and though I wanted to play, I was scared to leave. I went, though."

"They drove me up there, and just left me on the curb." She laughed. "I missed my family so much that I'd call all the time. My parents ended up unplugging the phone, so I'd quit calling. My little sis, she went and didn't like it and came home. My brother, he didn't like college, so they let him come home. But me? My dad told me, 'I knew you were stronger than the others. If you really wanted to come home, you would've found a way home.'"[8]

So many others who leave the reservation for school end up returning prematurely because their comfort levels have been stretched to the breaking point, but Laura wasn't as phased as most by the cultural gaps and by hanging around with white students. "My first roommate was a friend from Pine Ridge," Laura explained. "We were both Indian, but we were different. If anybody said anything about Native Americans, she was gonna take offense to it. I was the complete opposite. I'd think it was funny. I'm chilled about things. After two years, my friend returned home, but I got recruited to a four-year college [Mayville State]. My second roommate was white, and I remember that she started bowling, so I went along. We went shopping and hanging out, and before I knew it she was my best friend."[9] Definitely extroverted and definitely unintimidated by the white world, Laura Big Crow became very adept at handling relations between races.

It was at this point in my interviewing and document process that I began to have trouble figuring out how to cast Laura within the context of Pine Ridge. How would I situate her string of successes, her loving family, and her college achievements relative to the hardships and failures of so many others around her? In response to these questions, I gravitated toward the following conclusion: she was the exception that proves the rule. Obvious factors for her success leaped out: her family was intact and loving; Francis Big Crow, her dad, who died in 2010, had always been loving; she got along well with her siblings and loved her mom; and her parents both had jobs, which was not all that common on the rez—her mother worked in the tribal office and her father was a janitor at the Indian Health Service Hospital.

Appropriately, Laura cast their good fortune quite modestly, proving that happiness is relative. "We had just enough to be happy," she said. "We had one car. We had a home, clothes, and food."[10] In an environment like Pine Ridge, where most have so little, covering the basics was enough to be grateful for. But even in the larger world, sorrow and struggle are often the norm, so could it really be that Laura and her family had escaped it all? Where was the sibling resentment, the antipathy toward parents, the crossroads of life? It was so much easier to write about people who—like most of us—were a mixed bag of contentment and torment.

But as it turned out, not everything in her life had been so "chill." I discovered this when I told Laura how hard it was to write about someone as emotionally together as she was, and her face grew serious. "It wasn't always good for us," she said. "Growing up, my dad was loving, but an alcoholic. He completely missed my eighth grade graduation—almost drank himself to death." The pain caused by alcoholism is more than capable of derailing whole families, but the Big Crows' response was to draw closer—and, together with Francis's resolve, the family managed to escape intact. "So, we recorded the graduation and watched it a few days after he got out of the hospital. After I graduated eighth grade, that's when he started Sun Dance at Thunder Valley, and he was sober the rest of his life."[11] Francis Big Crow had been one of those who seized upon traditional spirituality to escape the clutches of this disease, and in doing so, saved his family.

There were other crucibles as well, but there too, the Big Crows tight-knit nature proved to make the difference in outcome. Many of the girls that Laura has helped and coached, however, haven't been so lucky. Many have stumbled and fallen, and some never got back up.

Resilience

There's an old anthropological adage I learned as an undergraduate student: "Women are the guardians of kinship." I took that to mean that women are the glue of society, that they keep the family together when centrifugal forces threaten its core. It's not the cliché that women are caring "by nature" so much as it is that, in the social complexities they face, women are more adept at figuring out how to survive bad situations because they grasp the impor-tance of kinship. They develop strategies to raise their children in part by keeping kinsmen close for mutual support; women also tend to see protect-ing kinship as a mission that helps the community survive.

Laura's aunt, Yvonne "Tiny" DeCory, is just one example of this kind of woman. This aging dynamo has fostered goodwill and aid throughout her life, whether by participating in women's causes, aiding in teen-suicide pre-vention, or tending to her family. In the wake of that uptick in teen suicides on Pine Ridge, DeCory has redoubled her efforts. "In the Lakota culture, we have a circle within ourselves and within our families," she explained. "When we neglect parts of that circle, we lose hope, we lose faith, and we lose spirituality. If families can strengthen that circle, hope, faith, and spiri-tuality can be returned. . . . I plan to be more visible than ever in the lives of our young people. We have to have continuity, and as adults we have to be consistent."[12]

In another poignant illustration of the adage about women, the documen-tary film *Kind Hearted Woman*[13] features the late Robin Poor Bear Charboneau, a thirty-two-year-old divorced single mother and Oglala Sioux woman living on North Dakota's Spirit Lake Reservation. Ensnared in a history of abuse and alcoholism, she struggled to hold on to her ties with her children after the tribal courts took them from her. She juggled hardships as if they were sixteen-pound bowling balls—deliberately, slowly, and always bracing herself. We watch her try to remain sober (which she does), battle in court for the return of her children, attend college classes, and even attempt a relationship. In the end, she was masterful at keeping it all together and, most important, at rekindling her relationship with her children.

Laura is cut from the same cloth. But, for every Lakota who withstands Shakespeare's "slings and arrows of outrageous fortune," there are many others that bend. Some even break.

"They're all different," Laura said about the girls who play for her, "but one thing I see a lot of in my girls is that they don't really have a home to go to. They don't have someone who's gonna be in the stands for them, letting them know how proud they are." Laura is talking about the unpaid part of her coaching job—the part where she tries to repair broken young girls. "This is where Corey (her partner) and I come in. We've talked about it a million times about getting a bigger house and taking in more kids—at least doing what we did with Santana (a former player of hers) getting her through high school. This is where we lose a lot of our children. High school is hard on them. Not just the work. It's hard to face the reality of growing up. What's next? Work? Babies? College isn't an option for many 'cause they don't have the confidence or don't wanna leave their siblings alone."[14] In any event, dealing with her players as girls in need is not part of her job description; it's just part of what she does—taking care of the *oyaté*.

Santana White Dress came into their lives when she made varsity basketball in her sophomore year at PRHS. An excellent player (scoring over 1,000 points and a second team All-State selection), she was confident, skilled, and tough on the court, yet off the court, she was insecure, fragile, and prone to bouts of despair. Her home life was always teetering on the edge of the violence that drinking creates. She'd been abused as a child, subject to all the dysfunction and craziness that swirled around her, so when it was time to go to high school, she immediately opted to be boarded at the dorm at Pine Ridge High School.

Laura felt that for Santana to get past some of her demons, it'd be better if she lived with a family where love and light-heartedness was the norm. While appreciative, Santana was, nevertheless, suspicious. She would, at various times, spend days holed up in her room. White Dress recalled, "When I first moved in with her, I was really quiet and I would stay in my room a lot. I was scared to tell her what was on my mind, how I was feeling at the time, what was bothering me."[15] Santana felt that her story marked her as broken, somehow unworthy of love. Despite this, Santana ended up being a beloved member of the Big Crow-Shangreau family.

Though only ten years older than Santana, Laura and her family tried to give her the parental influence that she had missed. But like so many victims of mistreatment, White Dress didn't completely know how to deal with an accepting environment. She would often backslide and sabotage good fortune because she felt she wasn't deserving of it. "If she had a good game, she'd find a way to bring herself down," Big Crow commented. "She'd score 20, 30 points and she'd cry in the locker room."[16] In Santana's senior year, as a finalist for South Dakota's highest basketball honor, Miss Basketball, she got drunk and almost didn't attend the awards event, a decision she rues: "I just wasn't thankful when I should have been."

But being part of Laura and Corey's family ultimately seemed to have an effect on her. On those increasingly rare occasions when Santana would go home to her biological family, it was likely that she'd call Laura early to get picked up (one time at 3 A.M. when people there had been drinking heavily). Clearly, she had begun to grasp the new normal.

In Santana's senior year, Laura got her ready for prom. She helped her fill out college applications. And, after a solid playing season, White Dress got an offer from United Tribes College to play basketball. "I really wanted her to get out of here," Laura said. "I wanted her to leave." But soon after, things began to unravel. In Santana's senior year, the Lady Thorpes went deep into the state finals, ultimately being runner-up. It was Santana's hope to bring back some kind of glory to her grandmother who'd she'd been so close to, but her grandmother died while the Lady Thorpes were competing, and Santana was distraught over not being told of her condition. "People just said, 'You have to worry about basketball. . . . It made me not like basketball there for a while," Santana said. "I was playing basketball when I could have been with my grandma for her last moments."[17]

Unbeknownst to others, the death of Santana's grandmother set into motion other sad scenarios. Santana's baby sister, Onyx, was being cared for by Grandmother Sylvia, and with her death the child was returned to her mother. In early summer, just after Santana graduated, she went to a workshop in Boulder, Colorado, during which time police picked up her mother, drunk and with the three-year-old in tow. The child was taken away and her status with her mother put in question before Santana could return. And over the ensuing weeks, just as Santana was starting her first year at United Tribes Technical College, the situation loomed over her like a dark cloud.

When Laura and Corey had driven her to start her freshman year, they thought once Santana started, momentum would carry her forward; but within a few weeks, Santana had decided to take the reservation jet-stream back home. The terror of knowing that her siblings could be in harm's way short-circuited any interest she had in school.

"Education should probably come first," Santana told me, "but it just came down to me wanting to come back (for my siblings), so I did . . . I made that decision for myself. . . . I know it's sad to say, but I don't trust my mom with having that role."[18]

All the work and worry and affection that Laura and Corey had poured into Santana's getting to college now seemed for naught; and for a time, perhaps because she felt guilty, Santana wasn't even in contact with Laura and Corey. The bond between the two women eventually reasserted itself, but in the end, White Dress became yet another young person unable to take advantage of an opportunity. And who could blame her? These teenaged young women are too often the only ones standing between their vulnerable siblings and tragedy. In this context, school, advancement, and planning for the future all seem indulgent.

Santana isn't especially unusual. As Laura noted, "Sarah, [not actual name of a current player] she's kinda like Santana. I don't see her playing after high school even though she could. She comes from a pretty rough family. Her parents drink a lot. Her little sisters were taken away last year. They're still in the system. Sarah is barely eligible now, but she gets by 'cause she's in the special ed program Fetal Alcohol Syndrome Kids."[19] This is an all too familiar tale since "roughly 70 percent of students in Pine Ridge schools drop out before graduating from high school."[20]

Life on Pine Ridge involves untimely losses of family and loved ones at a higher-than-normal rate. With a life expectancy of forty-nine years for men and fifty-two for women, surviving children have to bear these losses earlier than the rest of us. Another Lady Thorpe, Charlene, lost her grandparents and watched the dissolution of her parents' marriage all within her senior year. She went from being one of those kids who always had a ball in their hands to losing all interest in hoops. I remember her as a creative and confident point guard and outside shooter. I was even more impressed when I learned that she'd spent a summer playing AAU ball on a white border-town team—no small task for a Lakota. "My grandparents died in my last year, and it was hard," she told me. Quite the terse statement from this diminutive young lady.

Laura went on to fill in things a bit. "Charlene's grandparents were the rock of the family. That family is not complete since they passed. We were at the LNI, and her granddad was in the hospital and wasn't gonna make it. So her mother would drive her back from the hospital to play the next day. She'd have an amazing game and drive back [to the hospital] again. She came to my room crying the one night she didn't go back to see him 'cause he wasn't gonna last the night. That took something from her, and I don't know that she'll ever get it back. She used to talk about how she wanted to make them proud, and now they're gone and she doesn't have anyone to play for. Her parents also split, so she feels alone."[21]

Defining resilience through success in basketball isn't the tagline for everyone's story. But defining resilience through basketball is a theme that comes up at least periodically in the lives of rez ballers. So, even though Charlene seemed on a direct track to play competitively at a fairly high level and then her losses cut her basketball aspirations short, it was still the game that kept her on the straight and narrow all through her perilous high school years.

"Playing gave me focus," she told me, "and helped me a lot in my studies at school." It was also the game that positioned her to get into the college she's currently enrolled in.

Anissa Martin

Anissa Martin is not frivolous. She can laugh and joke along with the best of them, but there is a somberness about her. Like Santana and others, Anissa faced serious challenges growing up; but where others were derailed, Anissa prevailed. She took the help Laura and others offered and ran with it. She gritted out success.

The 2014 Lady Thorpes made a run at the state championship, and Anissa was one of its key players, later winning the prestigious Spirit of Su Award, given annually to the athlete who combines athletic accomplishment, academic excellence, and community involvement. I'd seen Anissa as a quintessential point guard, ready to do whatever was needed, but with a skill set that included deft 3-point shooting and hard boiled rebounding. Her coach,

Laura Big Crow, summarized her as "a feisty player who had an amazing work ethic. A big-time 3-point shooter and [she] led the team in rebounds."[22]

But for all of her presence on the court, it was her eyes that were hard to ignore; they were at once vulnerable and determined. And then Anissa graduated, and I didn't see her again until 2018, shortly following her graduation from the University of South Dakota. Those who knew her were especially happy for her because they knew the conditions that she had to overcome to graduate; however, not one of the women who talked to me about her told me what those conditions were. People, especially women, didn't talk about these things easily, and certainly not to outsiders like me.

But let's rewind a bit. I had set up a focus group to which head coach Laura Big Crow would invite several of her former players from the 2014 season, one of whom was Anissa. The former Lady Thorpes were loquacious, open, and full of mirth in talking about their time playing for Pine Ridge High School and their time since. Anissa contributed and broke up laughing at the stories being told. But a few days later I ran into her, and she quickly felt the need to explain that she had held back. I hadn't noticed, but apparently it had weighed on her. "I didn't get a chance to give you my story the other day, because I think it was so different from Shay and Shan," she said. "My background was harder. I didn't want to interrupt, 'cause my family puts a different perspective on it. I guess I struggled more."[23]

Ever the team player, she didn't want to be thought of as upstaging the other girls' stories, but she did want to talk about it. Her parents had divorced early, after which her mother began drinking heavily and, as a result, often ignored her six children. Tending to the siblings fell largely to Anissa. I asked her if she ever felt resentful toward her parents or the situation she was in, and while she said, "Not really," she readily admitted, "I'm not really close with my mom," going on to explain, "Like, when other girls would be going through puberty, they'd talk to their moms, and I couldn't go to her." That sounded a bit resentful to me.

The chaos at home, which she kept at arm's length, would always threaten to reach her, no matter where she was. When she would spend time at school or playing basketball, "there'd be times when my younger brother would call me, and my mom would be partying, and I'd get mad at my mom. I'd go back home and tell everyone to get out of the house."[24] That sounded resentful too.

Anissa worked hard to avoid being pulled down by the situation, so she denied its worst effects. Her weapon of choice was finding surrogates for what she needed: friends and grandparents. "So, it was about me finding support where I didn't really have it," she said. "I'd use my friends for support, and even Laura was my support, like I would always be over at her house." She made strategic choices and worked them into her very subjective needs. She even retrofitted basketball to work for her. "I developed a passion for the game because it was my getaway—me doing it for my sanity."[25]

Anissa went through school as a highly decorated achiever. She was a Gates Scholar. She was a key starter on the basketball team, guaranteeing her social standing. She was accepted to the University of South Dakota (along with her best friend). But many of the kudos she earned felt flat to her because she had no parents to share them with.

Going off to college is supposed to be a memorable day—a day when family gathers to send you off on a great adventure. But for Anissa, "It was kinda tough that first day I left. All my friends, their families dropped them off and helped them move in. That's what normal college kids do. When I left, I packed my car up, took my cell phone and a map. I said, 'Okay, this is kinda scary. My first big trip, and I'm by myself.' When I left, it was bittersweet, but when I got to school and saw all those families helping their kids, I thought, 'This kinda sucks, not having my family. But then I saw my best friend, and it was better. She was with her family, but they took me along with them to dinner, and they helped both of us move in.'" Once again, Anissa's friends came through, and she was able to avoid the worst of it. Otherwise, she admitted, "I would have sat there and sulked."[26]

Anissa's grandparents, but especially her grandma, also played a key role in her staying on track. Despite the accolades and accomplishments she had achieved in high school on Pine Ridge, Anissa was underprepared to replicate her performance at the University of South Dakota:

In class, I'd ask questions, and I'd go over the material I didn't know. Students around me would all know what the professor was talking about. I'm thinking, "I don't remember any of this." I'm thinking, "I'm not as smart as these people. I was the smartest one in my high school, and now I don't feel good enough." So, because of that, I felt inferior to a lot of those people. I was spending my weeknights in the library till 2 a.m. So, I really suck at writing and working every night to improve. In order for me to be at the same level as everybody else, I had to work so much harder than others.[27]

This was what separated Anissa from most: she owned her weaknesses more readily and was willing to do whatever it took to overcome them. This was Pine Ridge at its best. This was resilience.

But even Anissa hit the wall. One night, feeling frustrated and defeated, she hit a crucial low point—but again, her grandma was there to help. However, her grandma didn't do what many on the rez did when their children encountered obstacles in that white world, which was to let them come home. Instead, Anissa explained, the story went something like this:

Third-floor library. The quiet section. Just you and your thoughts. I was working on a paper, and I couldn't get it. I had writer's block, and I just broke down, thinking, "I wanna quit. I just can't do this anymore." I felt so alone. So, I called my grandma. "Grandma, I can't do it! I just wanna come home!" She said, "You know, Nissa, what are you gonna do if you come home? You're not gonna do anything. I know you wanna help your brothers and sisters, but you're just gonna be sitting here not really helping anyone." I told her that the young ones were texting me and begging me to come home: "We wish you were here. Mom's drinking again." When I broke down that night, all of it hit me at once. Grandma said that she wouldn't have made the choices she made if she could redo her life. She said that I reminded her of herself. Difference was, she stayed home and took care of the siblings. Some of them died, some were winos. She kinda resented that and didn't want the same for me. She talked about how she was living through me, like whenever I went anywhere, she'd tell me to take a lot of pictures to show her. She talked me through that night.[28]

Even the strongest, most resilient people have had someone else come through for them at the moment they most needed it. And while Anissa may have not had parents to swoop in and guide her, she had a special bond with her grandma, who guided her lovingly but firmly, telling her what she already knew but needed to hear—to stay the course.

While telling me this story, Anissa struggled to stay on point. She started to fight off the tears, but they came. And she let them.

"Sorry," she told me. "Every time I talk about my grandma, I cry. She passed in 2015. This whole time I've been talking about my grandma, I have a lump in my throat."[29]

Grandma didn't get to attend Anissa's graduation in 2018, but Anissa's convinced she watched. And anyway, Anissa took a picture to show her.

The Perils of Being a Lakota Woman

A good friend of mine who taught Native American Studies throughout her career warned me to be careful of "othering" Lakota women in talking about the issues they face. Othering involves depicting, and ultimately treating, people as sufficiently different, distinct, and foreign enough to see them not only as 'other' but also as inferior. Whether in regard to people of other nationalities, genders, or classes, with othering, one not only sees the differences and stigmatizes the differences; one also uses the differences to victimize.

That said, the issues most affecting indigenous women—sexual assault and domestic abuse—are by no means theirs alone. According to the National Sexual Assault Resource Center, one in every five women in the United States is raped at some point in her life. As for physical abuse, one in four women and one in nine men experience severe intimate-partner physical violence. But the National Coalition against Domestic Violence also reported that "American Indian and Alaska Native women experience assault and domestic violence at much higher rates than women of any other ethnicity."[30] The National Congress of American Indians policy center determined that "61 percent of American Indian and Alaska Native women (or 3 out of 5) have been assaulted in their lifetimes, compared to 52 percent of African American women, 51 percent of White women, and 50 percent of Asian American women."[31]) So, while domestic violence isn't only a Native American problem, it is a problem that disproportionately impacts Native women.

In avoiding the many pitfalls that affect them, young Native girls have to be counterintuitive: they have to trust others even when they have little reason or reserves to do so. An unstable family, an abusive relative, the death of a younger sibling are all disturbingly close, and agencies to aid victims or to prosecute their attackers are overburdened and underfunded. For many girls, escaping the trauma of such events might take the form of denial, fearful silence, or in some cases, the mental fabrication of a utopian world: one that is unreal and in direct opposition to the jarring reality that they hope to escape.

For some, the idea of meeting Mr. Right and establishing your own family might be the lure—a way to create meaning in your life. For example, Robin Charboneau (Poor Bear) was molested and raped throughout her childhood, and conjuring up a savior was her way of trying to escape. "I've always looked for that great big guy that would protect me," she said. "I never, ever in my life thought that they would hurt me . . . but that's what happened."[32]

The poverty that envelops Lakota life and limits most people's hopeful vistas limits women's even more. Sunny Clifford, a young Lakota, had a matter-of-fact way to describe this shrunken world of possibilities, which was terse but powerful: "We're not expected to do much. Have kids and raise them and take care of them."[33] So, the utopian future is too often thought of as young people falling in love and having kids in lieu of planning for a more responsible future. The result is that Pine Ridge has an inordinately high amount of single-mother households (20 percent of all households between 2011 and 2016). To boot, over 40 percent of its population is under twenty years of age.[34] Keeping girls clear of this cycle is an additional benefit that can come from being a Lady Thorpe.

Abused and Missing

In 2015, at President Obama's insistence, Congress passed a ruling that allowed Native tribes to prosecute non-Natives for committing domestic violence. It was a long time coming and plugged a loophole that had allowed a non-Native partner to abuse his Lakota spouse and children and evade prosecution. Most of the violence against Native women comes from partners, and in most cases, from non-Native partners.[35]

"A lot of women have simply stopped reporting incidents of domestic violence," said Kim Clausen, executive director of Wild Horse Butte Community Development Corporation in Martin, South Dakota, a town that belongs to Pine Ridge Reservation. "They just live with it because there is no safe place for them to go here on Pine Ridge."[36] That said, some women and their supporters have banded together in grass roots organizations, like the Sacred Shawl Society, to provide such safe places.

The Lady Thorpes team, while not created for that purpose, also provides a measure of safety for some girls. Shaevan, who lived with Laura and Corey and their family was a case in point. "She came from a bad place out there in Oglala," Laura said. "And, she was sexually abused as a young girl. So, being out here (at Pine Ridge High School's dormitory) and then with us was best for her. But the damage had already been done."[37]

Given the vulnerability of these situations and the relatively weak institutional support structure for such women, the safe space that basketball at Pine Ridge High offers is badly needed. When Laura gets girls committed to playing ball for her, she is also accounting for them, documenting where they are, at least for the time she has them. As part of this, Laura and Corey pushed to get the high school gym opened for their teams all through the summer, as much to give their players a place to be as to develop them as ballers. It was almost as if by becoming a Lady Thorpe, you were somehow allowed to be a "girl" for a bit longer, allowed a few more days to be carefree.

It would be tempting to think that prepubescent girls are exempt from such vulnerability, but they aren't. Sexual abuse is a threat in some of the most dysfunctional families. And even when such abuse is ruled out, the instances in which young girls are made to feel dehumanized are everywhere. Even in basketball. In a 1995 basketball tournament, a girls' team from Loneman School at Oglala was summarily humiliated.[38] The girls, all ten to twelve years old at the time, represented the Pine Ridge Reservation in a tournament sponsored by the Rapid City YMCA (Young Men's Christian Association). After the Loneman team won the semifinal against Hermosa School, the losing coach, a white man, complained that one or more of the Loneman squad's eight members were really boys. This was an outrageous accusation to make in this day and age, but as ludicrous as it was, tournament officials took it seriously. So before the championship game, the eight Loneman team members were taken into a restroom where they were examined by non-medical staff, to prove that each was, in fact, a female. The girls had their panty waistbands and bra straps inspected. Scott Ten Fingers, coach of the Loneman School team, said that he didn't know about the examination at the time and that no one had granted permission for it to happen. The court appeal read that "No other teams were subjected to the search. . . . The Indian coach's word that his players were female was not sufficient to end the matter when challenged by a white team and coach."[39]

The outrage among many who read the story in the news centered on the racism implicit in the case, but the scenario was just as much about gender humiliation. Being an Indian girl means living in a world that is dangerous, but also one that degrades; and the Loneman School case was especially egregious because, in the already sensitive situation of playing in a mixed-race tournament, these girls were singled out for special degradation. In front of people they didn't know—and white people, at that—these innocent girls had to, in a manner of speaking, strip down and be inspected. At an age when youngsters are intensely self-conscious, they were made to endure the stares of strange white faces.

The late George Carlin, a master at sociolinguistics, once posed an interesting question—one that may be well suited to understanding women's resilience. He quipped, "There are women named Hope, Faith, Joy. . . . Why not Despair, Guilt, Rage, and Grief?"[40] One is tempted to answer this question by saying that women don't give into the despair, guilt, and rage—or, perhaps, it's that they can't afford to, if they are going to survive.

In the preface, I talked about the ability of people on Pine Ridge to wail and laugh in quick succession. Experiencing loss is heightened on Pine Ridge, and to avoid being swallowed up in the vortex of grief, people need to find something life-affirming . . . and fast. And this is what Laura Big Crow does. For instance, while at a softball tournament in Nebraska in July 2016, Laura was enjoying family time and preparing a pancake breakfast for her children and Corey, when suddenly, she learned of the death of one of her former students. The student, now a twelve-year-old girl, had been walking in Pine Ridge village when she was shot.

Laura's grief was immediate and overwhelming, compounded by knowing the girl's sister had committed suicide just a few months earlier. I saw the post Laura made on Facebook: "Prayers to all the youth hurting right now . . . woke up to hear some awful news . . . former students of mine who I care about so much are leaving us way too early . . . my heart breaks for these young babies making their journeys like this."

Like so many others at Pine Ridge, Laura Big Crow's life vacillates, sometime wildly, between sublime and sad. But with the exception of her love of family, Laura's optimism is possibly her most valued trait. After all, she needs plenty of it to bolster all those who depend on her. We might call it a special kind of resilience.

Pine Ridge basketball legend Jesse Heart. At 38, he was still a stalwart playing for the Plainzmen—a group of all-stars from various Plains tribes who compete in all-Indian tournaments. (Photograph courtesy of Dominic Tiger-Cortez)

Santana White Dress playing as a Pine Ridge Lady Thorpe.
(Photograph courtesy of Jerry Matthews)

Laura Big Crow, winner of the Spirit of Su Award in 2004.
(Photograph courtesy of Jerry Matthews)

Bryan Brewer, co-founder of Lakota Nation Invitational and former president of the Oglala Sioux Tribal Council. (Photograph courtesy of Jerry Matthews)

Corey Brown, Pine Ridge Thorpe star in 2019. (Photograph courtesy of Jerry Matthews)

Anissa Martin, a Pine Ridge Lady Thorpe, winning the Spirit of Su Award. Giving a star quilt is a traditional form of honoring someone. (Photograph courtesy of Jerry Matthews)

6

Pine Ridge versus Red Cloud

Social Factionalism Posing as Sports Rivalry

Home court is supposed to bestow an advantage on a home team on two fronts: First, surrounded by family, community, and familiar turf, home teams are playing in their comfort zones. They sleep in their own beds, prepare in their own locker room, and are cheered on by friendly and familiar faces.

Second, home court should be intimidating to teams coming from elsewhere to compete.

In its own way, then, a team's home court and its fans can replicate the warlike atmosphere found in situations, where enemies coming into their midst—whether as captives, attackers, or negotiators—are fearful. In this kind of interface between foes, the home community takes on its most fierce expression of solidarity. In a perhaps unwitting imitation of the *Maori Haka*—a ritualistic display of ferociousness that precedes battle—your home court fans express your war cry with all of its grandeur and intimidation, radiating threats to the outsider through sounds, colors, and smells. Sports rivalries feed on this atmosphere. Think Barcelona versus Madrid. Or New York versus Boston.

The Pine Ridge Thorpes court typifies this kind of community space. Murals, each close to 100 feet, span both long gym walls. Celebrating Oglala history, one side depicts the mid-nineteenth century northern Plains, when the Lakota hunted buffalo and roamed as lords. The scene, which depicts men and women in their camps, tending to their children, horses, and teepees, is drawn in a style reminiscent of nineteenth-century Lakota art. The other side depicts the changes brought about in the reservation era: missionaries, little Lakota children having their long hair lopped off, and so on.

Separate from the murals, banners commemorating championships hang high on the walls, like war trophies or totemic community expressions. Of course, school colors are also central to a team's identity, so the Thorpes gym bristles with red and black. If the décor doesn't command your attention, it nevertheless frames your field of vision, insisting this is Oglala space—so tread lightly. At game time, fans claim their seats bedecked in Thorpe gear of one sort or another, and they act loud and proud, owning the space. They want the opposing team to be more than a bit disconcerted. They want them, as one Thorpe fan delicately put it, "to shit themselves."

On this night, the opposing team was the Red Cloud Crusaders. The crowd arrived especially early to get seats. No one was really sure how the event would play out. The relationship between the two schools hadn't been cordial for a long time. "Old ones" came first and sat courtside, bundled in down coats. It was four degrees and snowing, and it would only get colder, so these old-timers would stay wrapped in their coats throughout the game. It's hard to warm up in this weather and harder still when your home heating is questionable and you're sixty, seventy, or older. One old woman in her wheelchair is checking out the Thorpes' warm-up drills. She's holding her cracked glasses, which have only one arm, up to her eyes, as if she might have something to say to these young men, one of whom is no doubt a distant relative.

Small packs of children were running up and down the stands as if they were hillsides. Infants were passed around from one "auntie" to another—and I mean passed around with ease and familiarity, as if each woman were the baby's mom. Here, there was no freaking out when a parent couldn't see his child. Most everyone was a relative of sorts, so children were casually accounted for rather than constantly monitored as they would be in a suburban counterpart to this event.

Former ballers, viewing current editions, were shouting encouragement or making comparisons: "They don't find the open man like we did, *enit* (right)?" A few wore T-shirts memorializing the famous 1987 Thorpe team that went undefeated en route to the state championship. And among the dialogue in the stands, there were all the recollections of games between these two bitter rivals. They could remember when things were so rancorous that games between them couldn't be played on either home court, even though the schools were just a short ten-minute drive apart; instead, they had to drive two hours away to Rapid City to play. But, they all said, things had settled down since then.

The crowd noise settled as Tiny DeCory, the aunt of Pine Ridge Girls Coach Laura Big Crow, announced the game and called for a moment of silence for two lifelong Thorpe fans who had "gone to the Spirit World recently." A uniformed color guard ended the moment of mourning, marching onto the court carrying three flags (of the United States, South Dakota, and the Oglala Sioux Tribe). They played the national anthem as a preamble to singing the Lakota Flag Song. Sung in Lakota, the latter was the meaningful piece to this ritualistic display of flags and marching.

When I mentioned to Dusty LeBeau that this would be my first Pine Ridge versus Red Cloud game, he said, "You'll hear things tonight all right, but a few years ago there used to be fist fights. There was one year we almost locked the crowd out and played in an empty gym." For all of tonight's pregame hype, nothing happened. Pine Ridge won. There were no fights. Nothing even close. And everyone felt grateful that things had gone so smoothly, because this trouble-free, tensionless game was virgin territory in the history of these two schools.

But to me, to characterize a game as "trouble-free" (rather than "exciting," "an outstanding performance," or "hard-fought") was more than curious.

School Rivalry

The meaning of the sports terms *home* and *away* are most fully revealed in rivalries between schools. When the relationship between schools is built on social acrimony involving class, race, or cultural distinctions, these rivalries galvanize communities and their teams. The games cease being merely heated sport competition. In the most intense rivalries, the vitriol is palpable as enemies seethe in each other's presence. Games then become incubators for insults, intimidation, and displays of domination—all designed to exalt, sting, and be mulled over—and over time, those incubators produce a history, amplifying the terms *away* and *home* into notions of danger and safety.

The Pine Ridge versus Red Cloud game that night epitomized all this and more; it was a high school rivalry that went right to the heart of who the Oglala Lakota of Pine Ridge are. Because the two schools endure the same hostile environment of South Dakota and serve the same people—the same tribe—they shouldn't have been rivals at all. They should have been staunchly defending each other, and even extensions of each other, in this state that has isolated all Lakota and hated them since before its statehood. In fact, belonging to the same reservation, which was roughly the size of Delaware and Connecticut combined, Pine Ridge and Red Cloud high schools were so close in proximity to each other and worked with so few resources that they should have been regularly playing each other—scrimmaging each other weekly and even sharing each other's equipment and staff. But, they may as well have been 5,000 miles apart. With an erratic history of competition, which included several stretches when play between them was suspended and even whole decades when they could play each other only in third-party facilities located hours away from both schools, one can only surmise that there was a level of rancor here that couldn't be explained in sport terms, even if that's how it got played out. This was a rivalry that had been experienced as much in the breach and bitterness as it had in engagement and respect.

Oddly, the origins of this mutual bitterness seemed to elude people on both sides. Whenever I asked about it, the response I often got was denial: that relations may have once been rocky but were now unimportant; or that any rivalry was strictly about sports. And those who admitted to the acrimony might soften it by saying, "It wasn't ever the kids. It was only the parents," or "It was never as bad as they say." But no one denies that, for many years, the two teams did not play each other, regardless of the different leagues they may have been part of at various times.

In what follows, it becomes clear that Pine Ridge versus Red Cloud is a sports rivalry resting on a volatile tectonic fault line over a century old—a fault line of compressed resentment between two social-political reservation factions. Today, those factions are known as "full bloods" and "mixed bloods," but in the past, they went by names like "hostiles" and "friendlies." Despite sharing a history and culture, these modern-day factions are also divided by culture, language, and most of all, by their orientation toward whites.

Paul Robertson, who spent years on Pine Ridge, wrote a book examining the ways in which mixed bloods had, both through chicanery and through legal and bureaucratic wiles, usurped control of tribal land on Pine Ridge.[1] The book details the insidious manner in which certain mixed bloods found common cause with white ranchers to harm the Lakota land base beginning in the 1880s and lasting to the present. To the rest of the Lakota, this has amounted to collaboration with the enemy.

To be clear, the terms *full blood* and *mixed blood* have little to do with biological purity and almost everything to do with orientations to traditional Lakota life; so one may look light-skinned but be considered full blood if they engage in traditional activities, live in certain areas, or speak Lakota. Regardless, for almost a century and a half now, mixed blood plus full blood has equaled "bad blood."

The school rivalry I look at in this chapter is only a sporting reflection of this longstanding mutual distrust—a mere embodiment of a division that dates back to the reservation's very beginnings.

The Latest Round

In an engaging article in the *Los Angeles Times* written in 1999, sportswriter Bill Plaschke detailed this hostile rivalry between the two schools.[2] He reported that the latest round of hostilities was prompted by a brawl late in 1991, between Pine Ridge basketball legend SuAnne Big Crow (along with her family and friends) and a group of girls from Red Cloud. The brawl had erupted at Big Bats, the gas station and convenience store in the center of the Pine Ridge community. It was a mélange of girls punching, scratching, swearing, and ripping at each other's clothes, and everyone involved was arrested on disorderly conduct charges. It came to nothing *in court*, but it had serious repercussions *on the court*: after that incident, Pine Ridge and Red Cloud would not play each other for more than a decade (1992–2005), and when play resumed, they would not play in each other's schools for yet another decade. They considered it safer to drive an hour and a half through bone-chilling winter nights, risking occasional whiteout conditions, to see games in Rapid City than to brave the hostile crowds only a few miles away. And even then, games were marred by fights in the stands, lobbies, parking lots, and streets of Pine Ridge—anywhere passions pulsed. They'd battle with fists, stones, and, on one occasion, screwdrivers.

"It went off the court. It was heated," says Narcisse Heart. "Parents mostly, Pine Ridge, Red Cloud, even Little Wound. Even though we're on the same reservation, we're the same people, we'll be battling each other."[3]

It was as if there was a basketball civil war in the tribe, with once close families or relatives now set against each other. You were identified as being with one school or the other, and people were going to ridiculous lengths to influence game outcomes. In one game in the mid-1990s, when the teams played in Rapid City, the Red Cloud Lady Crusaders' best player was pregnant. When she missed school just prior to a game, her grandmother had her arrested for truancy, and a Pine Ridge judge (and fan) decided to jail her for the tournament. Red Cloud fanatics got wind of this and got one of "their" judges to order her release. Dusty LeBeau was the Red Cloud coach back then and was driving the team bus to Rapid City when a "Red Cloud-identified tribal policeman" pulled him over and informed him that he should take all back roads to Rapid City because the main road out of the rez was patrolled by Pine Ridge cops looking to put her back in jail. Red Cloud Police and Pine Ridge Police? Not Oglala Sioux tribal police? At the game, Pine Ridge supporters tried to convince the refs to prohibit the girl from playing because she was pregnant. She played and Red Cloud won, but the entire affair was colored by this highly toxic partisanship.

Brandon Ecoffey attended Red Cloud from first grade through his junior year in high school. He played on the Red Cloud Crusaders varsity team for three years but did the unthinkable when he transferred to Pine Ridge for his senior year. When I asked him whether he'd come in for his share of recrimination for switching schools like that, he explained, "I avoided a lot of the outsider problems in transferring to Pine Ridge, because I had played sports with all these guys my whole life. We played Little League baseball together, so it wasn't a big deal. I left because Red Cloud was filled with freshmen, and they weren't very competitive. Some of the older people, though, they wouldn't talk to me ever again."[4] When viewed in community terms, Ecoffey's shift was more than a basketball decision; older folks saw it as perfidy, and it affected relationships within and between families.

The mutual animosity also affected other areas of life. If a Red Cloud supporter were running for office, he might be defeated by a solid Pine Ridge block of votes cast against him. In the area of jobs, Robert Yellow Hair, a former tribal vice president recalled, "Jobs here are sometimes handed out by tribal officials on the basis of where the prospective employee attended school. Red Cloud people won't give jobs to Pine Ridge people that quickly, and vice versa."[5]

This malicious sporting relationship, however, actually predates the SuAnne Big Crow incident. Writing about Pine Ridge basketball a half century earlier, in the 1940s, Lakota journalist Charles Trimble singled out the rivalry between Holy Rosary (as Red Cloud High was then called) and Oglala Community High School (as Pine Ridge High was then called) as, "the worst and roughest."[6] That rancor between the schools foreshadowed the cessation of play in the 1990s. Trimble wrote that "The competition between the schools was officially suspended for a decade through the 1950s because of the violence."[7] And when describing the atmosphere leading to that decision not to play each other, Trimble wrote, "The games were as hotly contested in the stands and on the streets as on the court and resulted in many fights among adults. A group of high school girls from Holy Rosary— who were transported to the game in a stake-rack truck for lack of a bus— was bombarded with rocks following a victorious game, and one girl was knocked unconscious."[8]

Trimble's reports make two things are clear: The rivalry's acrimonious origin was not initiated by the Big Crow fight but started at least a half century earlier. Second, a rivalry that elicits such extreme behavior and over such a long time period has to be rooted in something bigger than sports.

Religious Divide

At a distance, there are broad commonalities between Pine Ridge and Red Cloud. Both campuses comprise fairly contemporary buildings and hire certified teachers. Both claim to be dedicated to serving the children of Pine Ridge. But scratch the surface, and you become quickly aware that the most powerful difference between the two schools lies in their academic performance. Red Cloud is a stellar example of a high-functioning school, while the vast majority of the other twenty-four schools on the reservation are chronically struggling. Students at Red Cloud students typically score high on state tests, graduate, and go off to college, while students at the others schools generally fail to meet state proficiency requirements,. Red Cloud High boasts the distinction of having produced more Gates Millennium Scholars (72) than any other school of its size in the country—a remarkable achievement. Pine Ridge High, on the other hand, is chronically under-performing. This difference may have some bearing on the depth of ill will swirling around their sports rivalry, but it isn't the ultimate source of acrimony. The ultimate source is found in the role that the Red Cloud school has played in Oglala history.

Staunchly Jesuit, the school these days builds its brand by peddling academic rigor and homage to Lakota culture. It has been on Pine Ridge for almost a century and a half, beginning as Holy Rosary before taking on its current name in 1969. But, as progressive as Red Cloud High is today, its origins were ignoble and abusive. Holy Rosary was once as committed to cultural genocide as it is now to resurrecting and protecting Lakota culture. It was as driven to training Indian children to take menial positions in the local economy as it now is to get them to excel in college and beyond. Established as part of a pincer-like educational movement at the core of Indian assimilation policy, in which federal and religious boarding schools were combined, Holy Rosary opened its doors in 1888. Pine Ridge's government school—Pine Ridge Boarding School—had already opened its doors five years earlier, in 1883.

Holy Rosary is fond of claiming that they were asked to minister to the Lakota by none other than Chief Red Cloud himself, one of the West's most famous figures. In a meeting with government officials on White Clay Creek in 1876, and later in a White House meeting with President Rutherford B. Hayes, Red Cloud was reported to have said, "We would like to have a schoolhouse—a large one, that will hold plenty of people. We would like to have Catholic priests and Catholic nuns, so that they could teach our people how to write and read, and instruct us."[9] It seems incongruous that an inveterate foe of whites such as Red Cloud would be so eager to have the "black robes," as Jesuits were called, settle among his tribe. Additionally, why, with a government school already in place, would Red Cloud so openly court another? We know that quite a few indigenous resistance leaders became convinced of the futility of opposing the U.S. government, but Red Cloud had always been politically savvy. He had never been one to hesitate to oppose the U.S. Army or government policy. So why the turnabout? We can understand the strategic, if sobering, point he would have arrived at— that the old ways would be inadequate to prepare future generations—but white schools already existed, so why lobby for another? Perhaps an answer comes from the rancor that occurred between Red Cloud and the Indian agent at Pine Ridge.

During most of the 1880s, Valentine T. McGillycuddy, an impatient and arrogant administrator with little respect for the Lakota, was the Indian agent in charge. He made an instant enemy of Red Cloud, and the two worked overtime at undermining each other.[10] One can't help but link Red Cloud's strategic request for Jesuits to his gaining the upper hand with the government in ridding Pine Ridge of this agent. Ultimately, Red Cloud's efforts paid off, and the agent was replaced. The Jesuits have been leveraging Red Cloud's request for them to come to Pine Ridge ever since, and particularly now that they've been able to cash in on the "new" Red Cloud school's cultural affinity for the Oglala.

For its first eighty or so years, Holy Rosary's intentional and severe suppression of all things Lakota and Indian was an extension of the federal government's far-flung boarding school program. The architect of that program, Captain Richard Henry Pratt, started the nation's first Indian boarding school—Carlisle Indian School in Carlisle, Pennsylvania—in 1879. His guiding principle was one of forced assimilation and total immersion. It was Pratt who coined the famous dictum "Kill the Indian to save the man," the meaning of which is patently clear in cultural terms. Carl Shurz, secretary of the interior under President Rutherford Hayes, shared this sense of bringing Native populations into the American cultural domain. In his words, Indian policy was built on "a stern alternative: extermination or civilization."[11] All of this was in keeping with the basic beliefs of the Jesuits as well.

Combined with the Allotment Act of 1889 (which took Indian reservation land out of the tribal collective domain, apportioning it as private property to Indians while, at the same time, opening up more Indian lands to white settlement), these policies were hoped to give Indians an economic and social stake in the American system. Instead, however, they amounted to a sweeping governmental effort at cultural genocide.

Assimilation was thought to be wasted on adult Native Americans, whose ways were set; conversely, youngsters were ripe for turning into, as Pratt called it, "imitation white men." Total immersion was Pratt's modus operandi, so, children were prohibited from speaking their language, sporting their long hair, wearing their clothes, eating their food, and of course worshiping their gods. Pratt's affinity for carrying out all things in a military fashion was also adopted, meaning children were coerced into a daily regimen of discipline, regimentation, and surveillance, all while learning skills that reinforced white Christian society. Punishment, often severe, was considered essential to combat backsliding and instill white values.

The callousness in this view of assimilation was, in part, explained by Pratt's original experiment in Indian assimilation. In the 1870s, he had been appointed warden of a prison that housed Kiowa and Cheyenne prisoners who had fought against the United States. His charge included resocializing them so that they might eventually fit back into a world that was radically different than the one they grew up in, and his canvas consisted of incarceration and education—complete control of mind and body. The notion that a model for the assimilation of children had been built on a like model used for an adult prison population was never questioned.

While the physical abuse in these boarding schools was often inhumane, the psychological dimension was at least as bad and maybe worse. Being socially torn away was hard enough on adults, but for children to lose their social bearings was much more damaging. Oglala journalist Tim Giago recalled, "We lost the connection to our parents and grandparents that is so vital to the continuation of our culture and spirituality. From our parents and grandparents, we learned about all the things that made us Indian."[12] At boarding and government day schools, these children were stripped of that link to Indian culture. It was total immersion, so that upon boys' and girls' entry into the schools, their Indian identity was removed.

At Pine Ridge Boarding School in the 1880s, for instance, the staff marched newly arrived children into a room, one at a time, to cut off their braids. In one instance, some of the children waiting outside happened to catch a glimpse of what was happening and responded with shock. "Like a war hoop rang out the cry: '*Pahim Kaksa*! . . . They're cutting the hair! . . . Through the door and windows, the children flew, down the steps and over fences in a mad flight toward the Indian villages. . . . They had been suspicious of the school from the beginning; now they knew it was intended to bring disgrace upon them."[13]

As the cultural onslaught continued, their clothes were taken from them, replaced by uniforms that were coarse and scratchy. Stiff leather shoes encased and tortured their feet. Indian names went wherever their Native clothes were taken, a move that guaranteed confusion and identity loss. A young eight-year-old Pattwin Indian, Tah-rruhm, became Bill Wright with a stroke of the pen. His first visit home caused his family consternation as he recalls, "I remember coming home and my grandma asked me to talk Indian to her and I said, 'Grandma, I don't understand you.' She said, 'Then who are you?'" Wright says he told her his name was Billy. "'Your name's not Billy. Your name's TAH-rruhm,' she told him. "And I went, 'That's not what they told me.'"[14]

Dietary changes followed, often with dangerous results. Luther Standing Bear, an Oglala, was in the first class at Carlisle and summarized the trauma and tragedy they went through: "Of all the changes we were forced to make, that of diet was doubtless the most injurious, for it was immediate and drastic. White bread we had for the first meal and thereafter, as well as coffee and sugar. Had we been allowed our own simple diet of meat, either boiled with soup or dried, and fruit, with perhaps a few vegetables, we should have thrived. But the change in clothing, housing, food and confinement combined with lonesomeness was too much, and in three years nearly one half of the children from the Plains were dead and through with all earthly schools. In the graveyard at Carlisle most of the graves are those of little ones."[15]

Quite often, children referred to themselves as "survivors" of these schools, and since then, some have written about their experiences.[16] Some expressed their boarding school experience in terms that parallel concentration camps. Others thought of it as getting through an unpleasant experience, while acknowledging that they gained skills that helped them. And one, Luther Standing Bear, a Lakota who left Rosebud for Carlisle Indian School in 1879, thought of his experience in a most revealing and unusual way: He looked forward to school as a life-and-death challenge to prove himself a warrior. Standing Bear saw modernity as an extension of Lakota tradition. In his autobiography, he claimed, "I was thinking of my father, and how he had many times said to me, 'Son, be brave. Die on the battlefield, if necessary away from home . . . it occurred to me that this chance to go East would prove that I was brave.'"[17] But no matter how one felt about boarding schools, the connection to culture and family was seriously ruptured.

The person most completely committed to critiquing the boarding school experience has been Tim Giago.[18] As a student at Holy Rosary for ten years, in the 1940s and 1950s, he experienced and later chronicled many of the soul-wrenching cruelties propagated by the clergy at Holy Rosary Mission School before its dramatic makeover. The worst of it was the sexual abuse perpetrated upon little children who, as a result, felt doubly powerless: first as Indians, then as children. The scars they bore reverberated beyond their generation, noted Giago. "My eight-year-old sister was raped at the mission school [Holy Rosary] by a pedophile. My younger sister told me about her abuse on her deathbed and I, along with her three children, finally understood why she had become a violent, alcoholic woman for so much of her life. She died angry at the world and all alone. If only she had spoken sooner maybe we could have helped her."[19]

In 2003, one hundred Lakota who had attended Holy Rosary and St. Francis on the Pine Ridge and Rosebud reservations during the 1960s and 1970s filed a class action suit in which they alleged that they had been sexually abused as children by clergy. One of the plaintiffs was Sonny One Star. He was taken from his family in 1963, at age six, in part because he only spoke Lakota. "One day here comes a car, my father gets out and talks to my grandmother, and off I went," he recalled. "That's when my ordeal started. . . . My grandmother started singing a death song. People had lost relatives at other Indian schools, so she looked at it as a one-way death sentence."[20] One Star's grandmother's reaction summarizes the feelings of most traditional Lakota that the confiscation of children constituted a brutal cultural act.

In his interview with a *Washington Post* writer, One Star continued his story with his arrival at the mission boarding school. The sexual abuse started shortly thereafter, One Star said, and included fondling, oral sex, or rape by two nuns and five priests or brothers.

"I was quiet," he said. "I never spoke up. I never said anything." He dreaded one nun's repeated advances at recess. "I can still smell her, feel her grip. A terrible woman." When during a school vacation, One Star told his grandmother what was happening, she refused to send him back, he said. When school officials came to fetch him, she hid him under the bed.

"But my father and mother, they wouldn't believe me at all, whatsoever," One Star said. "It's very hard to have someone believe stuff like that. And no one wanted to bring something like that into the open. My dad might lose his job."[21] The shame and the refusal to process all this is understandable, as is the self-destruction that follows. One Star became alcoholic; many others became suicidal or abusers themselves.

Daily, run-of-the-mill slights and punishments may have been more easily born, but their cumulative weight took its toll. Stories of sadistic punishments by nuns and priests make up the memories of many children—Native and non-Native—who attended Catholic schools through the middle of the twentieth century, but Indian kids were more scarred than others, if for no other reason than they were brought there against their will and raised in an alien and unfamiliar manner. Even parents who felt that getting a white education would make life easier for their children in the long run also understood that boarding schools were antithetical to Lakota ideas about raising children, and those parents must have wondered from time to time whether they'd made the right decision.

For Indian children, the initial shock of their physical transformation was followed by a regimen of surveillance and coerced foreign practices. Many boys and girls sought to run away; however, those who did were, like fugitive slaves in the antebellum South, hunted down, returned, and made to face greater punishments.

Witnessing one of his classmates being punished in such a scenario, Tom Gannon decided to act. "I saw him beaten interminably by the Brothers, by a paddle several inches thick; and on one occasion they struck his buttocks so hard that his head was propelled into the concrete wall several feet away. So, we ran away, once, my brother and me. We were also too young and stupid to realize that home—Rapid City—was almost a hundred miles away. And we only got about two or three miles, I figure, through the semi-desert, cactus-ridden terrain before we gave up and lay down on the side of the highway, waiting for the Jesuit van to find us and take us back. To another nice paddle-beating, as you can well imagine."[22]

In comparison to the experience of other runaways, however, Tom Gannon's outcome was fairly benign. Tim Giago recalls, for example, a boy at Holy Rosary who everyone called Omaha. The boy escaped from the school and ran straight into a sudden winter storm, suffering severe frostbite to his feet. Upon finding him, the school took him to Omaha where both of his feet had to be amputated. Despite his brush with death, the wonders of this big city so captivated him that he wouldn't stop talking about it. The other boys at Holy Rosary ended up calling him Omaha, and his life became one of being pulled around the school seated on a red wagon while brandishing a whip and a cruel smile.[23]

In fact, schools would have their own trackers, whose job it was to hunt down escaped children and return them. Punishment for this violation ranged from having one's hair completely shorn to receiving a beating. This practice continued into the 1950s, indicating the punishments meant little to Native children.

Former Oglala tribal president Bryan Brewer recounted his experience at Holy Rosary School in the 1950s: "I was always fighting this one boy, and this priest got tired of it and he took this baseball bat to the two of us. All over my back and legs, he beat me . . . and he told me I'd have to stand against the wall every free time I had 'til school ended (three months away). I said, 'I can't do that. I'm taking off.' One of my cousins said he'd go with me. . . .

So we ate breakfast, and walked behind the school, crossed the highway and went up into the hills. Guys would run away, and they had 'chasers,' and when they caught you they'd take you back and shave your head. We watched the high school door open and they come running out . . . so we ran all the way to Pine Ridge (four miles away)."[24]

Most times, runaways who made it home would be returned to school by intimidated parents, but Bryan's father, a tribal policeman, was outraged at his beating. "My dad came home and saw me. 'What happened?' [he asked.] I told him, and he says, 'Show me.' I took my shirt off and pulled my pants down. Solid bruise up my back. He says, 'Get in the car.' My dad was so mad he went after that priest. Couldn't catch him though, 'cause dad had all his gear on and he was older. Don't know what would've happened if my dad woulda caught him."[25] Bryan's father had him clear out his locker, took him home to get some lunch, and then drove him over to Lakota Community School and enrolled him. These memories inform much of the Natives' current lack of faith in Christian institutions.

Not everyone's memories of these schools were so fraught with trauma and pain as to scar them completely. Many kids just endured it and even toyed with it. I read several recollections of a boarding school student, Charles Trimble, a highly accomplished Lakota journalist who attended Holy Rosary in the 1940s and 1950s. He detailed his experiences there, and, in stark contrast to many others', his recollections, while acknowledging punishment, were absent of the mutilating memories.

"Last week, June fifth, I attended an all classes reunion at the Indian boarding school from which I graduated fifty-eight years ago. . . . At a picnic lunch a microphone was passed around so that people could tell about the old days when things were much different, more difficult, and harsh. Many identified themselves as boarding school "survivors;" however, even the stories about harsh discipline, including physical punishment, were told with humor. Horror stories of terrible beatings and feelings of bitterness were absent."[26] But cruelties of all sorts did, in fact, occur and even characterize the school—a reality borne out in the widespread attitudes on Pine Ridge to Holy Rosary.

The Great Makeover

The Oglala Community School (today's Pine Ridge School System) also punished students for transgressions but never garnered the reputation for cruelty that the Jesuit school did. For many at Pine Ridge, the Catholic school and its nuns and priests continue as a potent symbol of twisted foreign overseers who terrorized generations of Oglala. For older generations, Red Cloud School's name change and personnel makeover from clergy to laymen wasn't sufficient to completely change their attitudes toward the school. The school's current emphasis on academic accomplishment and prep school pretentions is seen by many as a continuation of the outsider's imposition of culture and serves to maintain the social divide that previously existed on religious grounds. The religious divide, in turn, morphs into a social, quasi-class divide.

Bryan Brewer "survived" Holy Rosary; and while he disliked it, he came back to Red Cloud as a coach after serving in the navy and finishing college. The odious clergy were gone, he noted, replaced by lay people and a sense of social exclusivity:

> It was hard for me at Red Cloud. Though there were nice people there—all white—there were only three or four of us Indians who worked there. They just had their own community down there. Other churches mingle more, but not the Catholics. Also, it was hard to listen to their attitudes towards Pine Ridge High School and Little Wound. When I went there (Holy Rosary), they took everybody—all the pitiful ones, special needs—but now you gotta take a test to get in there. And at Red Cloud you get parents dropping kids off in their cars 'cause they're working. BIA money.[27]

Brewer's reference to special-needs kids refers to the many families on the reservation who have been scarred by the high rates of alcoholism, which results in mothers giving birth to children who suffer from fetal alcohol syndrome (a condition caused by a mother drinking when she is pregnant, which results in much higher rates of learning and behavioral disabilities). The rising number of children born with this condition additionally burdens the ability of schools to educate, and the Red Cloud Schools want nothing to do with them; they end up funneling these students into the reservation's other schools, swelling the numbers of students with learning difficulties at those schools while leaving Red Cloud's academic profile unblemished. Add to this the number of babies now being born to meth addicts, who also have learning disabilities coupled with aggression, and schools like Little Wound High may have upwards of 20 percent of the student body that is learning impaired. So, while Red Cloud may tout itself as being in sync with Lakota values, its student enrollment policies are anything but.

In addition, Brewer's comment about parents dropping off their children in cars might easily slip by unnoticed, but it is a subtle socioeconomic marker. The vast majority of parents on the rez don't have the reliable cars or the gas necessary to ferry their children to and from school; however, most Red Cloud parents are from among the roughly 20 percent of those who are employed. Red Cloud also demands that parents take a hands-on role in their children's education, something commonplace in middle-class homes but not remotely part of the working culture of most Oglala.

So, in the minds of many at Pine Ridge, Red Cloud people display a sense of social superiority that, mixed with their Catholicism, makes them hard to take for others. Anything that is attributed to Red Cloud will often elicit comments like, "Yeah, well, you know how Catholics are," or, "Yeah, they think they're better than anyone else."[28]

As such, Brewer's return to Red Cloud might have been to a less Catholic-feeling place, but it was one that had simply supplanted Catholic authoritarianism with class privilege. Brandon Ecoffey echoed Brewer's view. He attended Red Cloud through almost all of secondary school. When I asked him what was different about Red Cloud, he responded, "Some people are driven by community. They're the ones that go with Pine Ridge High School. Red Cloud caters to a population looking for upward mobility. They have a little bubble over there, separate from everyday people. It's pretty segregated."[29]

He goes further, linking Red Cloud's current persona as a protector of Lakota values to poverty porn. "There's a tension between agency folks who have access to resources and others who don't. Red Cloud was geared toward attracting those with more resources. It's developed a marketing strategy that uses the poverty here to generate donations. So, they profit from the problems we have here."[30]

This tension between upward mobility and a departure from traditional values begs the question: Is the converse true? That is, are authentic Lakota values to be found only in impoverishment? Success shouldn't be equated with abandoning Lakota culture. Red Cloud sits in a very precarious place in Lakota society—perched between rupturing with its past and being a steward of that past; between changing conditions that have plagued the reservation and protecting much of the culture that has been closely linked to an anachronistic past. The critiques of Red Cloud are based on its building exclusivity, but the school's effort to break with past failures (both its cultural insensitivity and the history of academic failure on the reservation) are welcome. It seems the divide has shifted axis rather than disappeared.

In trying to understand where this relationship is going and where it came from, we can view it in terms of peeling an onion. What initially looked like a sports rivalry revealed a layer of divisiveness built around either acceptance or resistance to white education. This, in turn, revealed additional factional divisions going back to the beginnings of the reservation system.

The Early Reservation Factions

Even before boarding schools and religion became issues splitting the Lakota, there were internal social rifts at work. The Lakota didn't move onto reservations as a tribe; rather bands and parts of bands haphazardly straggled in as buffalo herds dwindled to the point where they couldn't feed their families. The first groups settling on the reservation were those who had grown most comfortable around white traders and administrators. These bands were derisively referred to by other Lakota as "Loaf-about-the-Fort Indians," but the U.S. government liked referring to them as "friendlies." The last to enter the reservation were those who clung to their autonomy—called "hostiles" by government officials. U.S.-appointed Indian agents or superintendents in charge of maintaining the reservations inherited the problem of keeping order among a combination of hostile and friendly bands. The problem for white administrators became one of minimizing the disruptive potential of figures like Sitting Bull and Crazy Horse. The government felt they would likely incite young men all over the reservation to fight. This fear was often fueled by rumors emanating from the friendly camp. As noted by Black Elk in his autobiography, the surrender of Crazy Horse elevated fears: "the Hang-Around-the-Fort people said that he [Crazy Horse] was getting ready to tie up his horse's tail again and make war on the *wasichus* [whites]."[31] This perception of Crazy Horse and Sitting Bull played a key part in the U.S. government's soliciting the reservation's Indian police to arrest and kill both leaders when they offered even the slightest hesitation. Both friendlies and Indian agents, uneasy about living amid unruly elements, readily spread such misinformation. By 1889, the Lakota were grimly certain that U.S. policy and the agents on the reservation were undermining the treaties. The hostile Lakota embraced a renegade religious movement that had come out of the Western Plains, known as the Ghost Dance. It preached apocalypse: a dance that hastened the end of their world on the reservation and the subsequent rebirth of the halcyon days—a world free of whites and a return to buffalo-hunting days. Hostiles enthusiastically took to this revitalization movement, heightening the sense of panic in the eyes of already nervous Indian agents and their friendly allies.

Administrators on reservations both sought to contain the threat by getting more troops to the area and to undermine the authority of traditional chiefs by elevating the status of lesser leaders (treaty chiefs).[32] By giving these lesser chiefs control of the annuity goods for distribution among their people, they hoped to increase economic dependency on these treaty chiefs while diminishing the influence of people like Crazy Horse or Sitting Bull.

In the early days of the reservation, Indian Agent Douglas Cooper claimed that favoring compliant Indians was an effective political strategy: "The best method for settling trouble is to use the good element against the bad and quiet the matter."[33] Reservation politics have followed this strategy ever since. By the twentieth century, friendlies became known as "mixed bloods" while hostiles were renamed "full bloods." This was a misnomer derived from the idea that blood quantum was a valid predictor of which faction one belonged to, though it had little to do with blood and everything to do with cultural and political orientation: if you followed the older cultural ways, you were full-blooded no matter what you looked like.

When, later in 1934, the Indian Reorganization Act was enacted, it set in motion a modern tribal governmental organization based on elections, with a president, a vice president, and councilmen from each of nine political districts. It was done with an assimilationist eye, promoting "democratic" elections and a government free of kinship and old-time values. But, as with all such policy, the friendlies were poised to take advantage of the new system. They were more open to attending and completing white schools, spoke English better, were more likely to be Christian, and had control of the relatively few jobs that were around. They, their families, and their friends continued their political control of the reservation by taking over the tribal government. Meanwhile, the traditionalist-oriented full bloods were more reluctant to get involved with this new form of governance, and as a result they were, until recently, virtually powerless.

Kathleen Pickering's work on Pine Ridge noted that traditional factions showed their disapproval by not engaging in the process at all. One Pine Ridge traditionalist she spoke with stated, "No one believes in voting. It's only those people who have positions that go to the poles. Everybody else stays away. That was the traditional way of expressing your disapproval."[34] Disapproval by "flight," is something we see in many traditional egalitarian societies that lack coercive authority. But of course, this only perpetuated mixed-blood control over reservation politics.

The Impact of the Hide Trade

The halcyon days of Plains Indian culture centered on the material affluence accompanying the buffalo hide trade. Metal goods (from sewing needles to knives, guns, and ammunition), dress goods (fabrics, beads of every kind, European paints), American foods (coffee and sugar), and, by the 1840s, alcohol, were all introduced as trade goods. The lure of so many exotic and technologically remarkable goods increased the degree to which Indian groups hunted buffalo, which would allow them to secure trade goods.

But imbedded in the newfound affluence and political expansion of the Lakota was a growing dependence on these trade goods. The robust economy carried within it the eventual loss of autonomy. As such, bands that kept a respectable distance from the trade (coming in to trade but not to lose autonomy) also used the derogatory term "hang-about-the-fort-Indians" to describe those who had succumbed to the trade. Black Elk noted this dependent status to his biographer John Neihardt. Black Elk, whose band followed Crazy Horse, considered Red Cloud a hang-about-the-fort-Indian.[35] Early nineteenth century fur traders, such as Edwin Denig of the Upper Missouri, used this term as well. Tribal leaders like Sitting Bull cautioned their people against overreliance on the trade and, by extension, overreliance on whites. Traders, however, preferred Indians who were friendly and considered them trustworthy. Groups that were leery of whites and the trade were considered very dangerous to do business with, so it was fairly common for traders to attempt to marry into bands (e.g., the Bent brothers among the Cheyenne or Edwin Denig among the Dakota) to promote the security of trade.[36] These strategic marriages often resulted in an increasing reliance of native bands upon the traders that they could now count on as kinsmen.

Dividing Indians into friendly and hostile factions had also become common military strategy after 1876, when Indian conflict was a matter formally transferred to the secretary of war, who codified it. This divide was a quick and dirty way to wage the U.S. campaign of pacification. As the terms suggest, those like Crazy Horse or Gall, who preached distance from whites, were declared hostile to U.S. interests. They became legitimate targets for the U.S. Army. Friendlies, on the other hand, were amenable to U.S. interests, and after being empowered as treaty chiefs, assisted the pursuit of government policy of every stripe.

Undergirding these divisions was the position each faction took toward assimilation. Embodied in everything Red Cloud School currently has and promotes, assimilation included upward mobility, more education, control over reservation resources, and a Catholic (or Christian) leaning. It was also found in the economic control of grazing lands on Pine Ridge by a certain cohort of mixed bloods and white ranchers.

Opposing assimilation were those (hostiles, full bloods) who preferred to distance themselves from white institutions; they remained traditionalist, were unlikely to hold tribal government jobs, and were eager to continue separation. To this day, those living at a distance from the governmental center (the town of Pine Ridge) are more likely to practice traditional religion and speak Lakota and less likely to send their children to Red Cloud School. Bryan Brewer attended Holy Rosary but graduated from Pine Ridge High School because his father was willing to remove him from the physical beatings of the priests. So despite being well-educated, Bryan identifies with traditional Lakota ways and looks critically at the role that Catholicism (and, by extension, Red Cloud) plays on the rez:

> There's the church. Our Lakota religion has been too influenced by the Christians in big and little ways. If I'm going to a Sun Dance, I got my eagle feathers. I gotta take it to a medicine man to get 'em blessed? I'm a traditional dancer! The bustle I make, I gotta have em blessed!? We never did anything like that before. No man can make an eagle feather holy! They're already holy! It's the Catholics that do that. They bless everything! So now its our [Lakota] spiritualism that gets affected.[37]

The divide between traditionalists and assimilationists isn't hard and fast. Many people who were educated at Red Cloud and raised to be Catholic found it easy to forsake it. However, if we see this longstanding and layered division as an ideological split among Lakota as to how they will deal with being enmeshed in a white world, then the two schools are symbols of a century and a half of factional dispute.

Conclusion

SuAnne Big Crow wasn't aware of the historic depth of this factional divide when she got into that fight with the Red Cloud girls. Rather, the fight was understood to have been generated by their envy of her dominance on the court, which was acted out as heat-of-the-moment trash talking, which led to punches being thrown. But I've tried to show that the rivalry between the two school teams is an unconscious manifestation of longstanding factional resentment, which dates back to the era of the buffalo-hide trade and, through every decade since, has created a chasm separated by two main streams: culture and economics.

Rooted in the Lakota response to white intrusion into life, this deep social chasm within Oglala society now poses as a sporting event. And since the tribe has never been able to create consensus on these matters, it's now up to *tiyospayé* and smaller family units to consider what adapting to white culture represents to them. As it was in the beginning, those who feel there is more to be gained than lost favor accommodation, and those who see white culture as antithetical to Native ways seek to avoid close proximity.

There is a catch however: since the issue arose so early in Indian-white relations, the assimilationists/friendlies/mixed bloods have been able to control political and economic life on the reservations. They were reinforced early on by traders and Indian agents and later took the reins in tribal political office-holding. Meanwhile, hostiles/traditionalists/full bloods removed themselves from the scene but, in so doing, disenfranchised themselves.

And so today, by comparison to Red Cloud School, the three public high schools on Pine Ridge are where the less intelligent, less privileged, and more traditional children tend to go; and the lack of funding and staffing, along with the profusion of learning-disabled students, guarantees that the divide between them and Red Cloud will continue. These economic and educational differences between the schools plays out in unfortunate, frightening, and humiliating ways, from gang incidents in hallways, to exposed asbestos, to the basic needs of children not being tended to. The divide is tangible at the level of the everyday experience of these children, but it too often gets missed in general discussion about the issues. Eleanor Goldberg's *Huffington Post* article provides an example of the disturbing and immediacy of this social divide I'm referring to. Goldberg noted that female students in Pine Ridge schools live with regular anxiety about whether they'll be able to attend classes during menstruation. Not being able to afford tampons haunts many of the girls in the school system and also aggravates many of the larger issues they negotiate: like being teens, functioning in a school setting, and thinking about the future. Julia Chipps, the nurse at Crazy Horse School, recalls one young student who "was considering getting pregnant. That way, she wouldn't have to worry about buying tampons for a while."[38] How's that for a disastrous short-term solution? Adding insult to injury, the cost of tampons is roughly twice as high on the reservation than off of it: $7.39 on the rez as compared to $3.97 ninety miles away at Walmart in Rapid City. Because she couldn't afford tampons, Dominique Amiotte's cousin was dropped from school after missing too many classes her freshman year. And re-enrolling requires meeting with a truancy officer and signing a slew of contracts. "We're living in poverty and we're trying to keep up with school and we're trying to maintain our personal issues," Amiotte said. "But it is very hard."[39]

This is such a specific issue that is so personal and so inaudible, but once voiced, it illuminates how poverty and schools replicate the divide between the vast majority of students on Pine Ridge and those who might be attending Red Cloud. Young girls in Pine Ridge High or Little Wound would likely be the ones considering dropping out of school and/or getting pregnant as an answer to being unable to afford tampons. This expands to include the many kids who refuse to attend class because they don't have clean clothes—it embarrasses them. Crazy Horse School has bought a couple of used washers and dryers and keeps them on campus to allow kids to wash their clothes.

All of this should also make us stop to think about how Red Cloud School, in comparison, is cocoon-like, relatively removed from such issues. To reiterate, however, it would be wrong to simply paint Red Cloud High as some reservation version of a preppy, entitled, suburban program. These are Lakota families and children who are not content to succumb to the numbing environment that Pine Ridge can easily become. These are Lakota who are prepared to demand more and have a school on their own reservation that can develop potential in their children. They have shown that Lakota students can perform as well or better than any white kids in the state (and beyond). And that Red Cloud has redefined itself away from its ignoble origins is also quite laudable. The school is at the vanguard in its commitment to preserving the Lakota language; and its insistence that parents make a serious commitment to the school is cutting edge on this reservation.

The ultimate challenge for the tribe, then, is to maintain the accomplishments of Red Cloud while trying to expand the infrastructure that allows Red Cloud to succeed in the reservation's other schools. That is easier said than done. Until some of the differences between the schools is evened out, the invidious comparisons will continue to rankle and be sublimated into the sports rivalry that is Pine Ridge versus Red Cloud.

7

"Crabs in a Bucket"

Envy and Egalitarianism in
a Lakota World

The Lakota have always been at their collective best when facing the outside world. Confronted with an endless stream of whites coursing through their lands and aggressively trying to take it, the normally autonomous Lakota bands joined forces to defend themselves. For three decades, they inflicted pain on the U.S. military as they continually recombined under the leadership of various chiefs. Today, the Lakota are still most unified when being challenged by whites. They are relentless in their legal battle to reclaim the Black Hills. In 2016, the Standing Rock Sioux, in their fight against the Dakota Access Pipeline, were reinforced by Lakota from everywhere. Two years earlier, every corner of Lakota Nation had expressed outrage at the racist treatment of Pine Ridge elementary school students at a hockey game in Rapid City; they demanded a police investigation, bringing the incident to an international audience, and when the courts saw fit to charge only a single white man, who was acquitted, they banned his attorney from their reservations, threatening to move the lucrative LNI out of the city.

But while the Lakota demonstrate solidarity when facing others, among themselves, they can on occasion turn nasty. Even the name *Oglala*, translated as "to scatter one's own," suggests an inclination to disperse in response to discord; and there is a vague understanding among certain tribal historians that the name emanated from a disagreement of some sort (although this is a fairly frequent explanation in tribal societies everywhere for groups that split up). Speaking the same language, Dakota neighbors interpret the term *Oglala* (pronounced *Okdada*) has a contemptuous connotation. In Dakota, the name "scattering one's own" is accompanied by a hand movement among the Dakota "You take your thumb and bring it to the tips of your fingers, to make a group of five. Then you flick your wrist quickly outwardly. This means throwing sand or dirt at someone. Upon receiving the sign, the old-timers went for their knives."[1]

On the everyday level, discord among the Lakota can come out in spitefulness, envy, and backbiting. In this chapter, I look at bitterness and resentment as something that earlier both harmed and safeguarded cohesiveness, but in contemporary Lakota society has become less functional. When people are sharing widely and level out economic differences, an atmosphere of well-being pervades the community. But should inequalities arise, it is felt to be the outcome of people hoarding at which point Lakota begin to disparage those they feel have not taken care of the community. People often express the feeling that the reservation is a place where "haters love to hate," and this is often expressed in social media. As poor as people may be at Pine Ridge, they have a hypersensitivity to anyone around them that might appear to have it better.

In small-scale hunting societies, sharing was a way to ensure against food shortages, and enhance survival. He or she who gives freely is entitled to receive readily, and that constitutes survival in a land that is erratic in its largesse, but in addition promotes goodwill. In our society, where accumulation and materialism reign supreme, this concept might sound counterintuitive, but it isn't. It's really a variation of the Golden Rule, and as the Swedish doctor Axel Munthe stated it, "What you keep to yourself you lose, what you give away, you keep forever."[2]

In line with this dynamic, some of humankind's more base behavior served to guarantee loftier ends. Ridicule, spitefulness, and gossip were used to level a person who showed signs of rising above the group. However, as essential as such behavior was among the traditional Lakota, how does it play out today?

Between brief stints, either in college basketball or in the All Indian Tournament circuit, Jesse Heart was repeatedly drawn back to Pine Ridge. His returns were, of course, met by a mixed sense about how Pine Ridge viewed him. He was certain that people had admired him when he was a high school star, but he was less sure how they saw him in the years after. So, when he was at home, he was always recognized and approached with smiles by fans who had watched him play. But Jesse also knew the pettiness of his small community. "Crabs in a bucket" is the analogy he and others used; it is a widely traded expression in Indian Country to refer to how people on the rez seek to level anyone deemed too rich, adept, talented, or high in social standing.

Jesse explained the concept of the crabs. "Yeah, they're all fightin' to get out. Especially when they see someone like me, who was king around here. You know, I got nothin' but basketball, but still that's what people hate. 'How come he's not in the NBA?' I have to be in the NBA to be successful in this game? . . . I mean, this is what people do to each other, bring people down!"[3] Here, Jesse was complaining about the denigrating or sarcastic remarks made *about* him but not *to* him, comments that painted him as a failure. The same people who'd made these remarks knew full well that he was the best player to come out of Pine Ridge in the past thirty years but felt that putting him down was necessary to restore balance and egalitarian relations.

This hardly differed from Lakota relations of the past, which placed a premium on social unity by fostering a social world in which no one was elevated above the others. Such relationship ideals are echoed not only in Jesse's situation but also in basketball in general.

"Crabs in a Bucket" Syndrome

This is one way the story gets told: "Two fishermen, one white and one Indian, are sitting on a dock. The white fisherman would catch crabs and put them into a bucket, but they would still manage to climb out of the bucket. He noticed that the Indian's crabs stayed in the bucket. He finally asked, "How come the crabs you catch stay in the bucket?" The Indian replied, "Those are Indian crabs; every time one tries to climb up, the others reach up and drag him back down."[4]

Coach Rick Sanchez, who teaches and coaches basketball at Alchesay High School on White River Apache Reservation, used this metaphor to characterize reservation life.

Having grown up there, he lamented, "It's sad. Instead of helping someone get out and make a name for themselves, we just pull them back in. It's like crabs in a bucket. They're trying to crawl out, but the one right behind it is pulling it down."[5]

Envy and Leveling

What does it say about the Lakota that they insist that excelling of any sort must be accompanied by humility and/or distribution of gifts? First of all, their cultural resolve to foster equality is not just a Lakota thing; nor is it associated only with social or political infighting. Small-scale hunting societies have always been defined by their fierce determination to keep everyone economically interdependent. The idea is to avoid the social disruptions that can arise when individuals are elevated above the group; outward manifestations of such selfish rising can be found in hoarding, bullying, or boasting. People are socialized to sidestep this by sharing their good fortune or acting humbly. If humility and generosity aren't forthcoming, then the group will resort to gossip, ridicule, and in some societies (such as the Hopi) even witchcraft accusations, in an attempt to level him or her. In maintaining equality, the group is better prepared to survive individual shortages. Generosity begets generosity, but the failure to share unleashes a torrent of abuse.

The Lakota certainly understand sharing as a cardinal virtue. It was given to them by White Buffalo Calf Woman, a primary Lakota deity. Her call to be generous, compassionate, humble, and honest are among the seven hallmarks of Lakota virtue learned from an early age. Still, these values were only ideals, and societies needed to be prepared to rein in those who would act in their own self-interest, particularly where periodic shortages of food existed. Gossip, malicious accusation, and ridicule all played major roles in such reining-in and evening things out. Indeed, in the hardest-pressed communities, it was as Zora Neale Hurston said: "An envious heart makes a treacherous ear."[6]

Windfalls were as socially dangerous as unanticipated dearth. The propitious event—a good hunt, a successful raid, or a war honor—could easily be accompanied by a wary eye cast toward the fortunate individual. Gossiping about, mocking, or picking quarrels with those upon whom fortune had smiled could cast a pall over the group. The peg that stuck up must be somehow hammered down. Whether it was a traditionally daring deed in warfare or quilting or, today, in passing the bar exam or being selected to an All-Star team, announcing the deed had to done in a way that made it "safe" for the victor, by distributing any wealth earned or by behaving modestly.

One of the most utilitarian concepts in anthropology is that of "leveling," of making certain that no individual rises too far above others.[7] Individuals can avoid the unpleasantness of being leveled by leveling themselves. Still, it is a delicate task. To accomplish it, people engage in rituals of modesty that diffidently and positively bring one's achievements to the fore. If done right, one's accomplishments are accepted and enjoyed by the group. To this end, a family or clan might downplay any semblance of boasting or distribute whatever wealth they came upon to the community in a giveaway ceremony. Ceremonies for honoring, ghost-owning (memorials for the departed), and naming young children are all Lakota occasions marked by giveaways of property. Honoring is all-purpose, in that it can occur any time a family wants to publicly take pride in something done by one of its members (win a title, advance in education or work, achieve military success, etc.). In the past, to make honoring more palatable would involve an outlay of goods, at times resulting in the family liquidating a good portion of their worth. Emil Her Many Horses recounted what his grandmother told him of this:

> Grandma used to say, "Grandpa Pourier would have been a rich man, but Grandpa Pourier kept giving the horses away." Hosting a giveaway today involves tremendous preparation, including the gathering of gifts, such as brightly colored star quilts, Pendleton blankets and handmade shawls, as well as feeding the whole community. . . . My grandmother also remembered that women would give away dresses made of tanned deer hide, with the yoke of the dress completely covered with beadwork. They would take off their beaded dresses right there in the dance arbor and give them away. Giving away a fully beaded dress in honor of a relative was a tremendous act of generosity.[8]

In these giveaways, the generosity of the conveners triggered the applause of the community for the individual being feted. Envy was averted and praise was heaped.

Novelist Sherman Alexie discussed the use of leveling techniques in his Spokane tribal culture thusly: "White folks love to think that Native American culture is liberal. But it's actually repressive. Indians are quick to socially judge one another. And even quicker to condemn and ostracize. . . . Disruption was not tolerated. And I think I know the source of the intolerance. For thousands of years, we Spokane had endured and enjoyed subsistence lives. We'd lived communally. . . . So, inside a subsistence culture, a socially disruptive tribal member [one with more wealth or good fortune] would have been mortally dangerous to everybody else."[9]

Anthropologist Richard Lee, who studied Namibian Ju/'hoansi people, published a famous anecdote about how, during one Christmas, he sought to repay a group of people who he had stayed with for their kindness. He bought the fattest cow he could find to be slaughtered and cooked for the entire encampment. Ignorant of the leveling safeguards of Ju/'hoansi social cohesion, Lee neglected to belittle his contribution to the Christmas celebration and was roundly ridiculed. One after another, man and woman complained about how scrawny the cow was and how little Lee must think of them to bring this to the encampment. Properly chastened, Richard Lee learned firsthand how leveling worked.[10]

These traditionally rooted social mechanisms to ensure a smooth-functioning society are much harder to successfully pull off in a contemporary society that is based on class and private property, and in a society in which the Lakota exist in rural poverty. Instead of shortages being met by widespread sharing, they end up severely straining tribal government's capacities and cutting people's magnanimity short. Marion Billbrough-Dreamer, a white teacher at Pine Ridge's day school in the 1930s, noted that, back then, feeling pressure to share and griping about inequality went hand in hand. "Indians always complain if some other Indian has something better than he has," she said. "If you have money, the relatives come and live with you until it's gone."[11]

In an atmosphere of deprivation, it becomes easy for complaints to grow louder. Traditional giveaways remain invaluable in cutting short this carping by allowing the sharer to accumulate social capital. That kind of self-leveling (sharing out) is a bit more strained in contemporary society and is further compounded by white attitudes toward accumulation and self-promotion that have filtered into Lakota life. The divide between self and others used to refer to Lakota versus other tribes as well as Lakota versus whites, but it is now experienced primarily between Lakota individuals.

The "crabs in a bucket" reflex can be triggered in a variety of situations, but especially when Indian students seek an educational path to a better life. "Instead of encouragement to do better, often American Indian students who try to excel academically off the reservation experience negativity from peers back home. They may get accused of 'acting white,' or 'too good' for their reservation roots."[12] In this context, Indian identity is linked to educational failure, which creates a powerful downward thrust in efforts to better the community.

Sherman Alexie described the same marginalizing when he recounted being abused by other Indians while growing up on the Spokane Reservation. Medical issues early in life made him somewhat frail and hence marginal. "I was a kid somewhere on the Spectrum when the spectrum was only "normal" or "not normal," he wrote. "I was the Official Tribal Fool living one hundred years after fools were last thought to be holy. I was a mess, a mysterious casserole slowly going bad in a half-assed freezer."[13] How was he being marginalized? By being called ugly and being laughed at, yes, but what really set him off from other youngsters was his love of books. And Alexi's quasi-banishment was neatly tied up in his being called white. "So, if one Indian wants to inflict a grievous emotional wound on another Indian, then "white" is the Big Fucking Gun of insults . . . I was called white, not because I was white, but because I was the frail kid. I was the easiest target."[14] And, as he repeatedly called up from memory, "I didn't belong because maybe I never wanted to belong. When everybody else danced and sang, I silently sat in my room with books."[15]

Kyle Goklish, an Apache, experienced this as well. As a stellar athlete and solid student, he went off to college in 2002, hailed by some but viewed suspiciously by others: "It's hard when I go home for summer break. . . . They look at you differently, talk to you differently. They think, 'Oh, you're better than us.' Just because I go to school and I've gotten an education, they call me white boy. They say, 'You're not really an Apache.' That's what hurts the most."[16]

Sometimes athletics, and particularly basketball, can short-circuit the social isolation that often accompanies studious kids. This was certainly the case for Brandon Ecoffey (see chapter 6), whose family valued education above all else. "Basketball was always the leveler," he said. "Whether you grew up as a gang member from East Ridge or from the District of Oglala, once you got on the court, it didn't matter. What happened at home last night didn't matter. You were gonna play until you lost, and then you got off the court."

The idea that hoops can promote egalitarian social relations is an important one, and it plays off of the democratic value of a level playing field embedded in sports. Ecoffey noted, "I wasn't one of those 'smart kids' who was better than everyone. I was a smart kid that balled and ran with the stoners."[17]

Still, while sports may be a leveler, sporting acclaim and excellence threatens to upset notions of equality. Consider Jonathan Takes Enemy of the Crow tribe, for example. In the long line of remarkable ball players that have come out of the Plains, Jonathan Takes Enemy was typical. Playing in the 1980s, he dominated the state in high school basketball only to badly flame out afterward. In a masterful article on Plains basketball by Gary Smith, the tugging of the community on Takes Enemy's lofty accomplishments was discussed, again in reference to education:

> "Jonathan Takes Enemy. Where are you going to college?" people asked Jonathan everywhere he went. "He'll be home by Thanksgiving," they told each other. "Like crabs in a bucket, that's how we are," says Dell Fritzler, the coach at Plenty Coups High. "Whoever tries to get out, we yank him back down." Even Jonathan's own Indian name—bestowed upon him during his senior season after it had come to the medicine man in a dream—tugged downward at the boy. *Iiwaaialetasaask*, he was called. Does Not Put Himself Above Others. Go off to college? That would definitely Put Himself Above Others. No, white people couldn't understand this; Jonathan himself could barely grasp the code: It was OK for an Indian to clench his teeth and compete as part of a team, especially an Indian team. But to do it alone, to remove yourself from the dozen people in your living room at midnight and go sit over a chemistry or algebra book—in many families, that tainted you. "We want our young people to go off and show the world how great a Crow can be," says Fritzler, "but as soon as someone does, as soon as anyone starts trying or studying too hard, a lot of us say, 'Look at him. He's trying to be a white man.'"[18]

Poverty and failure have, unfortunately, become too linked with what it means to be authentically a tribal member. And, as such, anyone seeking to escape, to accomplish something, is viewed as a threat, garnering the ultimate social putdown—trying to be white. Those who leave for good can leave the reservation and its small-mindedness behind, but those who occasionally return can rekindle the group's ire each time they come back—and malevolent gossip ensues.

Jesse Heart said he feels it when he comes back and his friends let slip what people said about him in his absence: "People always talk. Not to my face, but they talk." His father affirmed this. "He wouldn't a got treated like that if he wasn't such a high-profile player. Just because he didn't make it to the D1 schools, didn't get drafted to the NBA, he's [treated like] a bust."[19]

The decision to demean rather than celebrate Jesse Heart was most typically made by people who felt his success somehow reflected their own lack of it. And it seems that no amount of modesty by Jesse changed this. "After college I was hardly ever home, so I couldn't catch flak from people around here," he said. "I'd come back to visit mom and dad and stay a couple of months 'til I found some more tournaments. . . . People here (Pine Ridge) think I'd fallen off 'cause they don't see me. My closest friends would know. They'd hear people talkin' smack about me. They'd let those people know, "Oh, Jesse is still playin' here and there. Comin from here, I try never to run my mouth about what I done. I let it show on the court. But I know people thrive on the shit-talk."[20]

On the rez, one's absence is interpreted as success. To leave, is to be portrayed as being superior to the group. Perhaps if Heart had ever had the wherewithal to hold a giveaway, this portrayal could be avoided, but he's never made that much money from the game.

Further, even when he experienced failure, returning to Pine Ridge somewhat chastened, attempts by others to level him continued at every turn. "That shit (gossip) happens all the time. Even when you're not working, it's there!" Jesse told me. "After I stopped playing in college, when I wasn't working, people would be cool with me [stopped gossiping], but the second I started working and doing my own thing (getting ahead), people would start talkin'. "Aw he has this job 'cause of this person or that person—which might be the truth—but they don't care that I'm providing for my family when I can."[21]

It seems the bar for abating envy, then, is absolute failure, with any good fortune setting tongues back to wagging.

The crab syndrome has even spilled over onto legend SuAnne Big Crow. It might come out more subtly, but it is certainly still present.

"SuAnne Big Crow was good, but Red Cloud beat them, and there were players at Red Cloud as good as her. She's the only one mentioned though. Because she died young, people thought she was so good,"[22] said someone familiar with her.

This comment didn't seek to destroy her reputation so much as to take it down a notch. And this wasn't the only comment about her I encountered. Another person, one knowledgeable about the basketball scene, noted, "See, like SuAnne, she's not what they're proclaiming. I know the mean things she did in the rivalry (with Red Cloud). I could say more negative things, but that's all I'm gonna say."[23]

Addressing an audience gathered for the twentieth anniversary of the SuAnne Big Crow Boys and Girls Club at Pine Ridge, Tim Giago noted the treatment she and her family received from some quarters. "I recalled vividly the struggles endured by the founders and current managers of the club, Chick, Cee Cee, and Pigeon Big Crow, not only financially but politically, to keep it going these twenty years. They were often the targets of vicious rumors and unfounded gossip by some local residents, and getting the financial support from the tribe that the boys and girls of the reservation deserved was often very iffy."[24] Subtle, but these kinds of attempts at disparaging are corrections and all part of a Lakota (and generally Native) sensitivity to elevating individuals above the group.

Ironically, the very nature of contemporary sports is antithetical to the modesty that communities like those in Pine Ridge demand, because individual sports acclaim ends up taking a person out of the local communal realm and catapults them into a state of stardom. Winning All-State honors, garnering the interest of college teams, scoring titles, achieving glowing statistics—all elevate an individual above his or her teammates and their community. Even when athletes are modest about their own awards, the media and fans elevate them. So it becomes imperative to conduct oneself in a humble manner to try to short-circuit the community's leveling responses. Maybe that's what Jesse Heart was thinking when, after winning a tournament with his team in which he garnered All-Tournament honors, he posted a picture of it on Facebook, prefaced with "In a humble way."

As detailed in chapter 2, back when Dusty LeBeau coached, he brought two state championships to Pine Ridge. Did LeBeau strut around on stage like Mick Jagger or brag about these accomplishments either publicly or privately? Definitely not. Yet some circles read this success as being LeBeau's personal social ascent—not the tribe's—and they couldn't let this fellow Lakota's accomplishments go unsullied.

Knowing that LeBeau often invited players to the sweat lodge at the beginning of the season, these Lakota expressed the feeling that LeBeau sweated and smudged with players only to win. Dusty, a bit peeved that people would accuse him of subverting his religion purely for extraneous reasons, said, "People think that we go to ceremonies for wins. That's not what you do. You're asking that everything will be good with these kids. That nobody gets hurt. Some people even say, 'Oh, he's winning 'cause he's using bad medicine' is how they think of all this. No way! We want the kids to be okay and safe. We just walk with our heads held high and don't get caught up in all this bad stuff."[25]

Further, the public criticism spreads to Dusty's family. The LeBeau family's efforts to tend to the spiritual needs of the community, while appreciated in many circles, are still disdained in others.

When I asked Dusty if he'd ever personally encountered not only leveling criticism but outright jealousy, he didn't hesitate to respond with, "Boy, you hit it right on this one. I listened to Joel Osteen say that 'jealousy creates hate.' Some guy told my daughter, 'You guys [the LeBeau family] are like celebrities down here. Everybody watches your moves and they wanna see you fail because of what you did in sports and what you did in the Sun Dance. You turned it into something powerful, where people came up here and left healed. Even the educated people who are here are jealous of you guys!' Yes, it's jealousy, big time!"[26]

So back to the original question: How important are leveling behaviors in modern Lakota society? Today, in the absence of the Lakota's traditional, fully-functioning economy, leveling, especially if by way of envy, no longer has a positive effect. It comes off less as functional and more as plain old carping.

What's the difference? Back then, leveling had an effect that more closely resembled the old New England adage made famous by John Fitzgerald Kennedy: "The rising tide lifts all boats." That is, an individual's windfall helped *everyone* to eat or live better. But now, more than a century of rural poverty and living in an environment of racial hostility has eroded that functionality, because people have less material wealth to distribute and have adopted more anglo-individuality—leaving only residual mean-spiritedness. Ridicule and gossip just don't work well anymore, except to inflame emotions and set people further against each other. If anything, they serve to heighten endemic divisions. No amount of leveling could soften that.

Siege at Wounded Knee, 1973

The social divisions that threaten groups everywhere must be judged not only by their presence; a second criteria is a society's ability to soften these divisions enough to enable the group to work together when it's most beneficial. In the previous chapter, we saw that deep social divisions are certainly nothing new to the Lakota: we saw them in the halcyon days of the buffalo-hunting era, where political rivals would create rifts, and we saw them in the early reservation era, where hostiles and friendlies vied with each other. But early on, factions could put aside their differences in defense of the people as a whole—a practice that happens less often now.

Case in point: the Siege at Wounded Knee in 1973 brought together all of the worst and most divisive tendencies of the Oglala. Because of the massacre of hundreds of Lakota by U.S. Army troops in 1890, Wounded Knee is now the emotional center of Lakota culture. The tragedy is undoubtedly seared into the memory of every Lakota, but people from around the world also visit to pay their respects. Yet, even in this consecrated place, social divisiveness and animus threatens.

The key to this divisiveness lay not in the original massacre but in what has become known as the Second Wounded Knee—a two-month siege by an array of U.S. forces against the American Indian Movement (AIM) who took over the town on February 28, 1973. By that time, AIM had grown from being a sprinkling of disaffected and politicized young Indians in Minneapolis led by Lakota Russell Means and Dennis Banks (Ojibwa) to a pan-Indian movement across many reservations.

As a movement, AIM was forged out of the societal upheavals springing up everywhere in the country in the late 1960s, but Indian activists were a bit different than their white civil-rights counterparts. Indian activists were primarily urban, removed from their cultural roots back on the reservations. While this made them politically charged, it also meant they were in need of cultural remediation. In their thirst for authenticity, they bonded with tribal elders throughout Indian Country but especially on Pine Ridge. It was in this context that AIM leaders Russell Means and Dennis Banks came to Pine Ridge to seek mentorship from Leonard Crow Dog and other traditional elders. In doing so, however, they ultimately widened the rift between full-blood traditionalists and their mixed-blood antagonists.

At the time, Pine Ridge was under the sway of the corrupt tribal government of Dick Wilson, who many locals felt should be impeached but who was particularly repugnant to traditionalists. On the other side, AIM vowed to defend their interests. This put Dick Wilson and AIM on a collision course.

After a series of high-profile political actions, which included the forced takeover of the BIA in Washington DC (one of the most reviled institutions in Indian country), AIM determined to take over Wounded Knee in the name of the Traditional Lakota who were most alienated from Wilson. Armed with their newfound authenticity and an array of weapons, AIM occupied the town of Wounded Knee in the middle of the night on the February 28. Their blitzkrieg tactics saw them rounding up people, emptying the main store, and fortifying their position in anticipation of what they knew would be an official response; in fact, they expected nothing less.

The two-month-long siege involving an array of government forces (tribal police, state police, FBI, and reservists) became an international story and emboldened all sides. Mistakes were made by both AIM and the pro-Wilson side, making the rift so deep that, once the siege ended, open conflict ensued. Scores were killed. In the end, it was the Lakota who lost, as the outside world watched Wilson goons and AIM hack away at each other.

Built on the old traditionalist-versus-friendly/mixed-blood-versus-full-blood split, it became the worst outbreak of factionalism in American Indian history. And while the divide has softened over the four decades since, it is surprising how easily it can rise to the surface.

Protecting Wounded Knee

More recently, a dispute has emerged over what the tribe should do about the long-neglected Wounded Knee massacre site. Though couched in the politics of "who is most concerned with protecting" the site, this dispute continues the tribal propensity for internal fighting. The publisher of the *Native Sun News*, Tim Giago, has been pushing to honor the site by buying it (as it is currently owned by a white man) and building a museum on the land to commemorate its history. His plans also call for ways to cater to the many visitors who come there. The current owner has agreed to sell the site for $3.9 million, and Giago is actively trying to raise the money to buy and develop the 40 acres.

Opposing Giago are a number of people at Pine Ridge, most importantly the group known as the 1890 Wounded Knee Massacre Descendants Society. Their claim to the site is the most direct and psychologically compelling, and they feel that using the site for anything other than a sanctuary for cultural mourning is inappropriate. Laurie Black Shawl, the group's spokesperson, argued, "Tim Giago is coming into the picture with plans for our sacred site . . . for our sacred grounds. . . . To develop it into a tourist attraction. . . . Which is all fine and great . . . but not at the Wounded Knee Massacre Site. Not where our relatives' and ancestors' blood has been shed and sanctified that ground."[27]

Even though Giago has put forward a plan that aims both to honor the memory of the place and to generate badly needed money for the tribe, he is being portrayed as an opportunist. One can't help but wonder how much of this portrayal was forged in the political past and in his accomplishments and successes as a journalist and businessman. Giago has always been committed to honoring the site, but he also understands that it doesn't preclude economic development for the tribe. "Can you imagine a really beautiful holocaust museum and a big trade pavilion for Indian artisans and craftspeople?" he said. "They could set up booths year-round and sell their arts and crafts to the tourists. We would have tourists come from all over the world and stay in Rapid City, go to the restaurants and hotels, take buses to Wounded Knee. It would create over two hundred jobs for the people down there. It would also be a boost financially to Rapid City, South Dakota."[28]

Jobs and income *are* in short supply, of course. The descendants of the massacre, however, are angry that Giago did not consult with them, perceiving his snub as being contrary to the Lakota consensus method traditionally used to arrive at agreements. Both sides want to honor the site but don't share a vision of how that should happen. Both sides agree that Wounded Knee is virtually a holy site. Does anything that economically benefits the Lakota constitute a violation of its sacredness? Would having a tourist gift shop attached, say to Auschwitz, somehow violate the moral volcano that is that place? I think many Jews would be outraged.

Though he didn't start out that way, Giago eventually become one of the most outspoken foes of AIM and its 1973 Wounded Knee takeover. Early on in the battle, Giago and AIM leaders like Dennis Banks had acknowledged differences but sought to find common ground. That ended when AIM "occupied" or "took over" (depending on who you talk to) the town of Wounded Knee. From Giago's perspective, the trading post where his father had worked and where he and others had grown up was looted by outsiders with little connection to the community: the Gildersleeves, who owned the store there, were tied up; dozens of people were displaced; and the life that he and many others had known was destroyed.[29]

AIM, however, had sought to improve conditions on Pine Ridge by ridding themselves of the oppressive political regime of Dick Wilson and the tribal government. To AIM members, the store at Wounded Knee was part of the problem, as they felt the owners took economic advantage of local Indian artists.

In this era of increasing direct confrontation—a point in time in which, if you weren't part of the solution, you were part of the problem—AIM's preferred strategy was also, unsurprisingly, direct confrontation. So, in contrast, Giago's more measured stance in the beginning was quickly perceived of as that of a "goon sympathizer." Because he refused to take ideological sides, in certain circles, Giago was seen as a turncoat who wouldn't unilaterally back the politics of AIM even though he was critical of Wilson and his goons as well; more specifically, he spoke out against tribal government while also speaking out against AIM's aggressive strategies. In the years after the takeover, the civil war that engulfed Pine Ridge ultimately resulted in Giago's newspaper office being torched in 1982. AIM supporters were thought to be responsible.

As the years peeled away, the excessiveness and violence of that era began to fade. "In the end, many AIM leaders like Vernon Bellecourt became my friends," Giago said, reflecting back on the experience. "In their own way, all of them tried to do what they thought was best for Indian Country. As Vernon said, 'Tim, we're working for the same cause; we're just coming from different directions.' My reply: 'Then quit firebombing my newspaper.'"[30]

But Wounded Knee is so loaded with grief, loss, betrayal, and anger that it isn't easily let go of. And, each time it surfaces, it does so as a divide in which each side maligns the other in every possible way. On the other hand, Pine Ridge has a long memory. For over a century now, Wounded Knee has been a powerful and contentious symbol of not only the Lakota's history of infighting but also its failure to heal their people's differences. And in this, the Oglala continue to resemble their name and risk "scattering one's own."

Caring for the *Oyaté*

Thankfully, there are many people in Pine Ridge for whom caring for the *oyaté*, the people, outweighs pettiness and callousness discussed in this chapter. They show this caring in big and little ways, and they do it daily.

Meghan Rae of Pine Ridge is an example of this dualism. Furious at what she felt was rampant indifference around her, she called out her people in a Facebook post:

> Tonight I'd just like to say a big FUCK YOU to humanity. Fuck every single one of you who drove by the young boy who was walking between Number 4 and Oglala. In -5 degree weather. Anyone of you could have stopped. He waved frantically and tried his damndest to get someone to stop. Guess what? I stopped! I made room for him and warmed him up and took him home to his doorstep. . . . He told me he thought he wouldn't make it. He told me his dad died frozen under a bridge. Just gave up and froze. I cried harder 'cause I heard it in his voice. It was real, he thought he would give up and freeze soon. You fucking heartless sons of bitches who drive by people in need of help.[31]

Meghan Rae was talking to her people when she screamed, "Fuck you to humanity!" She knew no whites would be driving down that reservation road at that time of night. More important, she knew that it isn't the Lakota way to ignore the plight of others. The boy's vulnerability hit her instantly— his certainty of freezing to death, his memory of his father's death, and the thought that no one gave a damn—it all got to her. And her one tiny act of kindness was one colossal gift of life. Mehgan had lost her little brother under similar conditions, so she could empathize with his helplessness, but she'd have done so regardless, her magnanimity is in evidence elsewhere as well. But her response to this situation can be construed as both a condemnation of and a model for morality on Pine Ridge.

Jerrold Mesteth is another example of hope and promise among the Lakota. He and a group of people who call themselves the Guardians patrol the roads of Pine Ridge each winter, ready to help people who are stuck in their cars and in danger of freezing to death. He got the calling for the job, because he was almost a victim himself.

"I was on the side of the road coming back from work, and my car overheated," recalled Mesteth. "I didn't have any water and no way to get it going. It was pretty cold out. The windows were frosting . . . and no one pulled over for me. And I had no way to call for help. . . . Because nobody stops for you here. They see you, but they just drive by you. I see that all the time."[32]

The two hours of waiting he endured before someone stopped to help him gave him ample time to fear for his life and grow angry toward his fellows. But rather than succumbing to the indifference, growing angry and numb toward the world, Jerrold, like Mehgan, responded by doubling down on compassion. He used his own money to buy cables and gas and other things that he could use to help get cars towed or running, and then he advertised his willingness to help others if they got stuck.

Jerrold recalled incidents when he'd encounter someone stuck on the road: "I'd say, 'You need help?' They'd say, 'No, I've got no money.' I'd say, 'That's fine. I've got it. I'll help you out.'"[33]

And, guess what? His kindness was contagious, and soon others contacted him, ready to help the *oyaté*. The group they formed, the Guardians, now has a fleet of trucks working the roads of Pine Ridge. They live off of donations, and thankfully the donations keep coming.

One Spirit is a non-profit organization that provides firewood to hundreds of people on the Pine Ridge Reservation. The Plains is chronically low on fire wood because there aren't many forests to be found. The native volunteers in One Spirit scour the countryside to get house bound residents firewood. It's this Lakota value of caring for the people that makes sense of the efforts by Corey Shangreau and Laura Big Crow to cram their house—which is already full—to overflowing, with players who badly need to escape a toxic home life.

These individuals acting on their own to help other Lakota are matched by an array of nonprofit organizations also working to improve relations and conditions at Pine Ridge. Of course, there are governmentally based organizations, such as those created to treat people with addiction issues or to help people find creative ways to get affordable housing. But there are others that are locally started by Lakota who want to fulfill the needs of their people. I came across a young man from neighboring Rosebud Sioux Reservation, for example, who was part of a group striving to empower youth. In the beginning, he, together with other teens and twentysomethings, had looked for a way to teach their generation life skills that could both serve them well going forward and rely on their link to the land. They settled on a honey-making enterprise and called it Honey Lodge.

This young man told me, "We sat around wondering what to call it, but one of the younger ones said, 'Why not call it Honey Lodge?' It was perfect! We overthought it. And a thirteen-year-old designed our logo."

These kids volunteered to learn bee-keeping and honey production, and as their promotional video points out, the young ones said, "We're gonna help the bees, but they're gonna help us too."[34]

Local non-governmental agencies exist on all of the Lakota reservations. Some travel around educating women on ways to survive domestic and sexual abuse, others help get Lakota into educational programs, and yet others teach specific skills.

In summary, in looking at the Lakota, as we would in looking at any other group, we must avoid one-dimensional perceptions of a people who are all-bad or all-good. In all of humanity, selfishness exists alongside selflessness. That said, given the degree of difficulty that so many Lakota face in reservations around the state or in places like Rapid City, dysfunction and the baser side of humanity seem to be more immediately visible. We are more likely to encounter the sordid before the heroic, the mean-spirited before the altruistic, but both sides exist. In real life, these opposing sides do not occur in an either-or fashion but live alongside each other to create the push and pull of life.

It is this push and pull that we see in everyday Lakota life, as the presence of recrimination and its cousins, ridicule and gossip, has been an essential part of maintaining a cultural commitment to egalitarianism and caring for all.

So, while "crabs in a bucket" cannot be anything but negatively understood from the vantage point of twenty-first century America, that analogy was valuable in the world of nineteenth-century Plains Indians buffalo hunting—coming off as communal rather than carping, generous rather than egotistical. It is this latter world that the Lakota come from, but what changed that world is the economic milieu: now, the Lakota must exist in a world of private property, of advancement at the expense of others, of concern with self. And they must endure all of these values being pushed on them while their moribund economic system twists in the wind. As such, the paradox for many in Indian Country, as for many in the developing world, is to find ways to retain their egalitarian institutions and concern for the general well-being, while still trying to advance into the future.

8

Race Relations, Hoops, and the Border in South Dakota

If border towns are places where social rancor is especially incendiary, sports is often the match that sets things ablaze. The NPR (National Public Radio) show *This American Life* aired an episode in 2001 on a particularly ugly incident that occurred following a South Dakota basketball game.[1] The NPR staff interviewed a teenage white girl from Miller—the town involved—who gave stark testimony to the racial rancor that existed between Indians and whites.

Her comments were noteworthy because people in Miller—and in other such towns that border reservations—usually stick together, denying to the world that there's a problem with their Indian neighbors while at the same time defending their own. But, for whatever reason, this girl broke the ranks, admitting, "When the reservation teams come down here, there's a lot of tension. . . . We've had to have kids get kicked out [of games] because of saying 'Indian,' or 'prairie nigger,' and stuff like that." She followed her unusual admission with a comment on the larger racist mosaic: "They were raised with it. Their parents taught them. I don't think that you have to say, 'Well, Indians are evil. Don't go near them. They're just taking their [welfare] money.' That's the big thing around here. That's another comment that was made at games that had Indians there. They'd say, 'Oh, you shouldn't even be playing on our damn court because we're paying for your shoes or we're paying for your uniforms.'"[2]

The Crow Creek Reservation in the center of the state is made up of Yankton Dakota (closely related to Lakota). Their girls' team, the Crow Creek Lady Chieftains, was at the center of this story. The night of the incident, they were playing a high school team from Wessington Spring in nearby Miller.

At the beginning of the game, as the Crow Creek girls made their way onto the court, they encountered what was, to them, a hale of all too familiar verbal assaults. Jessica Squirrel Coat recalled, "And then, as we were running out, we came on our side, we came under their hoop right by the Wessington Springs fans' area. And as soon as we went by their area, we heard those war whooping. I looked down. I was like, right now it's dirty in the beginning of the game. How you see it on cartoons, that's how you hear it."[3] In any hotly contested game, tempers flare, but since the winner of this game would play in the state championship tournament, the atmosphere was especially tense.

Later in the game, two girls collided—one from Crow Creek and the other from Wessington—and the Wessington player hit the floor particularly hard. Their fans spewed invectives at Crow Creek players. Jessica Squirrel Coat recalled hearing, "'She's dirty. She's a dirty Indian.' And I just looked at Chub [her teammate], and she looked at me. She smiled at me. She's like, 'Don't pay attention. Just don't pay attention.'"[4] There was little new here. Indian teams hear this all of the time.

After losing the game, most of the Crow Creek team loaded into the bus, but a few of the girls, including Squirrel Coat, left in a friend's truck. They had all planned to go the local Dairy Queen for post-game burgers. On the way there, the truck drove past a parking lot where some locals were hanging out, and Jessica Squirrel Coat said she heard boys hurling racist epithets at them. The girls circled the block so they could pass the lot again, determined to find out if they were really being targeted or if Squirrel Coat's ears had just deceived her. The second time past, the boys again swore at them, and that's when the smoothie that one of the girls was drinking got hurled out the truck window at the boys. The contents splattered all over one of the boys' prized white car. Incensed, he and several of his friends went in pursuit of the Indian girls. Catching up with them, one of the boys poked a shotgun out the window, causing the Indian passengers to dive, terrified, to the floor of the truck.

"And what happens next is unbelievable," Jessica's remarked. "You just don't hear of these things, even in South Dakota after a basketball game. There was four shotgun blasts shot from the car."[5]

The girls continued speeding through town, with the boys in pursuit, and even in their panic, they managed to get to the Dairy Queen, where they ran in, crying.

Police were called, and the Crow Creek parents got them to file a report. The boys, of course, claimed that they had made no racist remarks. Then later, after returning home to leave the shotgun, the boys went back to the police station to file their report of vandalism against the girls. They were not arrested. Miller townsfolk, especially teens, while regretting that gun-play was involved, rationalized that the girl's throwing of the smoothie triggered the incident.

One of the white teens present explained, "I know the reason that he did it [shot at the girls] is that he was drunk. And that's not an excuse to shoot a gun or anything. But his car is his baby. And they threw a milkshake right at it. As far as I'm concerned, they were asking for something. They were just asking for a good butt-whooping. I mean, if you saw a really sexy race car and you threw a milkshake at it, of course you'd be expecting the owner to be a little bit torked [torqued]."[6]

The Crow Creek tribe insisted that the incident be tried as a case of race hatred, but the Miller police saw it differently. Ernie Stirling, Miller's chief of police who ran the investigation, concluded, "Maybe for the Native American population, similar things [racially motivated violence] have happened elsewhere enough that they feel justified in saying this is the trend. This is the way we get treated when we go somewhere else. Maybe that's the case. I personally don't have any knowledge of that. All I can speak about is here, in Miller, South Dakota, where I've worked since 1979, this has never happened before."[7]

After that, for Miller's white population, the matter ended. The boys went on with their lives. But for the Dakota girls involved, a piece of their lives was thereafter disfigured. Jessica's mother told the NPR staff:

> that Jessica's personality changed. Jessica was the Crow Creek homecoming queen. She has so many friends that people say she's doing one of seven rights of the Sioux Nation, making relatives. But after Miller, she'd stay in

her dorm room, just lie on her bed and listen to her powwow CDs. She'd pray with her medicine bundle, which she made a couple years ago after she felt a sharp pain in her leg like someone was using bad medicine on her when she came down from making a layup during a basketball game.[8]

Another player, Arlene Weasel Bear, was also psychologically wounded by the incident. "I never told nobody my feelings about it," she told me. "I tried, but I can't—" she struggled, her anger seemingly ballooning "—I didn't want to see no white people. I just stayed home. My sister asked me to go to movies. But I didn't go with her because I would see white people. I didn't like white people." The trauma deepened until, one night, Arlene contemplated killing herself. She climbed a hillside and just sat. "I just sat up there and I was just thinking how we got treated. And I don't know how white people think they should be the only ones on this earth. I thought I'd make everyone feel better if we weren't here, if I wasn't. But then I thought how my family would suffer. So, I didn't. I came home."[9]

Schools, Borders, and Bigotry

School sports are central to so many of these incidents because sporting events, while combative, are democratically contrived to bring together teams (Indian and white, in this case) on a level playing field. Where schools border reservations, there is often an explosive mix of artificial and real social fears and recriminations.

Modern Lakota schools may bear little resemblance to the Indian boarding schools initially foisted on them, but both share a failure to educationally and socially advance Indian students. This failure is rooted in the racial, cultural, and class divides that form the cornerstone of race relations in this country. Because white border schools are often located in the same counties as reservation schools, they present options for Lakota families looking for better education for their children. That Indian families would risk sending their children to white schools where their children might not be welcomed speaks to two realities: the abysmal conditions of reservation schools and the resolve of certain Indian families to weather stormy race relations in order to pursue educational opportunities. For Lakota and other Indian students, today's reservation schools—as much as they seek empowerment—are still coming up way short. Twelve-year-old Carleigh Campbell, from

Little Wound School, may have tested as "proficient" on the 2014 South Dakota achievement test, but being the only student to do so out of the 150 enrolled speaks volumes about Indian educational shortcomings.[10]

The American Indian Education Study Group looking at native schools throughout the country concluded, "In South Dakota, which has the highest proportion of Native American students of any state, they lag on every academic indicator." This, according to the state's 2012–13 report card, where only 42 percent of American Indian students scored 'proficient' or 'advanced' on state math exams, while 80 percent of white students did so. In reading, 47 percent of American Indian students scored 'proficient' or higher, compared to 79 percent of white students. The four-year graduation rate for South Dakota's American Indian students in 2013–49 percent—paints an even grimmer picture . . . the four-year graduation rate at Pine Ridge High School, the biggest high school on the reservation, was 45 percent."[11]

Of course, poverty plays a significant role here; it means parents lack so many of the essentials that go into preparing a child to get the most that they can from schools and teachers. It also means Pine Ridge school buildings end up twisting in the wind, undergoing slow decay. "South Dakota has the third-highest number of BIE schools in poor condition, and the Pine Ridge Reservation has one of the largest clusters nationally."[12] At Crazy Horse School (on Pine Ridge), for instance, crumbling asbestos tiles on the floors along two main hallways pose health risks. After this was brought to the BIE's attention, the Lakota were told that the system was underfunded but would eventually be dealt with, "They tell us it's fine as long as it's not disturbed," said the school's athletic director with a wry smile.[13]

Nearby, American Horse School (K–8) is forty years old; not particularly old for a school, but it seems that in Indian years, school age mysteriously doubles. With 283 students, the school is "overcrowded, has broken asbestos tile flooring, and lacks the electrical and communications infrastructure needed to support the technology used in modern education. The building is also poorly insulated, resulting in high heating costs that eat up funding intended for other educational needs such as building maintenance."[14] Heating is a big thing in this part of the country where winters are long, cold, and treacherous.

Former tribal chair Bryan Brewer put a sobering spin on fixing broken down schools. "The central offices [the BIE], they take their big cut out . . . so by the time it gets to our children there's very little money left and that's one of the big problems. . . . We don't have enough money for facilities. If we need to buy something, a furnace, something like that, we have to cut out a teacher. It's that bad."[15] In other words, the cost of building maintenance can be devastating to furthering education itself; choosing whether to keep kids warm or hire a teacher becomes a *Sophie's Choice* situation between equally untenable needs. Factor in the social ills that accompany these hard-pressed communities—alcoholism, drugs, gangs, and abuse, along with a suffering healthcare system and high mortality rates—and educational advancement becomes something you do between crises. Too many Lakota students lack the stability needed to regularly do homework, study for Tuesday's test, or write the essay due in a week. That's why, to some Lakota families, white border schools seem like the answer.

Border Schools

Because Pine Ridge students live within a school district that uses a mix of BIA (Bureau of Indian Affairs) federal monies and county monies, they have the option of attending public schools off the reservation—schools with better resources and higher academic outcomes. Most times, however, these public schools have a majority white student body, which poses a different set of problems.

But for all of the lack of funds reservation schools offer students a rich cultural milieu that can bolster their sense of well-being. For instance, they can smudge and speak in their tribal language. This connection to culture is what many students don't want to lose, so in the end they often opt not to go off the reservation—or if they do, they quickly return to it. The choice: gain access to upward mobility or center your existence.

Paul Pawnee Leggings, an eighth grader at Wounded Knee School, had friends at these off-reservation schools, and he marveled that they had iPads to work with. He knew that his goal of being a video-game design student would be enhanced in neighboring school districts, but noted, "They only have Lakota (language instruction) once a week, and I would rather have Lakota every day, so we can learn it. We have to keep that alive."[16] This desire to hold on to culture in the face of modernist advancement is what keeps many of these kids close to home. They know that they're poor and that white schools can give them advantages, but they feel that being richer in spirit and life is more satisfying. One of the hardest lessons for outsiders to learn about the Lakota is that individualism, materialist satisfaction, and cut-throat competition is less valued than family and spirituality. This means that a lot of what may appear to be mired in poverty and non-forward thinking is actually about being grateful for Lakota cultural basics and surrounded by loved ones.

Laura Big Crow expressed this idea about as simply as anyone, when she made the following post on Facebook: "Well today was a great 4th of JULY we spent the day in K-Town with the Inlaws at the kids Grandma Bev's house and they loved it . . . it was so peaceful out there sitting on the porch (until the fireworks started)."[17] The post came with a picture of the family sitting around in beach chairs in front of a modest trailer home. The look on Laura's face as she held a niece on her lap was one of total joy and contentment. In other words, you don't have to spend the Fourth in a Newport, Rhode Island golf club or on the Esplanade of Boston to enjoy the holiday to the fullest.

Olrichs, White River, and Winner

In a previous study I did, which centered on the Texas/Mexico borderlands, I learned that borders can join as much as they divide.[18] However, the people along both sides of the Rio Grande River, which divides Texas from the Mexico border, are joined in spirit and history, both because they have race and history in common and because they perceive their problems as being ones that can be solved only if they work together. In contrast, when people in South Dakota talk about a "border town," their words carry undertones of pure difference, distrust, and venom. Even the problems that should join the two parties tend to be viewed differently by each group.

Back at the turn of the twentieth century, it would have been safe to claim that these towns had been built on a widely shared base of racial intolerance. Entering these white settings, Indians were commonly shunned or, at the very least, made to feel unwelcome, all of which reinforced Lakota determination to operate as sovereign nations making their own decisions. Whites have sought to do the same, with the result that white towns abutting the reservation—border towns—come off as being foreign. These border towns are often composed of fourth- or fifth-generation offspring of the original white people who wrested the land from the Lakota.

While some border towns, like Olrichs or Winner, have Indian populations (18 percent and 14 percent respectively) that are growing, the trend doesn't seem to be an indicator of white appreciation or even tolerance of

Natives living in these towns. At the very least, border communities today show a bit more range in their attitudes toward Natives who go to school and live in their midst. The day-to-day interaction between races, particularly that in which business is transacted—items bought or fixed, or services rendered—is, more or less, tensely cordial. But race always lurks in the background.

Below, I briefly look at three border communities to present some sense of the range that exists in regard to racial acceptance; however, it would be wrong to think that their stories are representative of all such border towns. In reality, border communities with healthy race relations number much fewer than those that remain hostile or guarded.

White River, South Dakota. White River, South Dakota, sits a few miles from the Rosebud Indian Reservation. It's a small ranching town with a population of 529, according to the 2010 census. Of that population, 48.9 percent are white, 40.6 percent Native American, and 9 percent biracial. A decade earlier, the town was both whiter (51.84 percent) and more Native American (43.48 percent). What changed in that decade was the biracial population. Though unusual in this part of the country, whites and Natives were willing to cross the racial divide and establish families, and this was an outcome of the Native world being more accepted. In fact, today, White River's most significant event, the annual Frontier Days celebration, which was begun in 1917, includes a Lakota *wacipi* ceremony, indicating a community with a relatively good sense of race relations.

In Eldon Marshall, the White River boys' basketball coach, we get a sense of these racial relations. Coach Marshall is somewhat modest and one of the state's most successful basketball coaches. He's taken his boys' team to the state tournament every year since 2005, winning the state championship outright in 2008, and all this with a total high school population of around 120 kids. The 2018 graduating class numbered 26. White River schools are officially considered "Indian schools," which means at least 50 percent of the student population is Indian.

Eldon, a Lakota, is from nearby Rosebud Sioux Reservation. He played basketball in high school and, later, at Black Hills State University, before graduating with an education degree. I asked him point-blank whether White River could be considered a town with racial problems. He didn't hesitate before responding. "We both know that if you're looking for racism, you can find it anywhere, but in my experience (his sixteenth year there),

I've never seen anything that I would call racist among the kids I work with every day in school. There's a respect there, where you know how things are. Natives know that non-Natives are different from them, just as non-Natives know that about Natives. I've never heard teachers or kids even say anything kiddingly that demeans."[19]

At least some of this racially accepting climate comes from the quality of the school. "It's small," Eldon said, "and kids get a lot of attention from our teachers." Also, the school doesn't have the problems with addiction, suicide, and so on that Pine Ridge has. When the White River basketball team encounters racism, it's when they travel elsewhere. "I've seen it with my kids. Some crowds will say something to 'em, or other kids will say things. That comes from family and community."

On my way back to Rapid City from my interview with him, I suddenly had one last question for Eldon. I called him and asked, "Eldon, what do you think the attitudes are in town and school about interracial dating?" While the absence of racist expressions between students was all well and good, their feelings about interracial dating would be a much more telling indicator of the school's race relations. "I've seen interracial dating among the kids," Eldon replied, "and it doesn't seem to cause any problems at school—no raised eyebrows or anything."[20] End of story.

White River, it seemed, had created a positive environment, at least from the perspective of Eldon, who said, "It's been good to me and my family, so we see ourselves as staying here."

Olrichs, South Dakota. Olrichs, on the western end of Oglala County, seems to tout acceptable relationships between the whites and the Lakota in their midst. Only 126 people live in the town; 100 of them are white (79.4 percent), 23 (18.3 percent) are Native American, and three (2.4 percent) are from two or more races. Ten years earlier, the census had reported more whites (83.45 percent), fewer Natives (15.86 percent), and others. In other words, demographics are trending in the direction of mixture, but very minimally. Olrichs schools are considered "Indian schools" (at least 50 percent of its student body being Lakota), because of the influx of Indian students from nearby Pine Ridge. As noted, these students represent a revenue stream, and a badly needed one for Olrichs. One superintendent told me, in passing, that federal monies might range between $10,000 and $13,000 per child. Over the past twenty-five years, however, Olrichs enrollments have steadily declined, and now it is on the verge of being closed. With little to keep young people there, the small town is steadily shrinking as students graduate and move away for work. One Lakota parent characterized Olrichs' predicament this way: "White kids are like a nest of birds. Raise 'em, push 'em out, and they're gone."[21]

Lakota parents have opted to put their kids in Olrichs schools for varying reasons. Many quickly point to the better quality of teaching. Some, however, cite personal reasons; for example, one student commented that had he stayed at Pine Ridge High, he'd have been bullied daily. But at Olrichs, he felt he had a safe environment.[22] This youngster was the kind of boy who, at Pine Ridge, might sit at the bottom of the social pecking order: he was scrawny and non-athletic. His parents hoped that certain border communities like Olrichs would less likely tolerate the bullying.

Ironically, a number of families sent their children to Olrichs because of the sporting opportunities. Youngsters who might have trouble making varsity teams on Pine Ridge can be starters elsewhere. "A lot of these kids who move didn't get a chance to play at Pine Ridge," noted one Lakota parent whose son played at Olrichs.[23] So, while Indians make up about 18 percent of the town's population and 50 percent of the school, in 2018 they made up 100 percent of the basketball team—and most importantly, the team was championed by the town as a whole. At games, you'd see a complete blend of races cheering for "their boys."

Parents also mentioned that racial tensions were absent at Olrichs. "I think it's good over there. Might be one or two [racists], but teachers and students are good."[24] Whether they admit it or not, most whites in Ohlrichs are beholden to Pine Ridge and their kids for having saved their school system and the town. All of this fosters a climate of overt acceptance; but that is somewhat, as Bryan Brewer shows. Now president of the county school board, Brewer has been active in education countywide, including in border schools. In summer 2018, Bryan presented some lectures to faculty and staff at Olrichs about Pine Ridge Indian Reservation, discovering in the process that none of them had ever been on the reservation.

Considering that Olrichs is less than ten miles from the reservation border, one would think that, at some point, something would have drawn them there. But, the state's social and racial divide is so pronounced that it never occurred to these teachers and other staff members, who cater to Lakota children on a daily basis, to visit these students' world. So Brewer arranged a tour for these people, who'd grown up just a stone's throw from the Lakota reservation.[25]

Winner, South Dakota. Winner has long been considered a kind of ground zero for racism. In 2010, Winner had a population of 2,861, of which 82.1 percent was white, 14.0 percent was Native American, and 3.2 percent was from two or more races. It's not only the whitest of the three communities, but it has consistently been the most unwelcoming of the three. Winnerians, however, think of themselves as welcoming, and its Chamber of Commerce seems to want to skirt the perception that it is perceived as racist (see chapter 9). On Winner's web site appears the following warm welcome: "Welcome to Winner, South Dakota! We feel we epitomize 'small town America' where everyone knows your name, where people are valued, and pride in our community is a way of life."[26] Sounds convivial, but for quite some time, Winner has been associated with racial intolerance and worse. If you're Indian, word has it, this is not where you want people to "know your name."

Playing for Little Wound High School in 1999, Corey Shangreau recalled a game against Winner. Indian teams traveling outside of the reservation to play aren't socially naïve. They know what to expect in these games. The exact form of racism they will face may not be predictable, but whether it's verbal taunts during the game, poor service in stores and restaurants, a melee with the other team, or a ref's singling out Indian players to call fouls, they will typically get something to take back with them.

But this particular game, Corey recalled, was a bit different. Their team was spit on. Their coach somehow managed to quell their anger and get them focused on the game, but when they went on to trounce Winner, "we made sure to wave our warm-up jackets with the dried-up spit to the crowd. Like flags," Corey said.[27] Waving Indian victory banners at a hostile crowd in their home court is a gutsy move. But while Corey and the others gained a measure of satisfaction from "kicking Winner's ass," they also succumbed to the race-hating game that relies on daily, weekly, and monthly doses of animosity.

Being spit on, though, was a singular statement of hate, especially since it happened before the game, when tempers hadn't even had the chance to be tested and people weren't yet riled up. The deliberateness and timing brought it even closer to that "hate crime" barrier.

Winner is a typical rural Plains community—the majority there are white, ranchers, and Christian. Why the town has developed a reputation as one of the most racist in the state is not fully known, but Winner has been singled out time and again as a nasty place for Native people to be. And, it's been that way for some time—at least since the late sixties. Deloris Taylor, actress and film producer of the seventies cult-film series *Billy Jack*—about a mixed-race, Indian-identified hero who stands up to belligerent, bullying whites—was from Winner. The town's Wikipedia page notes that, "Billy Jack films were due in part to the poor treatment Native Americans received by some of the residents of Winner."[28] Winner's Wikipedia page goes on to list her under "Notable People" (she is one of two). Either Winnerians are unaware of this Wikipedia entry, or they just embrace their racist reputation, but the history goes back at least forty-five years, and probably a good deal earlier.

While Lakota face prejudice throughout South Dakota, Winner has come to be thought of as the epicenter of the state's racism. And the lion's share of the attention given to Winner has been focused on the schools, which has a history of both zealously handling trouble involving Indian students and creating a toxic environment for them. In fact, through the first half-dozen years of the twenty-first century, Winner actively promoted one of the most egregious forms of racism—it tracked young Indian students into the state's prison system, and it used its schools to do so. The Winner School District was sued by the American Civil Liberties Union, which filed a class-action federal lawsuit in March 2006. The ACLU claimed that the school district systematically punished Indian students more harshly than whites.[29]

School-to-Prison Pipeline

The Chasing Hawk family thought they'd done the right thing when they had their son, Casey, attend Winner schools. The boy was studious, and they figured he'd thrive there. He was a middle schooler, and in middle school, incidents involving students who get into arguments and push and shove are not uncommon. As such, young Casey had an encounter with a white classmate, and when asked by a teacher about it, he said he was so angry that he wanted to kill him—an inappropriate response, but hardly a criminal offence. Except that it was. Winner's school superintendent personally came to Chasing Hawk's classroom and yanked him out. He was handed over to the police and promptly thrown in jail.

"He spent sixty-three days in a juvenile detention facility," Casey's father said, "sixty miles from home before the South Dakota Supreme Court determined that his misbehavior didn't even amount to disorderly conduct.

They claimed he was a monster, so they had to make him look like a monster. They did all these evaluations on him, and they found out that his only problem was what they had done to him at that school."[30]

It may be reasonable to assume that the educational system in the United States should reflect the same democratic principles and equal opportunity assigned to sports, but this was not the case in Winner, South Dakota—at least for Casey. It's also certainly not always the case for other school districts in the state. Otherwise, a veteran white teacher in the Rapid City school system, when referring to young Lakota students, would not have publicly declared, "We should just send all those kids straight to prison, that's where they will end up anyway."[31]

Treating in-school behavioral issues of Indian students as criminal offenses has been referred to as "the school-to-prison pipeline." By initiating a criminal record, it sets children on a track to prison. In 2006, a formal complaint filed with the U.S. Department of Education by the Rosebud Sioux Tribe and the ACLU, Winner, South Dakota's school department was accused of implementing such activity as unofficial policy.[32] The complaint also alleged that the Winner school administration had designed such systemic racist policy to drive away Indian students. To support this latter complaint, it was pointed out that in the 1998–1999 school year, fifty-one Indian students were enrolled at the beginning of the year, but by year's end only eleven remained. In 2007, the U.S. Department of Education officially stepped in, demanding that Winner had seventeen areas that needed to be fixed immediately. Since then, under the watch of a new superintendent of schools, Winner has ceased the most egregious practices. Still, it hasn't become an Indian-friendly environment in the manner of White River, and it probably never will.

Notably, South Dakota's criminal justice system mirrors the school practice of singling out Native Americans for almost every form of mistreatment: in 2011, Indians made up just under 10 percent of the state's population, but they made up 29 percent of the adult prison population and 38 percent of juvenile offenders.[33] And is it any wonder? After all, from the onset of U.S. efforts to educate Indians, the goal has never really been to elevate the students and, through that, to better the conditions of the various tribes. Boarding schools, BIE schools, community schools—all fall way short of this goal. However, as long as border schools continue to be an option for Native students, they have a special role to play in all of it.

9

Engaging Acrimony

Racism and Lakota Basketball
in South Dakota

"What they're doin' has to stop somewhere," Coach Dusty LeBeau fumed, disgusted at fans of a white school who were disrespecting Native culture during a basketball game. "We have to stop it in our own homeland. At Bennett County [High School], they were acting like they were praying to the Four Directions. Indians don't make a game of the way we pray, but it's nothing to them."[1] Often prayers are sent up in all four directions to solicit supernatural aid and these fans were laughingly imitating the Lakota ritual. His team did not play there again until they changed this "celebration."

In most ways, the racism faced by Lakota athletes is like that faced by Lakota in general, except that in sports settings racism can veer off in unusual and even antithetical directions. First, sports settings can amplify racism so that it is more directly experienced—not easily disguised as something else. Conversely, these settings can go in the opposite direction; that is, they can constrain racist expressions through the norms and formal codes that govern behavior during school sporting events. Finally, while sports works to curb racist behavior, it can also foster behavior that resists racist expression.

As such, racism is expressed as a mosaic (a complex of related traits) that Lakota athletes must deal with. In this chapter, I focus on this mosaic, drawing attention to a term I call *engaged acrimony*, a particular sporting relationship that occurs when groups that are socially antagonistic in everyday life play each other. For Native communities in particular, engaged acrimony creates opportunities to confront racist behavior, so the chapter will also explore the two most spectacular cases of such confrontation in the Lakota community.

Microaggression and Engaged Acrimony

Of the many racial outrages committed against the Lakota, the "mother" of them all was the Wounded Knee Massacre of 1890, in which 300 Lakota were murdered. Today, we acknowledge that it was a massacre rather than a battle, as the United States originally claimed, but something disingenuous remains: a fundamental sense of empathy among whites and the U.S. government, acknowledging just how despicable and ghastly the event was, is absent. Lakota journalist Tim Giago has spent decades attempting to capture both the horror and final humiliation experienced at Wounded Knee. In a 2014 editorial, on the December anniversary of the event, he wrote:

> One of the survivors, a Lakota woman, was treated by the Indian physician Dr. Charles Eastman at a make-shift hospital set up in a church in the village of Pine Ridge. Before she died of her wounds she told about how she had concealed herself in a clump of bushes. As she hid there, she saw two terrified little girls running past. She grabbed them and pulled them into the bushes. She put her hands over their mouths to keep them quiet, but a mounted soldier spotted them. He fired a bullet into the head of one girl and then calmly reloaded his rifle and fired into the head of the other girl. He then fired into the body of the Lakota woman. She feigned death and although badly wounded, lived long enough to relate her terrible ordeal to Dr. Eastman.[2]

Obviously, there was a perception by those soldiers that killing Indians was little more than political sport. This was confirmed when the U.S. government awarded the Medal of Honor to 21 of the 500 soldiers carrying out this slaughter. The nation's highest military award was handed out like candy for killing defenseless children and women trying to flee violence. I compared this to the 234 Medals of Honor handed out for the ten-year Vietnam War (1965–1975), which involved 2.7 million servicemen and women. If the U.S. government had awarded those medals for Vietnam in the same proportion as they had for the one day of Wounded Knee, they would have awarded 11,548 Medals of Honor. Giago's dismay that "Those medals will never be rescinded even in the wake of all the revelations occurring since that day," is made even more poignant when we realize that these medals, which were celebratory validations of barbarism, were handed out so liberally.[3]

Further, while the Wounded Knee of 1890 may have marked the most egregious and last of a string of murderous outrages by the U.S. military, it wasn't the end of racial murder or rights violations against Indian people. That, unfortunately, has continued. When you combine this reality with the altogether too-frequent current offenses against Indians in South Dakota, the disrespect of some white fans at a basketball game in Lakota territory might seem pretty tame. Still, these micro-aggressions, these everyday racial slights, are reminders to a people who don't need to be reminded—they already know what it means to get icy stares, to be followed around stores by white employees, to routinely get interrogated by police.

For framing racial insults, sports is particularly favored setting. Recent incidents that have garnered attention include one seasonably cold December night in 2018, when, following a game that Red Cloud High played at Hill City (in the Black Hills), Pine Ridge fans leaving town were bid farewell by a "sobriety checkpoint"—a gaggle of police with flashing lights reminding them just how Indian they were.[4] On another night, in February 2015, a group of Lakota fifth graders from Pine Ridge Reservation, on an outing with their teachers to a professional hockey game in Rapid City, had beer poured on them by drunken whites who also pelted them with racist insults.[5] And in October 2017, in the events leading up to their homecoming celebration, white students at Sturgis-Brown High School in Sturgis, South Dakota decided to resurrect a ritual that had been recently banned: They got a car donated for the sole purpose of demolishing it, thereby stoking student pride. That year, their homecoming game was against Pine Ridge High, so before trashing the car, they saw fit to spray-paint racist graffiti all over it, including,

"Go back to the rez." Someone then thought it a good idea to share their work with the world, posting a picture of the car on social media. Angry school officials responded appropriately by canceling the upcoming game and all other homecoming events, but of course, the damage had already been done.[6] Lakota students were admonished by their coaches and elders to remain calm.

Sporting spaces in South Dakota are a minefield for these kinds of slights and insults. When occurring between groups hostile to each other, basketball games can become settings for wildly unpredictable social dramas. For Indian nations, the exuberance and pride of competing is too often muted when their athletes are burdened by having to run a racial gauntlet. It often begins as their team bus enters a white town and ends only after their exit. In between is a collage of back-turning, suspicion, hard stares, questionable service, and the episodic confrontation. At games, Lakota players and their fans may be rudely ignored, taunted, or intimidated. And while the racist behavior or language is more often than not intentional, even when it isn't, it feels like it is.

Coach Dusty LeBeau remembers the insults that he and his players had to endure—everything from ridicule of Indian ceremonial behavior (as in the incident mentioned at the beginning of the chapter) to trash talk that was overtly racist or at least race-coded. Whites often dismiss such behavior as a way to "get into their (opponents') heads," a euphemism for psychologically rattling your opponents. Rattling the opponent with racially tinted behavior is often barely deflected bigotry, yet it is often sanctioned in sports. Indian players are, for the most part, inured to these racial insults, but not always. Lakota high school athletes will, on occasion, use the cloak of civility that the game's context provides to wreak vengeance on white teams that have a history of racism. In this way, the sporting venue provides a haven of sorts, a temporary reprieve from the more socially unsavory relations that frame these events.

As mentioned, *engaged acrimony* is my term for understanding this exchange between athletics and performance in a toxic milieu, which I'll talk about in more detail later. First, however, it's important to understand that while racism is particularly bad where youth sports is concerned, as racial outrages go, these incidents sit at the benign end of the spectrum of human rights violations in South Dakota, a state that is often referred to by Indians there as the "Mississippi of the North."[7]

Race Relations in South Dakota

"I have never been to a place that hated a group of people (my people) so much as they do here in South Dakota," Lakota James Swan said. "I used to think it was just ignorance, but it's not. It's just pure hate, passed from generation to generation."[8] This dire summation of Lakota-white race relations implies that life is significantly more dangerous for Indians there.

Dana Lone Hill, a Lakota writer, took it upon herself to gather data on hate crimes committed in South Dakota—no small task, since "hate crimes" disappeared from internet searches in South Dakota after 2003, undergoing a makeover there and emerging as "bias motivation." Lone Hill found that the incidences of such crimes in 2009 were 5.7 per 100,000. "This put South Dakota in fourth place nationally," she explained, "behind New Jersey, District of Columbia, and Minnesota."[9] Underpopulated South Dakota, with 833,354 people, was just behind New Jersey and its 8.9 million people in hate crimes? A state with one-eighth the population of New Jersey, but with enough hate to rank right up there with it? Now, that's hate! Underscoring this widespread racially violent mosaic in South Dakota is a Native victimization rate that is more than twice that of whites: 118.8 victims per 1,000 Indians and 45.4 per 1,000 whites.[10] Most important, 70 percent of the attacks on Indians are perpetrated by non-Indians.[11] And, in the socially explosive area of Indians being killed by law enforcement, the Center on Juvenile and Criminal Justice, a nonprofit organization that studies incarceration and criminal justice issues, concluded, "Native Americans make up three of the top five age groups killed by law enforcement."[12] These grim statistics all triangulate around the excessive vulnerability of Native peoples in the state.

The epidemic of suicide at Pine Ridge also links to the racist mosaic in South Dakota. Dominique Fenton, a Lakota journalist's examination of Lakota suicide noted that, "Between December 1 and March 23, 2015, Pine Ridge Hospital dealt with 241 patients under 19 years of age who actively planned, attempted or committed suicide. . . . At this rate, 37 young people in a county that only has 5,393 inhabitants under 18 will be gone by the end of 2015."[13]

Poverty, school failure, and overall angst over the future combine with racism to fuel this statistic, but racism looms large, becoming even more damaging once it gets internalized by Indian children. Davidica Young Man, twenty-three, articulated this psychological trauma when he said, "What's worse is that they slowly get used to it [racist behavior] and start thinking, 'It's no big deal that someone just called me a prairie n-word or a dirty savage.'" What's more, it is not uncommon for Young Man and her peers to hear horror stories from off the reservation of offenses that go well beyond racial slurs. They tell stories like, "Well, there was once a Native guy who was drugged by all these white dudes in a truck. He died, and they ditched his body." Fact or fiction, the stories have their desired effect. "All that stuff scared the crap out of me as a teenager," said Young Man."[14] The message sent to young Indian kids is that "You don't matter at all in the white community."

As discussed in chapters 6 and 7, Lakota children attending white schools must navigate daily through systems that range from indifferent to actively hostile.

In one of the worst-case scenarios, most Indian students attending Winner schools moved there to take advantage of the academically better non-reservation schools, but what they encountered, until several years ago, was a system that would criminalize Indian children for minor school infractions—a system that became known as the school-to-prison pipeline.

How Native children come to these ends is certainly not random or a matter of being inherently flawed; they are the result of formal and informal systems of oppression that especially target Native youth.

Two Lakota Ballers Engage Acrimony

At Pine Ridge, two stories involving Lakota basketball players have taken on a folktale quality. They are both accounts of individual Indian refusal to tolerate racism on the basketball court.

These two narratives are highly unusual as far as Pine Ridge stories go, and they differ from each other in the time era in which they occurred, in the gender of the player, in the schools involved, and in the meaning of each player's expressions. The two stories are alike, however, in that each is about a player who is widely known and talked about in the community, which means that these players' acts of racial defiance have been recounted often and, as a result, have undergone a certain amount of alteration.

In recounting these two stories, I use the notion of engaged acrimony—an idea that relies on the manner in which sports is understood to be a specific type of social performance—as a framework for understanding them better.

Story One: SuAnne Big Crow. SuAnne Big Crow was a remarkable young Lakota woman, and one of the best women to have ever played basketball in South Dakota. Big Crow's high school basketball career (1988–1992) actually started in eighth grade, when she began playing varsity and set state records for the most points in a single game and season. As a sophomore, she led her Lady Thorpes to a state championship with a last-second shot. That's Jordanesque! As a result, stories about SuAnne sprang up across the reservation, and one that was burnished over time was about something she did not during a basketball game, but before.

The most circulated account of the event comes from Ian Frazier's book *On the Rez.*[15] SuAnne is the centerpiece of this book, which has been widely read on the reservation but has also garnered a fairly impressive readership outside the reservation. Frazier claimed to have interviewed dozens of people who knew her.

In his account, Big Crow, against a white team from Lead, South Dakota, in 1987, and in the face of a hostile white crowd at the Lead High School gym, led her team onto the floor amid a torrent of racial abuse. Instead of quietly ignoring the toxic social outpouring, however, she suddenly veered off-course to deliver a performance that pushed Lead fans back on their collective heels.

The following account by Frazier depended heavily on his ties to SuAnne's mother and to Doni DeCory, a teammate of Big Crow who was playing there with her on that definitive night:

> She [SuAnne] was a freshman, fourteen years old. . . . Usually the Thorpes lined up for their entry more or less according to height, which meant that senior Doni DeCory, one of the tallest, went first. As the team waited in the hallway leading from the locker room, the heckling got louder. The Lead fans were yelling epithets like "squaw" and "gut eater." . . . The Lead High School band had joined in, with fake-Indian drumming and a fake-Indian tune. Doni DeCory looked out the door and told her teammates, "I can't handle this." SuAnne quickly offered to go first in her place. She was so eager that Doni became suspicious. "Don't embarrass us," Doni told her. SuAnne said, "I won't. I won't embarrass you." . . . She came running on the court dribbling the basketball, with her teammates running behind. On the court, the noise was deafeningly loud. SuAnne went right down the middle, but instead of running a full lap, she suddenly stopped when she got to center court. Her teammates were taken by surprise, and some bumped into

one another. Coach Zuniga at the rear did not know why they stopped. SuAnne turned to Doni DeCory and tossed her the ball. Then she stepped into the jump ball circle at center court, in front of the Lead fans. She unbuttoned her warm-up jacket, took it off, and draped it over her shoulders, and began to do the Lakota shawl dance. "I couldn't believe it—she was powwowin', like, get down!" Doni DeCory recalled. "And then she started to sing." SuAnne began to sing in Lakota, swaying back and forth in the jump-ball circle, doing the shawl dance, using her warm-up jacket for a shawl. The crowd went completely silent. "All that stuff the Lead fans were yelling—it was like she reversed it somehow," a teammate said.[16]

Once she tamed the crowd, SuAnne was reported to have picked up the ball and dribbled the length of the gym for a layup. Frazier concluded that this was "one of the coolest and bravest deeds I ever heard of."[17]

In her senior year, on a path to play D1 basketball in college, Big Crow was killed in a car crash while traveling to receive an award as the state's best player. Pine Ridge was beside itself with grief. Her passing brought together promise, performance, and passing, elevating her to an almost mythic plateau.

Story Two: Jesse Heart. At 6 feet 4 inches, Heart looked like a quintessential baller. Lean and long, he had been the best player to come out of Pine Ridge in decades. In 1999, his senior year, he was the first team All-State guard and a "Mr. Basketball" finalist (a statewide honor; see chapter 4). He attracted the interest of a number of D1 teams, particularly Kansas State University. One rival high school coach characterized Heart in the following terms: "I've seen a lot of basketball, but it seemed like he played with a passion that was unbelievable. I mean, I was awestruck." And one college coach, who had tried to tap Heart's potential, said, "I've talked to several coaches who think Jess Heart was big-time. . . . If Jesse had played four years of college basketball, he'd probably be known as one of the top five players who ever played in South Dakota."[18]

No one could deny his skills. Heart was a deft shooter from outside or inside. He could drive to the hoop or pull up and shoot at will. But like many at Pine Ridge, he was academically and culturally ill-prepared to play at the collegiate level. While he never made it through his first year at junior college, Heart still took his team to the national tournament, where he set the record for most threes in a game not once, but on consecutive nights.

The following story was the first one I heard about Jesse Heart. As SuAnne's story does, it has basketball and race at its core, and while not known by whites, people at Pine Ridge remember and retell it often.

The game took place in 1999, between Jesse's high school, Little Wound, and the high school in Winner, South Dakota. Winner hosted the game and, as mentioned, has a racist reputation among Indian tribes in the state. The Pine Ridge players knew what to expect coming to the town. The epithets started early and included the usual slurs, such as "prairie nigger," along with shouts to "Go back to the reservation."

With Pine Ridge maintaining a lead, the collective blood pressure among the opposing team's fans seemed to rise to dangerous levels. Winner's disdain for Indians had been seamlessly transmitted from parents to children, and one group of young whites at courtside was particularly dialed into the tirade against their guests. Jeering at the traditional long hair sported by one Little Wound player, they screamed with red-faced gusto, "Nice hair, Nancy!" along with an assortment of other racist phrases, laughing at their own verbal handiwork and thinking it clever. And though this may not have been particularly unusual, on this night Jesse Heart had had enough.

Defending against Winner's bringing the ball up-court, Heart quickly darted over to the fans making the racket, and since they were at courtside, he bent over until he was almost face-to-face with one of the loudest. He put three fingers directly up in front of the boy's face. Saying nothing, he then raced back to the action and quickly stripped the Winner guard of the ball. Then dashing toward his basket, Jesse stopped at the 3-point line, where he promptly drained one of his patented threes.

Next, he quickly returned to the same Winner boy, this time holding two fingers in his face, before returning to repeat his play, swishing a second three. Jesse again returned to the now quiet group who, at this point, didn't even want to make eye contact with him. But Heart, sporting an angry smile, knew what he wanted to do. He held up one finger before sprinting back to the game.

Trying desperately to get rid of the ball before Heart could humiliate him again, the Winner guard passed, but the ball was once again picked up by Jesse, who drove the final dagger into Winner.

It was then that the white boys and their neighbors ceased their taunting. It was as if this Lakota basketball warrior had sucked all of the bigoted oxygen out of the building. Jesse Heart had directed his fury at a white crowd and not only won the game but challenged them to do something about it. There are few places for an Indian to do that in South Dakota.

Debunking and Rebunking the Stories

Myth gets made in the retelling of a story, which gets morphed and embellished each time it's voiced. On Pine Ridge, these stories about Heart and Big Crow were told and retold many times over.

Marinated by memory and morphed by collective need, the games seized Big Crow and Heart, turning them into heroic figures—young athletes who flew into the teeth of white racism in ways that Lakota normally didn't. That these were public acts that whites couldn't immediately deny, and that it was whites who had to acquiesce and mutely endure Indian aggression, marked a momentary but real social reversal in Native communities.

In those ways, the two accounts were similar; however, the sudden passing of SuAnne before she even graduated from high school elevated everything associated with her story into the realm of folklore.

On the other hand, though the public rebuke Heart delivered was more direct and fraught with danger than SuAnne's, given South Dakota's racial climate at that time, his story was never written about as SuAnne's was. So the accounts I received of Jesse's game came from Lakota teammates and fans, from Jesse's coach and his father, and most important, from Jesse himself. Because I was fortunate enough to speak with him about it, I had the chance to get a closer look at what happened that night. And in his case, what wasn't talked about in the accounts of others, who had witnessed the event from a physical distance, paled in comparison to what had actually transpired.

The Other Story: Jesse. In the story according to Jesse, the high-level details were the same: the game was against Winner, and the outcome was the same, as was the racist climate. What spectators had observed—his animated behavior, his signaling to the fans, his putting up fingers—had indeed happened. But they got the significance wrong. The accounts claimed that Jesse was telling the fans what he was about to do, but Heart said it was about what he had already done and what *they* should do.

"They were hollering all right," Jesse recalled. "I remember them. I just went off! Hit five straight threes! After the second or third, I went over to them and flashed like this . . ." he extending the last three fingers of his shooting hand, indicating 3-point shots. "Then I went like this . . ." he pressed his index finger to his lips. With this last gesture, Jesse said, he was telling the rowdy boys in front to shut up.

What even fewer fans knew was what Heart actually said to the boys. "I told them each time I hit a three, 'You gotta be quiet, 'cause you're making it worse.' And 'Look at me, oooh, it's gettin' bad.' They got real quiet." He laughed at the memory.

He spoke to them in a quiet but threatening tone, as if they were errant children who needed to be chastised for their silly insults. There was nothing about Jesse that suggested restraint. If anything, he was emboldened. "They didn't bother me none," he said. "I like playing against those white boys. I get excited by putting on a show."[19]

Heart's version of the story added a layer of intentional verbal assault to the confrontation. It was a public repudiation in word and deed to a gym full of hostile fans in their own town—and by an Indian who didn't mind engaging their acrimony. His actions constituted a deliberate sense of confrontation that went to the very edge of what was tolerated. And these types of actions are what constitute engaged acrimony.

To explain further, the significance of Heart's performance lay in its being carried out in the particular space of a white high school basketball gym. The codes of conduct officially fashioned by the people of Winner for their sports activities were designed to curb inappropriate behavior. Winner High School's Student-Athlete Handbook states clearly, "Unacceptable behavior includes: trash talk, taunting, and other intimidating actions on behalf of players or spectators."[20] When playing against Indians, however, it seemed no one at the school felt particularly constrained, so what should have been a congenial place was taut with hostility from both sides. As such, the gym became a contested space: made civil enough to prevent violent outbreaks, while constantly pushing those same boundaries. By engaging acrimony, Jesse Heart took advantage of this space, effortlessly dancing on the boundary's edge.

To some Lakota, to have one of their own champion them in this way linked Heart to historic Lakota warrior heroes such as Red Cloud and Crazy Horse.

The Other Story: SuAnne. "Any time the subject of SuAnne came up when I was talking to people on Pine Ridge," Frazier said, "I would always ask if they had heard about what she did at Lead, and always the answer was a smile and a nod. 'Yeah, I was there,' or 'Yeah, I heard about that.'"[21]

It was the same when I first visited in 2014. Because Frazier's account of SuAnne Big Crow had jumped the reservation, so to speak, becoming widely known among whites, it further fueled the racial divide in South Dakota. Whites heartened by the Big Crow account could be found, but most who heard the account became defensive. Bill Harlan, a journalist from South Dakota, seemed to carry the banner for this latter group. He published a piece in the *New York Review of Books* accusing Frazier of shoddy journalism and, by extension, calling into question the events of that night.[22]

It so happened that Harlan's family was at the game on that notorious night. His niece had played for Lead in that game, and his brother and wife were in the stands. The first thing Harlan discovered was that the game wasn't even played in 1988; it was actually played in 1987. SuAnne was an eighth grader who played varsity at the high school that year.

Harlan also took issue with Frazier's neglect to interview a single person from Lead. This was important, because Harlan's Lead sources said they could not recall a racist climate in the game. They remembered no taunts or fake Indian music being played, and, most important, they remembered no center-court dance "that tamed an ugly crowd."

Their reaction isn't particularly surprising. It's entirely possible that Lead fans didn't feel their shouting and general demeanor were racist but that their guests simply interpreted them as such.

But maybe the most important part of the Harlan account was his transcribed conversation with SuAnne's teammate, Doni DeCory, who seemed to temper her earlier account. She acknowledged a group of "rowdy teenage boys" banging the bleachers, going "woo-woo-woo," but she did not remember hearing racial epithets, insulting music by the school band, or comments about food stamps that Frazier mentions in his book. Further, Harlan's Lead sources who claimed to have been at the game said they didn't see any such racism; and he cites Lena Norris, a Lakota who went to school at Lead, as saying, "There's no way that [racist displays] happened.... We had a really strict athletic director. He'd yank kids out of the stands for cussing. Besides, there is no way I would put up with that."[23]

To the Lakota, Lead epitomized racist South Dakota, part of the woof and warp of life in the state. Even those who denied the events of that day admitted that racial slurs regularly occurred on the Lead court. "There were also, as Mr. Harlan knows, other incidents of unruliness on the part of Lead players and fans in which racial slurs were involved," declared Frazier.[24] And even if we were to take Harlan's interview with DeCory as her only account of that night, she still claimed the presence of a "rowdy" group of boys that so rattled her with their actions and taunts that she froze at the gym's entrance. How could a player who had most certainly heard this kind of thing before be so unnerved as to refuse to go out on the court if it were so insignificant a matter?

More significant still, Harlan insinuated that the heart of the SuAnne story might not have happened. He wrote, "DeCory, a member of the Oglala Sioux tribe, told me the dance was 'highlighted too much' in Frazier's book." In Harlan's account, DeCory said SuAnne did a short dance at one end of the court as both teams warmed up, but she didn't sing. SuAnne was just clowning, DeCory said, as she often did before games to ease tension among teammates. The crowd took no notice. "It wasn't a big deal," DeCory concluded.[25]

What to make of these two very different accounts of the game? It seems Frazier hijacked the game, turning it into a heroic and romantic Western, while Harlan minimized Frazier's account and tried to cleanse the reputation of Winner. I was fortunate enough to converse with Dana Lone Hill, who was there as a young Pine Ridge cheerleader and who recalls SuAnne's performance. I asked her if she was there while SuAnne did her "famous dance at center court." Lone Hill replied, "Yes, but it wasn't 'famous,' like it wasn't 'a moment.'" It was just her messin' around. That's how she was . . . I remember her busting out a dance at the free-throw line. They were waiting for the ref to give her the ball, and he was getting mad at the crowd. They were being racist. Her and another girl did a dance to make us laugh."[26]

I revisit this story later in this chapter, but for now, what is clear is that some amount of racial intimidation occurred, despite Harlan's words to the contrary. Dana Lone Hill noted that the level of racism there was angering the ref, and DeCory admitted to not wanting to open the gym doors because of the racist din. Both DeCory's and Lone Hill's accounts also clearly state that SuAnne danced primarily to ease her teammate's nervousness. In Frazier's determination to make this "the coolest" thing he'd ever encountered, he never understood the way the Lakota use humor, a key point made by Lone Hill. "We all deal with it [racism] that way," she said. "Our humor helps us."[27]

At this point, then, we can only theorize about these seemingly irreconcilable understandings of the event. For starters, Frazier clearly failed to understand almost as much about the game as did Harlan. In addition, the story will likely never get the vetting it should, because SuAnne occupies such a special space in Lakota society.

In regard to Harlan's denial of so much of the story, however, maybe the white people in the crowd didn't know enough to take notice of a shawl dance. And maybe from that same white perspective, no racial epithets were observed because racism runs so deep that they regarded their shouting as little more than rattling an opponent or joking around. But even if that were the case, it doesn't mean the Lakota heard it that way.

Further, that SuAnne danced at the free-throw line rather than at center court and that she was known for clowning around to reduce tension when she felt her team was being attacked may be less romantic, but it is no less important and socially daring. In fact, the more I've thought about her clowning around, the more impressed I have become. Clowning to reduce tension is one thing, but doing so with a hostile crowd glaring at you is an ice-in-your-veins act.

As such, SuAnne had taken over on two fronts: first, she was looking out for her teammates and attempting to calm their rattled nerves, and second, she physically and psychologically performed with her back to the crowd, indicating that they and their taunts didn't matter. Now, *that's* a cool thing!

The Racial Mosaic

Seeing these stories as individual occurrences that constitute only one small part of the state's race relations conceals the perniciousness of a larger mosaic. A single play, a single game, an isolated comment may easily be explained away as "the heat of the moment" or "an unfortunate comment." Bigotry is, however, a social pattern, part of a complex that runs through and integrates an individual's or a community's thoughts, social views, and acts. It's not just fans or coaches, but the entirety of the event (all the actors and their props) that constitutes an amalgam, a racial mosaic. For example, a Lead fan may use a racial epithet and get away with issuing an apology in the spillover of a hotly contested game; however, that fan chose that specific expression to begin with, a choice that, in turn, was linked to his or her community's regular harassment of Indians who come to town. That town and its residents also likely hold a wider range of bigoted views of Lakota that extends to treating Indian children in their schools badly, censoring interracial dating, and allowing racist employment practices.

Earlier, I referred to the Lakota perception of playing in white towns as a "racial gauntlet." In this view, a string of micro events that begin and end in one space are linked together. The Dakota girls from Crow Creek who, in 2001, were shot at following a basketball game (see chapter 8), saw the gauntlet unfold even as they entered the town and played the game, and it lasted through post-game time and up until they left town. Conversely, the Winner community saw the whole event only in terms of girls throwing a drink on a boy's favorite car, thus stirring his anger—that is, they saw the drink-throwing as unconnected to events that had happened before that moment and to events that would happen after. They could not see that this moment with all of its social categories, along with all of the other moments that made up the trip—before, during, and after the game—were just pieces of that larger picture.

During the Game

To take a closer look at the individual pieces that make up the gauntlet, we need to take Lead and Winner out of our equation and look at the broader social context of Indian teams playing both against and in white-identified schools. As mentioned, the social environment of the game starts well before the opening tipoff, but its worst expressions are usually reserved for the game. Every Lakota player I spoke with has experienced racist behavior, either around them generally or directed toward them specifically, in game contexts—not at every game but in particular games. The experiences stay with them their whole lives, and they grow to expect such behavior.

One Lakota athlete recalled, "We were in our second game at a tournament in Aberdeen when we started pulling away. The fans on the other side began shouting the same old stuff at us, you know, like, 'Prairie niggers!' and stuff like that."[28] Another remembered, "Those little farm communities are pretty segregated, and they're the kind of places where racist attitudes are out there [expressed]. I've had coaches and fans use the term *prairie nigger*. That's a pretty common occurrence, and their players will say it too."[29] Laura Big Crow said, "I don't remember hearing that kind of thing until we were at the state tournament in 2004. We were being called prairie niggers and being told to go back to the reservation, that we didn't belong there."[30]

What's worse, these slurs and taunts give way to behaviors that are more difficult to quietly endure. A prime example of this is that famous game featuring Jesse Heart against Winner in 1999, in which Winner fans spat on the Little Wound players as they entered the court and ran past the crowd. Corey Shangreau, who played in that game, revealed the depths of the racism felt not only on that night but in the town in general. "Winner was a tough place. Tough place. One game . . . we saw that some of the guys had spit all over the back of their jackets from when they ran by. We were standing there looking at each other, and someone said, 'Damn. That looks like spit!' That stirred things up."[31] Spitting on the opponents *before the game*, when the crowds' passions about the game itself were still cool? That was not an isolated or spur-of-the-moment act; it was an act that could be fostered only by a history that had percolated over time. Due to that history and due to more heated games like this one, traveling to play at mostly-white schools creates psychologically taut emotions for Indian teams. They can never be sure whether what they are about to encounter will be one of those games that requires cooler heads.

Former coach Bryan Brewer recalls a game in Hill City where a player kept pulling the ponytail of one of his Thorpe boys' team players. When the player had had enough, he punched the white player, and a melee involving players and fans ensued. Coach Brewer managed to get his players into the visiting team's locker room as hundreds of irate fans swarmed around outside, blocking their exit. Then, in desperation, because Brewer didn't trust local police, he called the Pine Ridge police, a hundred miles away, to send cruisers to escort the team out of the building.[32]

Coaches and Referees

Players are not the only ones who have acted out their city's racist attitudes at games. Coaches and referees have also played a role. Although many coaches in the state, such as Rapid City's Dave Strain or Custer's Larry Luitjens, have worked their whole lives to promote respectful relations, coaches who openly express bigotry can still be found. One coach, having just lost to the Lady Thorpes, felt it appropriate to tell to the media, "It's a tough loss, but at least my girls have futures."[33]

Referees routinely and disproportionately call Indian teams for fouls. For some time now, there has been a tidal wave of objection to this trend all across Indian Country, because it has game-changing consequences and systematically puts Indian teams at a disadvantage. Natives are rightfully outraged at the thought that the very people who are defined as guardians of the game's integrity—those hired to work against impartiality—would penalize on the basis of race.

Many Native voices have expressed disdain at witnessing or experiencing racial bias by referees. Laura Big Crow said that, in some places, the refereeing is so blatantly biased that Natives say the game is "really five on seven. We have five on the floor, but they have two refs and their team. We could be in foul trouble in minutes, in the beginning of the game!"[34] Jesse Heart echoed this experience: "I remember at a regional tournament in Fort Pierre, and we played Winner, and the officiating was so bad that I got my fifth foul early in the second half, and I lost it. I got two technicals and got sent to the locker room."[35]

Brandon Ecoffey, head of Bad Face Indigenous Media Consulting, was so incensed at the officiating in the 2018 State Championship Tournament that he was moved to editorialize, "We have long recognized that when native teams take to the basketball court, fouls come quickly, aggressive play is labeled dirty, passion is interpreted as taunting, and subtle calls are made throughout the game that ultimately affect the final score."[36]

Dusty LeBeau remembered that, at a game in 1991 against Custer, "They made one field goal in the second half and beat us by five. [The] rest of their points were on free throws."[37] And that's not to mention the notorious acceptance speech LaBeau gave at his induction into the South Dakota Sports Hall of Fame: "Are you giving me this award for the two times I won championships or for the other times that I didn't because you took it from me?"[38]

What's more, Lakota basketball players weren't the only ones giving testimony to biased refereeing. Earlene Rooks, who worked for Pine Ridge's KILI radio, had similar complaints. Commenting on a 1999 game, she said, "The officials cheat us out of every game our teams play against white teams. . . . It's sad, but our teams are never allowed to make it out of the district." And in reference to a key playoff game that affected the possibility of a Pine Ridge team winning in the state championship run, she said, "Last winter [1999] there was outrage on Pine Ridge when Jesse Heart, perhaps the best high school basketball player in South Dakota, was ejected from a playoff game after being called for four fouls in the opening minutes of a contest against Custer High."[39]

Finally, Lakota journalist Jim Giago (nephew of Tim Giago) said he believes there is a pattern of referees systematically penalizing Indian teams, and he intends to capture this trend in an upcoming study that he's designed for that sole purpose.[40]

Before and After the Game

Of course, as discussed, the racial mosaic, or gauntlet, also extends to behavior both before and after the game. In the incident involving the Crow Creek girls team, for example, violence was presaged even as their bus entered town, continuing into the game, and fully erupting afterward, when a car full of girls were shot at.[41] But just in general, Indians in white towns know they are scrutinized when they walk into shops or restaurants, and some have even internalized the experience to the point that they have changed their expectations and behaviors accordingly. For instance, Davidica Young Man claimed, "I still don't carry a purse into stores, because they always used to ask me to open it before leaving." Indian athletes wanting a bite to eat after the game may also get shoddy service (like burgers with only the bottom buns or sodas only halfway full) or, at the very least, that subtle look from white employees that suggests "an attitude."

After a game, in particular, the culmination of all of these bits and pieces is the release of a panoply of feelings and behavior. The game is rehashed, or, in rare instances, anger is physically unleashed. Accounts exist of Indian athletes and teams being attacked by white fans following the game. Buses have been vandalized. In one instance, while getting gas on their way out of a white town, the Thorpe girls overheard the cashier inside the station say to another local, "Did they sell all their beers?" referring to their purchase. And finally, as pointed out, police often patrol the outskirts of town to do sobriety or car-insurance checks, delivering the final insult to Native teams before they leave to drive back home.

All of these moments—before, during, and after the game—are what comprise the complex of racism surrounding basketball.

Engaging Acrimony. Basketball has come to be, for the Lakota, a way of *engaging acrimony,* by giving sporting behavior expanded meaning. In an atmosphere of engaged acrimony, bad blood that exists between groups enters into game settings, where those feelings and relations are acted upon. These antagonistic relations may cause fans' or players' behavior to veer off-course, creating a sporting wrinkle that can exacerbate existing relations as well as test the civility espoused in sporting contests. We see it in both the racist behavior directed against Indian teams as well as in the examples of refusal to tolerate this behavior by SuAnne Big Crow and Jesse Heart.

The democratic ideology embedded in sports, which speaks to the level playing field—that metaphorical field on which contestants have equal opportunities—is often at odds with the reality of the social world that contestants come from. Winning the game symbolizes either a replication or a momentary upset in the existing order. The court, pitch, or field, then, is brimming with fears and phobias by socially dominant groups—trepidation that may give expression to ugly displays of rancor. And the sporting enterprise requires that they accept defeat by social underlings, all of which galls even more. In other words, fans of Winner or Lead, or any white teams fearing being beaten by Lakota teams, are more likely to seek to diminish their temporary loss of status by more vociferously and angrily demeaning their Lakota opponents with racial slurs or other behavior.

To fully grasp this concept, we should think of the game as having its own natural history in which there are things leading up to and following the actual game. Some of these pre- and post-game pieces were discussed in the previous sections, in regard to games played between Native and white teams in majority-white towns; however, pre- and post-game affairs that feed into engaging the acrimony surrounding a game extend beyond those "away" games, reaching, for example, those games played between rivals in reservation high schools if factionalism exists. In addition, pre- and post-game events that engage acrimony extend beyond the hours immediately preceding and following a game.

In the days leading up to a game, for instance, players get increasingly caught up in talking up their own team and demonizing the opponent. So, of course, one's own athletes are lionized as heroes, while opponents are depicted as epitomizing everything one's own team is not. But how one depicts the competition can, in engaged acrimony, exceed the bounds of what's appropriate and call on baser instincts of race and class; for example, when Sturgis high school fans, in preparation for their game with Pine Ridge, painted racist graffiti on the side of a car, vilifying the Lakota, and then proceeded to burn the car.

But Lakota engage acrimony as well. In the days leading up to their games, coaches echo the community sentiment, ramping up that ire. For example, legendary football coach "Pop" Warner (who was white) coached at Carlisle in the early 1910s. When his Indian teams played white college teams, Warner would actively encourage "racial spirit" to pervade the Carlisle locker room. His quarterback, Gus Walsh, recalled that in a 1912 game against West

Point, "Warner had no problem getting the boys keyed up for the game. He reminded the boys that it was the fathers and grandfathers of these army players who had fought the Indians. That was enough!"[42] Triggering Indian resentment took no effort, of course, but any reminder further fueled their existing sense of outrage against the white world.

When coaching middle schoolers, Brandon Ecoffey employed acrimony as well. "I coach my kids, the sixth grade team, and use resistance as a motivational tool. I tell 'em, 'Come on, these white boys can't run with you. We'll run 'em into the ground. They'll be throwin' up.'"[43]

In addition, passing conversations between people in the community in the days leading up to a game tend to focus on the game. The media also fan the flames by bringing up past slights, turning opponents into something undesirable. The hype may be couched as selling more tickets for the game, but it's selling rancor.

Once game day finally arrives, trash talk is a form of communication that goes on between players on the court, only pieces of which might be overheard by fans. Trash talk is a special bandwidth of communication filled with interpersonal insults, taunts, and rebukes that can appear to be said either to no one in particular, to one's teammates, or directly to one's opponent. Most often it is uttered so as not to be picked up by the referees or fans, but not always. It is often racist, but not always. It can appear misogynist (e.g., "You're my bitch!") or homophobic (e.g., "I'm gonna fuck you up the ass, bitch!"), but not always. The jawing can also be accompanied by glares between players, which can easily lead to brawls if unchecked by referees.

At times, these communications are punctuated by extravagant basketball gestures that are thinly disguised as play. Standing over an opponent who has fallen on the ground for just an instant too long is an expression of engaged acrimony. Dunking with vengeance and then hanging on the rim (especially if one's opponent's head is in the vicinity of one's genitals) is another form; called "baptizing" in some circles, it implies sexual dominance as well.

What places these gestures in the sphere of engaged acrimony is that brief instant when both players understand what locking in a mutual glare one millisecond too long means, or what having someone's genitalia too close means. If two players look at each other and move on, it's nothing. Or if a player hangs on the rim with his body close to another's face, but he doesn't linger for that extra split second, then it's just part of the game. Similarly, trash talk can be just part of the game and get easily dismissed—or it can catapult things into the realm of social animus.

Engaged acrimony also shows up in players' reactions to winning a game. Beating Winner, for example, is more than another notch in the collective belt of Pine Ridge sports teams, because of who Winner represents to the Native players and community. Recalling the words of Corey Shangreau, who played for Little Wound, "We felt really different when we played whites. We'd get so fired up to play their schools, wanted to beat them real bad."

For oppressed communities, sporting victories are especially savored. A state championship or even a victory over one's social nemesis is seen as proof that change is possible, resistance can pay off, and hope springs eternal.

In summary, in engaged acrimony, the game within the game is played out on a heightened arena of dominance, gender, social hierarchy, race, and so on. As such, any action related to a game can sit uncomfortably on the threshold between being an acceptable part of the game and being a part of the meta game of engaged acrimony.

Game as Performance

I've referred to SuAnne Big Crow's and Jesse Heart's acts of defiance as "performance," but as discussed in a previous chapter, every sporting event is a performance. A basketball game is essentially a competitive structured display of virtuosity that is best enjoyed with an audience. At its simplest, it entertains, though on occasion it can also elevate our existence, maybe even transform us in some way.

Anthropologist Victor Turner is generally credited with establishing the notion of "performance" as a socially revealing area of study.[44] In collaborating with theater professor Richard Schechner to consider the role performance plays, he began to develop the view that public ritual transforms people and social relations. For Turner, that meant looking at rituals that shuttle us between secular and sacred realms of being. Looking at coming-of-age rituals in Africa, for example, Turner was struck by the transformations that these ritual performances accompanied. Boys would be ushered into manhood by being sequestered and made to endure a rite of passage that acted as a threshold, a separation of their adolescence from adulthood. He called that time and place between boyhood and adult "liminal."

Sports makes another excellent example of Turner's sense of performance: they are mass public rituals that are transformative and liminal. Game day starts in a work-a-day secular fashion and moves to a heightened state of being, the team and the game both eagerly anticipated. Players and fans alike wear team-identified clothing and engage in special rituals shared with others, all in the hopes of garnering a win, vanquishing a foe, and bathing in the reflected glory of their team, their community. The stands become a place where people transform into fans, their moods elevated, many becoming euphoric. Resplendent in team colors and even face paint, many are even physically transformed. And at game's end, the fans begin to return to the secular, changing back to the office worker, insurance salesmen, UPS driver, and so on.

This idea of transformation receives added value if the game is one of engaged acrimony, because if the subordinate team defeats their betters, they symbolically upset the order of things, momentarily and euphorically engaging in as the seventeenth-century English ballad referred to, a "world turned upside down."[45]

Sports contain another very important difference from other forms of entertainment: the contest that serves to structure the event simultaneously threatens its tranquility and order. Even the anticipated outcome is thrown into question in sports: matches are enacted in accordance with strict rules of behavior under which the game can be played, but the game is open to turns, twists, and endings that neither athletes nor audiences can wholly predict or fully understand. What breathes life into sports is the chaos and artistic flourish that enters the game to jostle against its inherent order. The sports audience attends, excited for a hoped-for win but also brimming with trepidation—fearful of reversals that other performative audiences do not have to deal with.

Conclusion

In looking at Jesse Heart's and SuAnne Big Crow's stories, we see two individual performances within the context of the game of basketball. Their stories tell us very different things, but both draw on the sanctity and order of the game. Both players were capable of taking over games and could win them almost singlehandedly. What they did on these particular nights was engage acrimony within the context of a basketball game. Their enactments wouldn't exist without the sport, but their social implications were distinct from the game. Both performances highlighted refusal: rejecting the would-be abuse that emanates from their adversaries. Gerald Vizenor has characterized such narratives as "renunciations of dominance, detractions . . . and the legacy of victimry."[46]

These two refused to mutely accept insults, but they did so in ways very different from each other. As for Big Crow, whatever she did off the court was underscored by her dominance on the court. As with Heart, opposing fans and players all had to acknowledge SuAnne's excellence, and that had to affect their social perception of her. SuAnne engaged acrimony with a mock indifference: entering a hostile setting, she got ready to play and attempted to calm her teammates by dancing. And in turning her back to white fans, she simultaneously sent them the message "Mind over matter. I don't mind, and you don't matter."

Unflustered by the racism, SuAnne helped her teammates regain their composure by being lighthearted, just as she had the night their team bus was vandalized to read "Pine Ridge Hores." SuAnne's refusal to be victimized played out the same in both instances: her first concern was for her teammates, while the whites who pelted them with insults were, for SuAnne, a distant presence. In an oblique way of counting coup, Big Crow countered their attackers indirectly, remaining indifferent to the white gaze.

Conversely, Jesse Heart engaged acrimony directly. He identified the Winner fans making the most noise and punished them by shooting five 3-pointers and then telling them his scoring was their fault. As a result, Winner fans not only had to endure the loss of the game and the schooling by Jesse; they had to do so impotently—because even after his basketball performance quieted the crowd, Heart wouldn't let it go. His outrage was so all-encompassing that reengaged the crowd riling them up again. "Dusty was yelling at me to stop, but I wasn't havin' any of it," he said, laughing. "My dad was sitting behind our bench, behind where Dusty was, and he was clapping for me."[47]

The responses of Jesse's father and of Coach LeBeau reference the linked differences between basketball as performance (as LeBeau issued an edict to "kick their asses and get out") and basketball as a way of expressing Lakota identity (as Heart's father egged him on to "count coup" for the crowd).

Meanwhile, Jesse dodged the verbal barbs thrown at him, but he engaged the acrimony with a charge of his own, saying, "I liked it! They'd boo me, talk shit, call me names, and I'd look at 'em and light it up, and I watch those ugly white faces get quiet, get steamed."[48]

To so directly confront a racist crowd as Heart did was rare in Indian Country, as conventional wisdom dictated that Native athletes not inflame these situations. Compare, for example, a similar situation that occurred thirty years before Jesse Heart's time. Back then, Marty Waukazoo, playing for Rapid City High School Cobblers, was the most dominant Lakota ballplayer in the region. In their run at the state title, he led his team, putting his imprint on the tournament with a string of stellar performances.

But in the first-round game against Miller High, a game in which Waukazoo shone, he was taken out of the game after the Cobblers built a sizable lead. Leaving the floor, he was met by a wall of verbal abuse. His coach, Dave Strain, said, "He was booed by the near-capacity crowd. He was booed after delivering a performance of excellence for his team. I couldn't feel the emotion of those boos for Marty, but they must have hurt. They must have hurt a lot. Yet he never talked about it."[49] Strain said that upon getting to the bench, Waukazoo put a towel over his head to find reprieve from the verbal assault.

Years later, Marty Waukazoo recalled the moment. "At the state tournament in '67 in Sioux Falls, South Dakota, I think the arena held eight or ten thousand people, and it was packed for the state tournament, and I had an outstanding game. I did very well at the first game at the tournament and there . . . the crowd, rather than saying I did a good job, they booed me and there were all kinds of negative words that were said. I was seventeen years old. They would call you "prairie nigger," "dog eater" and this again was in the sixties and I think that kind of fueled me."[50]

But if it fueled him, it did so quietly, perhaps in the form of personal resolve. Jim Giago has written about both Waukazoo and Coach Strain that night, and Strain himself wrote about the event. Giago's accounts tend to support Coach Strain's sense that the effect of that wall of verbal abuse wounded Marty Waukazoo more than he might care to admit fifty years later. In any event, Marty Waukazoo, in typical Lakota fashion, bore the onslaught quietly. But Jesse Heart wouldn't tolerate any of that.

Heart's raw hatred of the Winner crowd and his decision to wage war on them was sanctioned by his dominant basketball performance. It was a liminal warfare: on the threshold between symbolic and real, in the spirit of George Orwell's quote that "sport was war minus the shooting." Heart was not intimidated in the slightest, and he also understood that his basketball performance gave him the caché to socially act: white fans would have to accept Jesse's excellence because, ironically, that's what they had come to see.

For Lakota, who'd endured all manner of ill-treatment by whites in these venues, the acts of Heart and Big Crow were seen as enduring acts of engaged acrimony—acts that emblematically vanquished their foes and psychologically fortified their people. As such, their stories, entering the world of Lakota lore, have been passed along from one generation to the next, at times mingling with other tales of heroism and at times amounting to mere idle sports chat, but always representing the strength of Lakota.

Epilogue

I wanted to look at the place of basketball in Lakota life, and do it without inadvertently claiming an inflated sense of its significance. Additionally, I wanted to show how seamlessly basketball is woven into contemporary life on Pine Ridge and, especially, how it helps reproduce traditional ways. (The easy way that Dusty and his sons moved between the sport and their traditional ways speaks to this; as does Bryan Brewer and his LNI tournament.) I also hoped to show through the stories of people like Laura Big Crow, Jesse Heart and others that the game has offered a heuristic path heading into adulthood for both boys and girls.

But as noted, I don't mean to force these conclusions by exaggerating the importance of the game. Maintaining a realistic sense of basketball's centrality was difficult simply because, in writing a book about anything, one becomes too focused on that thing—too close; and with that closeness comes a tendency to lose perspective. If you study birds, or the French impressionists, or Iraqi migration, the tendency to see birds, impressionists, or migration everywhere is strong.

So, for instance, how much credence should I give Dusty LeBeau's assertion that "They say the two hardest things to do here is be tribal president and the Pine Ridge head coach."[1] I know he realizes that equating coaching with the tribe's preeminent political position is not to be taken literally; one job is helping to lead a large community through perilous times, while the other is leading a small group of boys through a collection of games. Still,

Dusty and his family are in the thick of life at Pine Ridge: they know the infighting nature of tribal politics, and he sure knows what it was like to coach there. Is Dusty inflating the sporting side of his comparison?

Not entirely. Others have echoed LeBeau's view that coaching basketball at Pine Ridge is a high profile and thankless position that inspires legions of detractors. So, as tempting as coaching at his old high school is for Jesse Heart, he was adamant about never taking such a position because of the parental politics involved. Corey Shangreau grew so disgusted with it that he quit after two seasons. When thinking of his term as tribal president, Bryan Brewer shakes his head in recalling the thanklessness of that position; but, when thinking about his position as head coach, he remembers the pettiness and backbiting of parents. Dusty is so put off by this toxic drama that he smudges in his office. So as it would seem, because they incite familial passions, political office and coaching are identical at their core—weighted with people's energy, both ecstatic and neurotic.

In Dusty's original assertion—that the two hardest jobs on the rez are tribal president and head coach—he slipped in a very important insight. He noted that the game's protagonists, its players, may be invested in the game their whole lives but only briefly play it, "You know, for the majority of kids around here, high school ball is their Final Four. It's kind of like their career. There were quite a few who went on to college, but when they got there, they just didn't play."[2] So, basketball is not only a sport that the Lakota avidly follow through adulthood, but for most it's played, gets expressed, and dies only in high school and only within the confines of Pine Ridge.

Because players' basketball days are compressed into a mere four years of their lives, the game becomes a rarified and intense time for both the players and their families and friends. As such, growing up loving and playing the game, and then raising kids to grow up loving and playing the game, and doing it all within such a narrow time period and small cultural space, forms a kind of insularity: a basketball version of nuclear fusion, where energy, much of it euphoric and some of it toxic, gets created under intense compression.

Dreams of reservation youth are at once realized, deferred, and deliberated over through basketball and during long winters and hot summers, in part because basketball is transcendent (fosters dreams of escaping their conditions), but also because it fits snugly into daily life, like caring for one's family, repairing cars, finding work, as well as being light hearted. Additionally, when playing outsiders, the reservation's athletes allow the community to consider its relations with the outside world. As a result high school ballers may be a lightning rod for racial acrimony and/or bring back more recognition than anyone else. Together, these factors cause an artificial elevation of these teens' status in tribal life and that only adds to the cultural fixation on the game.

How different is Pine Ridge basketball, however, from other disadvantaged rural communities and their sports teams? Compare, for instance, Midland Texas High School football to Pine Ridge basketball. Both schools represent small, hard-pressed communities that seem to heavily—some would say overly—assign cultural importance to their high school athletes. And in both communities, the social standing of these athletes peaks early—while they are still in high school—after which they continue to live out life in their towns as only minor celebrities. Bruce Springsteen's "Glory Days," musically captured the pathos of this phenomenon. Communities that use high schoolers to momentarily rescue them from a humdrum existence is also a key theme in H. G. Bissenger's book *Friday Night Lights*.[3]

So, is Lakota Hoops just another example of this? The quick answer is yes and no. Insofar as sports plays a Band-Aid role by masking the misery associated with local myopia or community failure, yes, Pine Ridge is no different than Midland Texas High or Detroit's inner-city schools. But insofar as basketball is just another high school sport, no, rez ball is not exemplary of those schools that exist in hard-pressed communities. The difference? The Lakota infuse basketball with their culture, to make sure their world will persist. And striving as they do for survival alters the cultural calculus of Lakota sports, elevating its significance. Even those Lakota who just want to keep it simple—take in a game, trounce a rival, and nothing more—end up hearing their people sing in Lakota, watching their tribal flag be honored, and seeing their history depicted across larger-than-life murals on the gym walls. As such, even the most innocuous fan can't help but take in more than just a good game of basketball.

It makes me think of a relatively calm night in January 2018, when I drove to Red Cloud High School's gym to watch another game between Red Cloud and Pine Ridge. As mentioned, these are two schools linked by blood, culture, and resentment, and that history makes fans of each school want badly to beat the other. But on this night, none of the violence and anger that had marked these games in the past was in evidence.

And it said something about the feelings swirling around this game that by 5 P.M. the gym was filled for a contest that would start three hours later. Old-timers hobbled by arthritis and tiny children darting onto the court indicated that this was a tribal event. Tribal police officers had to turn away cars and crowds that continued pouring in. Officer Her Many Horses, a burly, imposing-looking tribal policeman with a handlebar moustache, stood by the door making certain nothing went awry.

The National Anthem was, as I've noted, sung in Lakota, during which a Lakota friend of mine observed that mostly only white people held their hands over their heart. Down in the front, four little girls were standing, facing the flag, one of them went to put her hand over her heart, but the others subtly let her know that this wasn't done. "We respect what the flag stands for," my friend explained, "but we also have reasons for being at odds with it."[4] Even if his explanation isn't the case often or at all, he explained this piece of behavior in Lakota terms, and so exemplifies how close the game is to Lakota meanings.

The game was a good one: loud and contested, played with great passion, and Red Cloud overcame a 10-point deficit late in the game to win. The players were focused on the win but managed to obliquely draw energy from the frenzy of the crowd. The compressed mob of reds (Pine Ridge) and blues (Red Cloud) in the stands visually reflected a partisan tension, using vocal combat, but it also forged a single collective expression. The boos, the cheers, the promenading, the eating and drinking, and the singing—all were stamped as being by Lakota and for Lakota. This was Lakota spending an evening together, celebrating who they are.

For a couple of hours, the gym and all of its disparate people became one heart, one soul. In their heated sporting opposition, they were joined by their love of the game, their joking and laughter, and the time of the year—and undergirding it all was their culture.

Looking around, I spotted a number of people I knew. They represented a spectrum of Pine Ridge: men and women, fit and frail, employed and unemployed, traditional and assimilated; one I knew was as young as three, and another was eighty. These people had all experienced that day in their own way. Some had gone to work or school, while others had been stuck at home huddling around their stoves. Some had visited the Indian Health Service hospital. Some had eaten well, while others went hungry. Most were sober, but some had had too much to drink that day. Some were planning their next sweat, while others had church prayer meetings on their minds. Given their different encounters of the day, were these people experiencing the game very differently, each colored by how good or bad their day had been? Or, was the game melding all of these varying daily experiences into a single, enjoyable event that leveled out the differences of the day? While it's probably impossible to answer that question definitively, the possibility that a game might have even a small capacity to create temporary amnesia, momentarily morphing disparate daily lives into a singular experience, is a tribute to the power of both sports and Lakota culture.

On Pine Ridge, the harder life is, the more one needs to fall under the spell of the game. At the same time, everyone knows that when the game ends, they've gotta walk back into the cold and hope their cars start and their homes are warm enough. Reality is more sobering than momentary euphoria.

The game can't ameliorate the most egregious cases of misery on Pine Ridge, of course. Clearly, if you're a meth addict or a late-stage alcoholic, you likely won't be at the game. If you don't have gas money, or are in dialysis, you have other things concerning you. And, while 2016 had been a sad year on Pine Ridge, I'm not sure that it was a completely unusual year. Major tragedies dotted the calendar.

Angela Shangreaux, for instance, doesn't attend any games. As little Kylen Shangreaux's foster mother, she was devastated and terrified when the tribal court told her she'd have to give two-year-old Ky back to his biological mother—a woman who, just a year earlier, had Ky taken from her because she was strung out on drugs. Now she wanted him back, claiming to be fit, and the court sided with her. When tribal police came to take away the little one who had grown attached to Angela over the past year, Ky cried, not wanting to leave her, and Angela could barely keep it together. Within two months, Ky was murdered by his biological mother; a fit of rage over toilet training would cause her to brutally kill her own baby. Courts had not seen it coming, and neither, actually, had the murdering mother. But Angela had, and she has been beside herself with grief ever since. News traveled through the rez via cell phones and Facebook, and people rallied behind Angela who spearheaded a successful campaign to remove the judges from their posts. Still, it was too late for little Ky.

Within a month after that incident, there was another murder, this time of a young man named Todd Little Bull. Originally a follower of a traditionalist family, he'd had a falling out with them, and was shot to death. Accusations, protests, and counteraccusations burned up Pine Ridge social media, but FBI investigations yielded nothing. Mutual anger ensued, much of it remaining to this day.

In between these bigger tragedies was a steady stream of smaller-scale crises causing consternation and suffering: Corey had his snowmobile stolen out of his truck, which was parked right in his driveway, a few feet from his bedroom. Sheila had to spend six hours waiting at the Indian Health Service hospital before she could get help for her sick child. Samantha posted an offer for a $200 reward for information leading to the arrest of whoever burned down her daughter's house. Bo got bit by a rattlesnake and, instead of waiting for questionable care at the Indian Health Service, he sliced his calf to drain the poison, and infection followed. Shaliya narrowly avoided getting sexually abused. And then, *pow!* a propane tank exploded, killing five—another big tragedy causing all of Pine Ridge to gasp. Nine days later, Vinnie Brewer, Jr. was pulled from a basketball game at Pine Ridge and murdered by outside drug dealers. Pine Ridge was incredulous . . . again.

In these instances, not much can offset the feelings of loss, and certainly not a profane game of high school hoops. Instead, these losses require the sacred hoop—a joining of Lakota everywhere to heal. The Lakota believe that all of life represents a sacred circle. To them, the sacred hoop is a powerful symbol—a metaphor that helps center Lakota and their culture.

In a world filled with random mishaps and deliberate tragedies, people often commit themselves to regaining stability, reason, and safety and distancing themselves from loss and chaos. They'll quickly move to reestablish small, familiar routines, and the more ordinary the better—grilling burgers, watching tournaments, or attending church socials or sweats. The more likely one is to suffer loss, the more he or she will embrace anything good that life throws their way. If they don't, they likely won't survive.

It is in those efforts to recalibrate life that one often finds basketball. As a profane manifestation of the symbol of the sacred hoop, basketball can help people not only regain their will to live in this rural, impoverished community but also to enjoy it as a part of this rural, impoverished community. As Anissa Martin said, with all of the despair she encountered at home, "I developed a passion for the game because it was my getaway—me doing it, playing the game for my own sanity."[5]

Unlike Anissa, some people may only vaguely grasp that the game works to displace their anguish and hurt, but almost everyone is aware of how the game fuels reverie. That's why former tribal vice president Tom Poor Bear's assessment of this writing project was positive—as far as he was concerned, it celebrated the people's joy. "We don't need another study done on our problems," he told me. "We know our problems. We'd like to see someone come here and talk about something positive, something we love, that makes our community happy."[6]

And for the Lakota, basketball brings not only that happiness but also the ability to maintain a sense of normalcy amid tragedy. They are two sides of the same coin: basketball for pure enjoyment and basketball for badly needed release and relief. As such, for Laura Big Crow, or Bryan Brewer, or Jesse Heart, or any number of others, Lakota hoops articulates the power of the every day to lend a deeper, specifically Lakota meaning to the slogan used by young basketball-crazed players and fans everywhere: ball is life.

Acknowledgments

Anyone writing about other people is intruding into their lives and so should be grateful to receive any kindness in this effort. I was blessed many times over in this study. Talking basketball with people on Pine Ridge Indian Reservation was easy, and I'm thankful to the dozens who shared their views with me. Several, however, were of immeasurable importance: Laura Big Crow started the ball rolling for me. She was the open and welcoming person one dreams will be there at the start of any ethnography. And Laura continued to be helpful at every stage of the project. Legendary coach Dusty LeBeau deserves a special thanks for taking the time away from his duties as athletic director and Sun Dance organizer to tell me his story and patiently explain things, sometimes more than once. The insights gleaned from the work of two Lakota journalists writing about sports were also invaluable. Brandon Ecoffey's incisive social commentary was so helpful in checking my sense of things in Pine Ridge. Jim Giago was always ready to have discussions and to provide me with context and insights derived from his, decades of work on the Lakota sports beat. He always directed me to look for the less obvious explanations. Bryan Brewer, a basketball luminary who created the Lakota Nation Invitational, was also generous and encouraging. As age mates, we shared history and life lessons. His knowledge of Pine Ridge politics, education, and basketball is unmatched, and it enriched my work immeasurably. And last but by no means least, Jesse Heart was the mercurial and essential core that drove the project in various directions.

Unguarded and always ready to express himself, he was as direct in his views as he was on the court for twenty years. As volatile as he could be, he was also capable of great empathy to anyone who was vulnerable. I'm deeply grateful to all of these people for their help, and for many others, and I hope this work reflects a good measure of their different lives and views.

Outside of Pine Ridge I found support from some of my dearest friends and colleagues, most notably Lindy Laub, Pat Albers, Nina Sylvanus, Doreen Lee, Carie Hersh, and Jay Meehan.

Finally, thanks also to my son Jordan, who, being the "baller" in the family, got me to shift my interests to basketball. His infectious spirit was much appreciated, and his aging dad often drew on his youthful energy and basketball acumen. My son Cody was always a great sounding board for ideas, and he was very valued here as well. I could rely on his thoughtful responses to anything I sent him. The rest of my family was an unwavering source of love and support of the kind that only a family can give, and that goes a long way when one is navigating unfamiliar waters. Knowing that my family (Mary, Benjy, Jed, Cody, and Jordan) would always be happy to see me when I came back, regardless of how any particular trip went, was the comfort I would need to see the project to its end.

Notes

Introduction

1 Patrick Sauer. 2014. "The Legend of Elvis Old Bull," *Vice Sports,* October 30, 2014, https://sports.vice.com/en_us/article/jpz9m8/the-legend-of-elvis-old-bull.

2 Bryan Brewer interview, 6/23/2017.

3 Corey Shangreau interview, 1/22/2016.

4 "Pine Ridge Statistics." American Indian Health Foundation. Brigham City, Utah. http://www.4aihf.org/id40.html.

5 Dana Lone Hill. 2012. "Racist State of Mind: South Dakota," *Last Real Indians,* April 13, 2012, http://lastrealindians.com/racist-state-of-mind-south-dakota/.

6 Brandon Ecoffey. 2014. "The Love of the Game and the Hope of the People," December 18, 2014, Indiancountrymedianetwork.com.

7 Vine Deloria, Jr. 1988. *Custer Died for Your Sins.* Norman, Oklahoma: University of Oklahoma Press, 78.

8 Ian Frazier. 2000. *On the Rez.* New York: Farrar, Straus, and Giroux; Sherman Alexie. 2000. "Some of My Best Friends," *Los Angeles Times,* January 23, 2000.

9 Gary Smith. 1991. "Shadow of a Nation: The Crows, Once Proud Warriors, Now Seek Glory—But Often Find Tragedy—in Basketball," *Sport Illustrated,* February 18, 1991.

10 Larry Colton. 2001. *Counting Coup: A True Story of Basketball and Honor on the Little Big Horn.* New York: AOL Time Warner.

11 Smith, "Shadow of a Nation."

Chapter 1   Landmarks in Lakota Life

1 Dana Lone Hill. 2007. "Remembering SuAnne," *Lakota Country Times,* March 22, 2007.

2 Dee Brown. 2014. *Saga of the Sioux: An Adaptation from Dee Brown's Bury My Heart at Wounded Knee.* New York: Harry Holt.

3 "Sitting Bull is Matched," *Pierre Free Press*, August 15, 1889. In the poem, "names enough" refers to a stipulation in the Sioux Bill of 1889, in which additional Indian land could be ceded if three-quarters of Lakota men signed off.

4 L. Frank Baum. 1891. Editorial. *Aberdeen Saturday Pioneer*, January 3, 1891.

5 William Byrd. 1733/2017. *The Westover Manuscripts: Containing the History of the Dividing Line Betwixt Virginia and North Carolina; A Journey to the Land of Eden*. Miami, FL: Hard Press. 2017.

6 Theodore Roosevelt. 1906. *The Winning of the West*. New York: Current Literature Publishing, 119.

7 Russell Means. 2009. "Khé Sapa and Paha Sapa: Russell Means Response to David Swallow," *Republic of Lakota*, July 29, 2009, http://www.republicoflakotah.com /2009/k%C8%9Fe-sapa-and-paha-sapa-russell-means-response-to-david-swallow/.

8 Peter Cozzens. 2016. "Ulysses S. Grant Launched an Illegal War against the Plains Indians, then Lied about It," *Smithsonian Magazine*, November 2016, https://www .smithsonianmag.com/history/ulysses-grant-launched-illegal-war-plains-indians -180960787/#RWDVwLakIyFxyrTq.99.

9 Ibid.

10 Alan Klein. 1991. *Sugarball: The American Game, The Dominican Dream*. New Haven: Yale University Press, 54.

11 Paul Robertson. 2002. *The Power of the Land: Identity, Ethnicity, and Class among the Oglala Lakota*. New York: Routledge, 49.

12 Ibid, 50.

13 John Ahni Schertow. 2006. "Oglala Sioux President Alex White Plume Sees the Old Ways as Better," *Indian Country Today*, August 28, 2006, https:// intercontinentalcry.org/oglala-sioux-president-alex-white-plume-sees-the-old-ways -as-better.

14 Robertson, *The Power of the Land*, 51.

15 David Bartecchi. 2010. "Range Units and the History of Leasing Lands on the Pine Ridge Reservation," *Village Earth*, landing.villageearth.org/pages/global-affiliate -network/projects-pineridge-reservation/range-units-and-the-history-of-leasing -lands-on-the-pine-ridge-reservation/.

16 David Rooks. 2017. "Can Raising Hemp Raise A Rez Economy? An Interview with Alex and Rosebud White Plume," *Indian Country Today*, June 29, 2017.

17 Charles Michael Ray. 2016. "White Plume Hopes to Plant Hemp in 2017," *South Dakota Public Broadcasting*, March 30, 2016, http://listen.sdpb.org/post/white -plume-hopes-plant-hemp-2017.

18 John Ahni Schertow, "Oglala Sioux President."

19 Editorial Board. 2015. "Pine Ridge Schools: Amid Beauty, Deterioration," *Star Tribune*, April 2, 2015.

20 Ibid.

21 "Draft Proposal to Redesign the U.S. Department of the Interior's Bureau of Indian Education," Bureau of Indian Education, accessed May 2, 2018, www.bie.edu/cs /groups/xbie/documents/text/idc1-026411.pdf

22 Brandon Ecoffey. 2016. "Wounded Knee School: $900,000 to Fight Suicide," *Lakota Country Times*, September 15, 2016.

23 John Bloom. 2000. *To Show What an Indian Can Do*. Minneapolis, MN: University of Minnesota Press, 38.

24 Ibid.

25 Scott Riney. 1999. *The Rapid City Indian School 1898–1933*. Norman: University of Oklahoma Press, 127.

26 Charles Trimble. 2012. *Iyeska*. Indianapolis, IN: Dog Ear Publishing, 46–47.

27 Jacqueline Gulledge. 2017. "American Indians Struggle to Survive Winter in South Dakota," CNN.com/2017/02/13. https://www.cnn.com/2017/02/13/health/iyw -american-indian-lakota-charity-one-spirit-firewood-program/index.html.

28 Bryan Brewer interview, 6/20/2018.

29 "U.N. Investigator Accuses U.S. of Shameful Neglect of Homeless," *The Guardian*, November 12, 2009, https://www.theguardian.com/world/2009/nov/12/un -investigator-us-neglect-homeless.

30 U.S. Senator Hon. Byron L. Dorgan from South Dakota, Chairman of the Committee on Indian Affairs. 1999. On the floor of the Senate (Congressional Record, February 25, 1999).

31 Natalie Hand. 2015. "FEMA Housing Delivery begins on Pine Ridge," *Lakota Country Times*, December 29, 2015.

32 Fieldnotes, 1/6/2016.

33 Ibid.

34 Ibid.

35 Ibid.

36 Thunder Valley Development Corporation, http://thundervalley.org/live-rez/our -programs/community-development.

37 "Mission Statement." Thunder Valley Development Corporation, http:// thundervalley.org/live-rez/our-programs/community-development.

38 Kathleen Pickering. 2000. *Lakota Culture, World Economy*. Lincoln, NE: University of Nebraska Press, 6.

39 "The Alex White Plume Story," Natives Unite, http://www.nativesunite.org/hemp /whiteplume/.

40 Jose Barreiro. 2000. "On Pine Ridge: Tiyospaye Talk," *Indian Country Today*, July 12, 2000, https://indiancountrymedianetwork.com/news/on-pine-ridge -tiospaye-talk/.

Chapter 2   Smudging, Sweating, and Sun Dancing

1 Dusty LeBeau interview, 1/8/2015.

2 Dusty LeBeau interview, 6/23/2017.

3 Dusty LeBeau interview, 1/8/2015.

4 Joseph Epes Brown (Editor). 1967. *The Sacred Pipe: Black Elk's Account of the Seven Rites of the Oglala Sioux*. Norman, OK: University of Oklahoma Press.

5 William K. Powers. 1982. *Oglala Religion*. Lincoln, NE: University of Nebraska Press.

6 Bryan Brewer, personal communication, 8/24/2018.

7 Fieldnotes, 6/23/2018.

8 Fieldnotes, 2/15/2016.

9 LeBeau interview, 6/21/2017.

10 "Drawing Lakota Lessons from an Anthem, *Thawápaha Olówaŋ* (Lakota Flag Song)," Red Cloud School, February 28, 2014, www.redcloudschool.org/news /2014/0228/drawing-lakota-lessons-from-an-anthem.

11 Ibid.

12 Paul Plume. 2004. "Lakota Flag Song." YouTube video, https://www.youtube.com/watch?v=d-xYnT3rUyM.

13 "Drawing Lakota Lessons" Red Cloud School website.

14 Alaina Adakai. 2017. "When You are a Veteran, You are Akicita," *Native Sun News*, August 11, 2017.

15 "Drawing Lakota Lessons" Red Cloud School website..

16 Ibid.

17 Eric Hobsbawm and Terrence Ranger (Editors). 1983. *The Invention of Tradition.* Cambridge, UK: Cambridge University Press.

18 Lyle LeBeau interview, 6/19/2018.

19 James Scott. 1992. *Domination and the Arts of Resistance.* New Haven: Yale University Press.

20 Valerie Taliman. 1993. "The Lakota Declaration of War," *News from Indian Country,* http://www.thepeoplespaths.net/articles/warlakot.htm.

21 Brandon Ecoffey. 2014. "The Hidden Tourneys: Independent Basketball in Indian Country," *The Last Real Indian,* April 4, 2014, https://lastrealindians.com/the-hidden-tourneys-independent-basketball-in-indian-country-by-brandon-ecoffey/.

22 Dusty LeBeau interview, 1/8/2015.

23 Dusty LeBeau interview, 6/22/2017.

24 Ibid.

25 Dusty LeBeau interview, 1/8/2015

26 Ibid.

27 Bob Drury and Tom Clavin. 2013. *The Heart of Everything that Is: The Untold Story of Red Cloud, An American Legend.* New York: Simon and Shuster.

28 Cedric Sunray. 2013. "Warrior Grounds: A Tornado Story," *Indian Country Today,* June 7, 2013, https://newsmaven.io/indiancountrytoday/archive/warrior-grounds-a-tornado-story-PUAszX8xGo-eGJ121ZzUFg/

29 Tim Giago. 1984. *Notes from Indian Country (Vol. 1).* Pierre, South Dakota: Keith Cochran.

30 Ibid.

31 Brandon Ecoffey interview, 6/20/2018.

32 Dusty LeBeau interview, 1/8/2015.

33 Jaylen Brown interview, 2/17/2015.

34 Dusty LeBeau interview, 2/4/2016.

35 Ibid.

36 Dusty LeBeau interview, 1/8/2015.

37 Bill Plaschke. 1999. "Little Big Rivalry: Bitter High School Feud with Vague Origins Has for Decades Divided a Sioux Community Along Athletic and Social Lines," *Los Angeles Times,* February 28, 1999.

38 Dusty LeBeau interview, 2/4/2016.

39 Nick Estes. 2014. "Chamberlain, South Dakota: A Border Town and Its 'Indian Problem,'" *Indian Country Today,* June 24, 2014.

40 Dusty LeBeau interview, 2/4/2016.

41 Ibid.

42 Dusty LeBeau interview, 6/21/2017.

43 Rich Anderson. 2014. "Pine Ridge Coach Calls it a Career after 26 Years of Teaching Life and Basketball," *Rapid City Journal,* March 22, 2014.

44 Dusty LeBeau interview, 2/4/2016.

45 Dusty LeBeau interview, 1/8/2015.
46 Ibid.
47 Ibid.
48 Dusty LeBeau interview, 2/4/2016.

Chapter 3   The Lakota Nation Invitational

1 Fieldnotes, 12/14/2018.
2 Ibid.
3 Bryan Brewer interview, 2/11/2016.
4 Kelli Anderson. 2003. "Hoops Dream: The Lakota Nation Invitational Honors the Sports Passion and Culture of American Indians," *Sports Illustrated*, December 22, 2003.
5 Kevin Woster. 2014. "Larry Luitjens and the Jimmy Gray Cloud Effect," January 26, 2014, http://kelolandblogs.com/tellkevin/tell-kevin/larry-luitjens-and-the-jimmy -gray-cloud-effect/
6 Woster, "Larry Luitjens."
7 Bryan Brewer interview, 6/23/2017.
8 Anderson, "Hoops Dream."
9 Tim Giago. 2014. "The Olympics of Indian Basketball," *Huffington Post*, December 16, 2014.
10 Bryan Brewer interview, 6/23/2017.
11 Ibid.
12 Bryan Brewer interview, 2/11/2016.
13 Fieldnotes, 12/13/2018.
14 Bryan Brewer interview, 2/11/2016.
15 Dusty LeBeau interview, 6/19/2017.
16 Fieldnotes, 12/15/2016.
17 Dusty LeBeau interview, 2/2/2015.
18 Bryan Brewer interview, 6/23/2017.
19 Ibid.
20 Bryan Brewer interview, 3/22/2017.
21 Bryan Brewer interview, 6/23/2017.
22 Dusty LeBeau interview, 1/8/2015.
23 Benedict Anderson. 2016. *Imagined Communities: Reflections on the Origin and Spread of Nationalism.* New York: Verso Books.
24 Eric Hobsbawm and Terence Ranger (Editors). 1983. *The Invention of Tradition.* Cambridge: Cambridge University Press.
25 Brandon Ecoffey. 2014. "Brandon Ecoffey: Tournament Shows Hope of the Lakota People," December 18, 2014, https://www.indianz.com/News/2014/12/18/brandon -ecoffey-tournament-sho.asp.

Chapter 4   Jesse Heart

1 Bryan Brewer interview, 1/3/2018.
2 Stu Whitney. 2002. "High School Star Took Three Tries at College Basketball but Left It Behind," *Argus Leader*, September 15, 2002, http://www.argusleader.com /sidebar/Sundayfeature.shtml 9/15/2002.

3 Whitney, "High School Star."

4 Carter Strickland. 2004. "Dreams Go as Quickly as They Come," *The Oklahoman*, July 4, 2004, https://newsok.com/article/2857767/dreams-go-as-quickly-as-they-come.

5 Strickland, "Dreams Go."

6 Smith, *Shadow of a Nation*.

7 Ibid.

8 Selena Roberts. 2001. "In the Shadows: Off-Field Hurdles Stymie Indian Athletes," *New York Times*, June 17, 2001.

9 Roberts, "In the Shadows."

10 Stu Whitney. 2002. "Indian Athletes Struggle to Make Transition to College," *Sioux Falls Argus Leader*, September 19, 2002.

11 Whitney, "High School Star."

12 Ibid.

13 Jesse Heart interview, 11/4/2016.

14 Whitney, "High School Star."

15 Ibid.

16 Fieldnotes, 11/6/2016.

17 Jesse Heart interview, 6/28/2017.

18 Brandon Ecoffey. 2014. "The Hidden Tourneys: Independent Basketball in Indian Country." *Native Sun News*, April 9, 2014, www.indianz.com/News/2014/013189.

19 Ecoffey, "Hidden Tourneys."

20 Jesse Heart interview, 11/3/2016.

21 Jesse Heart interview, 6/24/2017.

22 Narcisse Heart interview, 6/24/2017.

23 Jesse Heart interview, 8/20/2015.

24 Narcisse Heart interview, 6/24/2017.

25 Whitney, "High School Star."

26 Ibid.

27 Jesse Heart interview, 6/24/2017.

28 Ibid.

29 Ibid.

30 Ibid.

31 Ibid.

32 Gary Sandefur and Carolyn Lieber. 1996. "The Demography of American Indian Families." In *Changing Numbers, Changing Needs: American Indian Demography and Public Health,* G. D. Sandefur, R. R. Rindfuss, and B. Cohen (Editors). Washington, DC: National Academies.

33 Jesse Heart interview, 6/24/2017.

34 Ibid.

35 Ibid.

36 Ibid.

37 Ibid.

38 Jesse Heart, personal communication, 9/23/2018.

39 Laura Big Crow, "Corey jumped out of bed this morning . . ." Facebook, 10/12/2017.

40 Corey Shangreau interview, 6/20/2017.

41 Ibid.

42 Ibid.

43 Ibid.

44 Ibid.

45 Corey Shangreau, quoted on Laura Big Crow Facebook post, 7/9/2017.

46 Mercedes Osceola. "Happy Father's Day to Braxton's dad . . ." Facebook post, 6/19/2018.

47 Brandon Ecoffey interview, 6/12/2018.

48 Brandon Ecoffey interview, 2/19/2018.

49 Ibid.

50 Ibid.

51 William Powers. 1977. *Oglala Religion.* Lincoln, NE: University of Nebraska Press.

52 R. W. Connell. 2005. *Masculinities,* 2nd ed. Berkeley: University of California Press.

53 R. W. Connell and James Messerschmidt. 2005. "Hegemonic Masculinity: Rethinking the Concept," *Gender and Society* 19 (6): 829–859.

54 Alan Klein. 1983. "The Political Economy of Gender: A 19th Century Plains Indian Case Study." In *The Hidden Half: Studies of Plains Indian Women* (Pat Albers and Bea Medicine, editors). Washington, DC: University Press of the Americas.

55 Room existed for those who abandoned gender straightjackets. Men identifying as women (*winktes* or *berdach*) had a certain amount of social position, but, they were neither derided nor held up as role models.

56 First formulated by psychologist Alfred Adler to describe overcoming feelings of inferiority by emphasizing and exaggerating masculinity.

57 Mary Crow Dog. 1990. *Lakota Woman.* New York: Grove Weidenfeld.

58 Bea Medicine. 2006. *Drinking and Sobriety among the Lakota Sioux.* Lanham, MD: Alta Mira Press.

59 Kathleen Pickering. 2000. *Lakota Culture, World Economy.* Lincoln: University of Nebraska.

60 George Orwell. 1945. "The Sporting Spirit," *(London) Tribune,* December 1945.

61 Jesse Heart interview, 11/4/2016.

Chapter 5   Laura Big Crow

1 Laura Big Crow interview, 2/4/2014.

2 Fieldnotes, 6/28/2018.

3 Laura Big Crow interview, 2/4/2014.

4 Arthur Conan Doyle. 1927/2016 *The Case-Book of Sherlock Holmes.* Mineola, NY: Dover Books.

5 Laura Big Crow interview, 2/4/2014.

6 Ibid.

7 Ibid.

8 Ibid.

9 Ibid.

10 Ibid.

11 Ibid.

12 Mike Anderson, "Six to Watch in 2016: Yvonne 'Tiny' DeCory," *Rapid City Journal,* December 31, 2015, http://rapidcityjournal.com/news/local/to-watch-in-yvonne -tiny-decory/article_0ded6257-8e2e-5bfb-baff-c4f770f7a6c4.html.

13 David Sutherland. 2013. *Kind Hearted Woman* (film by David Sutherland), http:// www.pbs.org/independentlens/films/kind-hearted-woman/.

14 Laura Big Crow interview, 6/27/2017.

15 Brian Haenchen. 2018. "Rising above the Reservation: Hard Lessons Spark Signs of Hope," *Sioux Falls Argus Leader*, August 7, 2018.

16 Laura Big Crow interview, 6/27/2017.

17 Haenchen, "Rising above the Reservation."

18 Ibid.

19 Laura Big Crow interview, 6/11/2018.

20 Rebecca McCray. 2016. "Can a New School Help the Girls of Pine Ridge Indian Reservation?" *Take Part*, January 14, 2016.

21 Laura Big Crow interview, 1/11/2018.

22 Laura Big Crow, personal communication, 6/21/2018.

23 Anissa Martin interview, 6/19/2018.

24 Anissa Martin interview, 6/20/2018.

25 Ibid.

26 Ibid.

27 Ibid.

28 Ibid.

29 Ibid.

30 National Sexual Violence Resource Center. 2015. "Statistics," www.nsvrc.org/sites /default/files/publications_nsvrc_factsheet_media-packet_statistics-about-sexual -violence_0.pdf; and National Coalition against Physical Violence, https://www .speakcdn.com/assets/2497/domestic_violence2.pdf.

31 U.S. Dept. of Justice. 2012. "Protecting Native American and Alaska Native Women from Violence," November 29, 2012, https://www.justice.gov/archives/ovw/blog /protecting-native-american-and-alaska-native-women-violence-november-native -american.

32 Sutherland, *Kind Hearted Woman*.

33 Craig Phillips. 2013. "Young Lakota: Q&A with Sunny Clifford," November 21, 2013, http://www.pbs.org/independentlens/blog/young-lakota-qa-sunny-clifford/

34 NCAI Policy Research Center. 2013. Policy Insights Brief, Statistics on Violence against Native Women, 3.

35 NCAI Policy Research Center. 2013.

36 Mary Annette Pember. 2015. "'Praying Really Hard': Pine Ridge Needs Shelter for Abused Women," *Indian Country Today*, August 19, 2015.

37 Laura Big Crow interview, 1/11/2018.

38 "Degrading 95 Tourney Event Lesson for All," *Argus Leader*, June 26, 2000, 11.

39 "Girls Ordered to Prove Gender Lose Court Appeal," *Lincoln Journal-Star*, http://update.journalstar.com/stories/2.

40 George Carlin. 1997. *Brain Drippings,* New York: Easton Press.

Chapter 6 Pine Ridge versus Red Cloud

1 Paul Robertson. 2002. *The Power of the Land.* New York: Routledge.

2 Bill Plascke. 1999. "Little Big Rivalry," *Los Angeles Times*, February 28, 1999.

3 Narcisse Heart interview, 6/22/2017.

4 Brandon Ecoffey interview, 3/18/2018.

5 Plascke, "Little Big Rivalry."

6 Charles Trimble. 2012. *Iyeska.* Indianapolis, IN: Dog Ear Productions, 47.

7 Trimble, *Iyeska*, 48.

8 Ibid.

9 Thomas G. Andrews. 2002. "Turning the Tables on Assimilation: Oglala Lakotas and the Pine Ridge Day Schools, 1889–1920s," *Western Historical Quarterly* 33 (4): 407–430.

10 Nancy Hulston. 1995. "Federal Children: Indian Education and the Red Cloud-McGillycuddy Conflict," *South Dakota Historical Society* 25 (2): 81–94, http://www.sdhspress.com/journal/south-dakota-history-25-2/federal-children-indian-education-and-the-red-cloud-mcgillycuddy-conflict/vol-25-no-2-federal-children.

11 David Wallace Adams. 1995. *Education for Extinction: American Indians and the Boarding School Experience, 1875–1928*. Lawrence, KS: University of Kansas Press, 15.

12 Tim Giago. 1998. "Confronting a Legacy of Damage," *Baltimore Sun,* baltimoresun.com/1998-01-22/news/1998022146_1_indian-children-indian-boarding-canada.

13 Julia McGillycuddy. 1941. *McGillycuddy, Agent: A Biography of Dr. Valentine McGillycuddy*. Palo Alto, CA: Stanford University Press, 205–206.

14 Charla Bear. 2008. "American Indian Boarding Schools Haunt Many," National Public Radio, May 12, 2008, http://www.npr.org/templates/story/story.php?storyId=16516865.

15 Luther Standing Bear. 1960. *Land of the Spotted Eagle*. Lincoln, NE: University of Nebraska Press, 233–234.

16 Charles Trimble, "One Last Great Blast at Boarding School," *Lakota Country Times,* June 16, 2010.

17 Luther Standing Bear. 1975. *My People, the Sioux*. Lincoln, NE: University of Nebraska Press, 124.

18 Tim Giago. 2006. *Children Left Behind: The Dark Legacy of Indian Mission Boarding Schools*. Santa Fe, NM: Clear Light Publishers; Tim Giago. 1978. *The Aboriginal Sin: Reflections on the Holy Rosary Indian Mission School (Red Cloud Indian School)*. New York: Indian Historian Press.

19 Tim Giago. 2007. "Tim: Giago: The Dark Legacy of Boarding Schools," www.indianz.com/News/2007/04/02/tim_giago_the_d.asp.

20 Sharon Waxman. 2003. "Abuse Charges Hit the Reservation," *Washington Post,* June 2, 2003.

21 Waxman, "Abuse Charges."

22 Tom Gannon. 2014. "Immigration as Cultural Imperialism: An Indian Boarding School Experience," *Great Plains Quarterly* 34 (2): 111–122.

23 Giago, *Aboriginal Sin.*

24 Bryan Brewer interview, 6/21/2018.

25 Ibid.

26 Trimble, "One Last Great Blast."

27 Bryan Brewer interview, 6/21/2018.

28 Fieldnotes, 4/27/2017.

29 Brandon Ecoffey interview, 3/8/2018.

30 Ibid.

31 John Neihardt. 1988. *Black Elk Speaks*. Lincoln, NE: University of Nebraska Press, 141.

32 Thomas Biolsi. 2001. *Deadliest Enemies: Law and Race Relations on and off Rosebud Reservation*. Berkeley: University of California Press, 140.

33 James Fenelon. 1998. *Culturicide, Resistance, and Survival of the Lakota (Sioux Nation)*. London: Routledge, 214.

34 Kathleen Pickering. 2000. *Lakota Culture, World Economy*. Lincoln, NE: University of Nebraska Press, 117.

35 Neihardt, *Black Elk Speaks*, 80.

36 Edwin Denig. 1930. *Indian Tribes of the Upper Missouri*. 46th Annual Report of the Bureau of American Ethnology, 1928–1929. Washington, DC: Government Printing Office, 375–628, 460.

37 Brewer interview, 1/4/2016.

38 Eleanor Goldberg. 2017. "Why Many Native American Girls Skip School When They Have Their Periods," *Huffington Post*, August 25, 2017.

39 Goldberg, "Why Many Native American Girls Skip School."

Chapter 7   "Crabs in a Bucket"

1 John E. Koontz. 2003. "Origin of Oglala," http://spot.colorado.edu/~koontz/faq/etymology.htm.

2 Axel Munthe. 1929. *The Story of San Michele* (New York: EP Dutton).

3 Jesse Heart interview, 6/26/2017.

4 Tim Giago. 2012. "Divide and Rule Was the Unwritten Rule of the Indian Agents," *Huffington Post*, June 3, 2012, https://www.huffingtonpost.com/tim-giago/divide-and-rule-was-the-u_b_1566477.html.

5 Selena Roberts. 2001. "Off-Field Hurdles Stymie Indian Athletes," *New York Times*, June 17, 2001.

6 Zora Neale Hurston. 1937/2006. *Their Eyes Were Watching God*. New York: Harper Perennial Modern Classics, 42.

7 Morton Fried. 1967. *The Evolution of Political Society: An Essay in Political Anthropology*. New York: McGraw-Hill: 34.

8 George Horse Capture and Emil Her Many Horses (Editors). 2006. *A Song for the Horse Nation: Horses in Native American Cultures*. Washington, DC: National Museum of the American Indian, 12.

9 Sherman Alexie. 2017. *You Don't Have to Say You Love Me*. New York: Little Brown, 146.

10 Richard Lee. 2013. *The Dobe Ju/'hoansi*. Belmont, CA: Wadsworth, 245–252.

11 Laura Woodworth-Ney. 1994. "The Diaries of a Day-School Teacher: Daily Realities on the Pine Ridge Indian Reservation, 1932–1942," *South Dakota State Historical Society* 3–4 (194–211): 207.

12 Adrian Jawort. 2009. "Elephant of Indian Racism Discussed," *Indian Country Today*, October 23, 2009.

13 Alexie, *You Don't Have to Say You Love Me*, 425.

14 Alexie, *You Don't Have to Say You Love Me*, 426.

15 Alexie, *You Don't Have to Say You Love Me*, 374.

16 Roberts, "Off Field Hurdles."

17 Brandon Ecoffey interview, 2/19/2018.

18 Gary Smith. 1991. "Shadow of a Nation," *Sports Illustrated*, February 18, 1991.

19 Narcisse Heart interview, 6/26/2017.

20 Jesse Heart interview, 6/26/2017.

21 Ibid.

22 Field notes, 6/2/2017.

23 LB, personal communication, 12/15/2018.

24 Giago, "Divide and Rule."

25 Dusty LeBeau interview, 2/15/2016.

26 Dusty LeBeau interview, 6/23/2017.

27 Jim Kent. 2017. "Wounded Knee Survivors Group Objects to Developing Massacre Site," *Lakota Country Times*, December 28, 2017.

28 Vincent Schilling. 2015. "Wounded Knee SOLD? Tim Giago Has Plans to Buy It for $3.9 Million," *Indian Country Today,* December 29, 2015.

29 Tim Giago interview, 2/15/2017.

30 Ibid.

31 Meghan Rae. 2018. "Tonight I'd just like to say a big FUCK YOU . . ." Facebook post, February 10, 2018.

32 Jim Kent. 2018. "Guardians Ride Pine Ridge Reservation Roads," *Lakota Country Times,* February 8, 2018.

33 Liz Gauthier. "Guardians Protect and Serve Everyone on the Rez," Kumeyaay.com, accessed November, 18, 2019, https://www.kumeyaay.com/news/350-guardians -protect-and-serve-everyone-on-the-rez.html.

34 Toyacoyah Brown. 2017. "Young Lakota Entrepreneurs Create Sweet Business Ideas—1400 lbs of Honey Sold!" Powwow.com, March 21, 2017, https://www .powwows.com/young-lakota-entrepreneurs-create-sweet-business-idea-1400-lbs -honey-sold.

Chapter 8   Race Relations, Hoops, and the Border in South Dakota

1 "High Speed Chase." 2002. Episode 219, *This American Life*, Washington, DC: National Public Radio, August 16, 2002.

2 Ibid.

3 Ibid.

4 Ibid.

5 Ibid.

6 Ibid.

7 Ibid.

8 Ibid.

9 Ibid.

10 Trymaine Lee. 2014. "Pine Ridge: A Broken System Failing America's Most Forgotten Children," MSNBC, May 28, 2014, http://www.msnbc.com/msnbc /failing-americas-most-forgotten-children

11 American Indian Education Study Group, "BIE Students Perform Worse than American Indian Students Attending Public Schools," Preliminary Findings and Recommendations Prepared by the American Indian Education Study Group for Purposes of Tribal Consultation.

12 Editorial Board. 2015. "Pine Ridge Schools: Amid Beauty, Deterioration." *Star Tribune*, Minneapolis, MN, April 2, 2015, http://www.startribune.com/part-3-pine -ridge-schools-amid-beauty-deterioration/284902601/.

13 Ibid.

14 Ibid.

15 Lee, "Pine Ridge."

16 Ibid.

17 Laura Big Crow. 2017. Facebook post, July 4, 2017.

18 Alan Klein. 1997. *Baseball on the Border: A Tale of Two Laredos.* Princeton, NJ: Princeton University Press.

19 Eldon Marshall interview, 6/15/2018.

20 Ibid.

21 Gummer Garnier interview, 2/12/2017.

22 Ibid.

23 Ibid.

24 Ibid.

25 Bryan Brewer interview, 12/13/2018.

26 Winner Chamber of Commerce website.

27 Corey Shangreau interview, 1/25/2017.

28 "Winner, South Dakota," Wikipedia, https://en.wikipedia.org/wiki/Winner, _South_Dakota.

29 *Antoine et al v. Winner Schools.* 2007. https://www.crin.org/en/library/legal -database/antoine-et-al-v-winner-school-district.

30 Tracy Dell'Angela. 2005. "Dakota Indians Say Kids Trapped in School-to-Prison Pipeline," *Chicago Tribune,* December 5, 2005, https://www.chicagotribune.com /news/ct-xpm-2005-11-29-0511290157-story.html

31 Hazel Bonner. "Sioux Addition Today: 47 Years of Struggle, Part V of V," *Lakota Journal,* NatNews Msg# 12303H, http://www.lakotajournal.com.

32 ACLU. 2005. "South Dakota Schools Discriminating against Native American Students, Charge ACLU and Tribe," June 23, 2005, www.aclu.org/news/south -dakota-schools-discriminating-against-native-american-students-charge-aclu-and -tribe; American Indian Society of Delaware Forum. 2005. "Dakota Indians Say Kids Trapped in 'School-to-Prison Pipeline,'" November 29, 2005, http://udaisd .proboards.com/thread/2278/ndns-trapped-school-prison-cycle.

33 Lisa Desjardins and Emma Lacey-Bordeaux. 2012, "Problems of Liberty and Justice on the Plains," CNN, updated 11:36 A.M. EST, August 10, 2012, www.Lisa Desjardins and Emma Lacey-Bordeaux.

Chapter 9   Engaging Acrimony

1 Candy Hamilton. 1995. "Where a Tomahawk Chop Feels Like a Slur Indian: Reservations Sound Off on the Culture of Sports Mascots." *Christian Science Monitor*, 10/25/1995; http://www.csmonitor.com/1995/1025/25032.html

2 Tim Giago. 2012. 'Wiping Away the Tears' at Wounded Knee," *Huffington Post*, December 31, 2012.

3 Giago, "Wiping Away."

4 James Giago Davies, "Sobriety Checkpoint Mars Red Cloud-Hill City Games," *Native Sun News,* December 12–18, 2018, B4.

5 Georgianne Nienaber. 2015. "Native-American Kids Doused With Beer at SD Hockey Game," *Huffington Post,* February 5, 2015; Simon Moya-Smith. 2015. "Suspects Who Hit Native American Kids With Racial Slurs, Beer Identified, Police Say," http://indiancountrytodaymedianetwork.com/2015/01/29/suspects -who-hit-native-american-kids-racial-slurs-beer-identified-police-say-158936.

6 Mark Anderson. 2017. "Sturgis Cancels Homecoming Game as Fallout from Insensitive Message Continues." *Rapid City Journal,* October 13, 2017. http://rapidcityjournal .com/news/local/sturgis-cancels-homecoming-game-as-fallout-from-insensitive -message-continues/article_045d8a27-8c39-5129-95be-3f24dce27aac.html.

7 Luke Warm Water. 2005. "South Dakota is the Mississippi of the North," *Aborigi-nal Performance* 2 (1), 2005, http://hemi.nyu.edu/journal/2_1/warmwater.html.

8 James "Magaska" Swan. 2012. "They hate Indians in Rapid City . . ." Facebook www .facebook.com/notes/james-magaska-swan/they-hate-indians-in-rapid-city-south -dakota-8912/466623556695801.

9 Dana Lone Hill. 2012. "Hate Crimes and the KKK in South Dakota." *Last Real Indians,* https://lastrealindians.com/hate-crimes-and-the-kkk-in-south-dakota/.

10 Callie Rennison. 2001. "Violent Victimization and Race, 1993–98." Bureau of Justice Statistics Special Report. March 2001, NCJ 176354.

11 Rennison, "Violent Victimization."

12 A. J. Vicens. 2015. "Native Americans Get Shot By Cops at an Astonishing Rate. So Why Aren't You Hearing About It?" *Mother Jones,* July 15, 2015, www.motherjones .com/politics/2015/07/native-americans-getting-shot-police/

13 Dominique Alan Fenton. 2015. "Racism at Core of Native Teen Suicides in Pine Ridge," April 2, 2015, http://www.colorlines.com/articles/racism-core-native-teen -suicides-pine-ridge.

14 Fenton, "Racism at Core."

15 Ian Frazier. 2000. *On the Rez.* New York: Farrar, Straus, and Giroux.

16 Frazier, *On the Rez,* 208–209.

17 Frazier, *On the Rez,* 209.

18 Stu Whitney. 2002. "High School Star Took Three Tries at College Basketball but Left It Behind," *Argus Leader,* September 15, 2002.

19 Jesse Heart interview, 8/15/2014.

20 The Winner High School Athletic Handbook, 2014–2015 states, "All spectators, officials, and participants are expected to conduct themselves in a manner that promotes good sportsmanship and fair play. Behavior that is a detriment to the contest and the spirit in which it is held is greatly discouraged." Winner High School Athletic Handbook, 2014–15, 11.

21 Frazier, *On the Rez,* 211.

22 Bill Harlan. 2000. "The Game at Lead," *New York Review of Books,* May 11, 2000.

23 Harlan, "The Game at Lead."

24 Ian Frazier. 2000. "Reply to Bill Harlan." *New York Review of Books,* May 11, 2000.

25 Frazier, "Reply to Bill Harlan."

26 Lone Hill interview, 1/21/2018.

27 Lone Hill interview, 1/21/2018.

28 Brandon Ecoffey interview, 1/19/2015.

29 Corey Shangreau interview, 6/21//2016.

30 SuAnne Big Crow interview, 2/4/2018.

31 Corey Shangreau interview, 6/21//2016.

32 Bryan Brewer interview, 1/31/2016.

33 Stu Whitney. 2002. "High School Star Took Three Tries at College Basketball but Left It Behind," *Argus Leader,* September 15, 2002, http://www.argusleader.com /sidebar/Sundayfeature.shtml 9/15/2002.

34 SuAnne Big Crow interview, 2/4/2018.

35 Jesse Heart Interview, 11/21/2016.

36 Brandon Ecoffey Facebook post, March 16, 2018.

37 Dusty LeBeau interview, 6/21/2017.

38 Dusty LeBeau interview, 1/15/2015.

39 Jon Lurie. "Harvest of Death," http://www.dickshovel.com/lsa27.html.

40 Jim Giago, personal communication, 3/28/2017.

41 National Public Radio. 2002. "Episode 219: High Speed Chase," *This American Life*, August 16, 2002, Washington, DC: National Public Radio, http://www .thisamericanlife.org/radio-archives/episode/219/transcript.

42 Robert Wheeler. 1975. *Jim Thorpe: The World's Greatest Athlete*. Norman, OK: University of Oklahoma Press, 128.

43 Brandon Ecoffey interview, 3/2/2018.

44 Victor Turner. 1988. *The Anthropology of Performance*. London: PAJ Books.

45 "Digger's Song," Wikipedia, https://en.wikipedia.org/wiki/Diggers%27_Song.

46 Joelle Rostkowski. 2012. *Conversations with Remarkable Native Americans: Gerald Vizenor*. Albany, NY: SUNY Press, xlvll.

47 Jesse Heart interview, 6/26/2017.

48 Ibid.

49 Quoted in Jimmy Davies, "Rapid City's Urban Indian Basketball Legacy," *Native Sun News*, March 27, 2013.

50 Mica Valdez. 2013. "Basketball, Motivation, and the Making of Relatives," June 16, 2013, https://malinallimedia.wordpress.com/2013/06/16/basketball-motivation -and-the-making-of-relatives/.

Epilogue

1 Dusty LeBeau interview, 1/8/2016.

2 Ibid.

3 H. G. Bissenger. 1991. *Friday Night Lights: A Town, a Team, and a Dream*. New York: Harper-Collins.

4 Ibid.

5 Anissa Martin interview, 6/19/2018.

6 Tom Poor Bear interview, 1/3/2014.

Index

About the Author

ALAN KLEIN is a professor of anthropology at Northeastern University in Boston, Massachusetts. He has examined the intersection of sports and culture for forty years. Author of six other books and scores of articles and chapters, his studies have delved into such topics as the contested terrain of baseball in the Dominican Republic, nationalism and sport on the U.S.-Mexican border, masculinity among California bodybuilders, and globalization and sports.